The
Biggest
Company
on Earth

The
Biggest

Company
on Earth
A Profile of AT&T

Sonny Kleinfield

An Owl Book

Holt, Rinehart and Winston
New York

To My Mother

Copyright © 1981, 1982 by Sonny Kleinfield
All rights reserved, including the right to reproduce
this book or portions thereof in any form.
Published by Holt, Rinehart and Winston,
383 Madison Avenue, New York, New York 10017.
Published simultaneously in Canada by Holt, Rinehart
and Winston of Canada, Limited.
Library of Congress Cataloging in Publication Data
Kleinfield, Sonny.
The biggest company on earth.
Based on a series of articles published in 1978
and 1979 in the New York Times.
Includes index.
1. American Telephone and Telegraph Company.
I. Title.
HE8846.A55K57   384.6'065'73   80–13095
ISBN 0-03-045326-7
ISBN 0-03-061483-X (An Owl book) (pbk.)

First published in hardcover by
Holt, Rinehart and Winston in 1981.

First Owl Book Edition — 1982

Designer: Constance T. Doyle
Printed in the United States of America
1 3 5 7 9 10 8 6 4 2

ISBN 0-03-061483-X

Contents

Preface

This is not meant to be either a definitive or an investigative treatment of AT&T, but rather an exploration of the variegated faces of the modern-day phone company, a sort of serendipitous odyssey through its numberless corners. Much has been written about the phone company, but it seemed to me at my outset that remarkably little had been devoted to an understanding of its actual workings.

It was at the bidding of John Lee, the editor of the business section of the *New York Times*, that I embarked on a nineteen-part series of articles on AT&T that appeared at frequent intervals in the paper, beginning in early 1978. It seemed a particularly fitting time to take a close-up look at the doings at the phone company. Its bitterly protected monopoly had been slowly crumbling, and it was finding itself faced with its most brutal competition since its nascent days. Moreover, spectacular technological progress had spurred a convergence of the computer and communications fields that was producing a parade of new products and services. In short, a lot was cooking at AT&T.

This book is an outgrowth of that series, and I am therefore indebted to John Lee for his wise counseling and unalloyed enthusiasm for the project. Also, I have thanks to give to Fred Andrews, the deputy business editor, for his suggestions and support, and to the *Times* itself for sponsoring such a lengthy series, one of the longest it has ever run.

AT&T was generous in accommodating my needs (with the notable exception of the Southwestern Bell brass), and I am grateful to the several hundred employees who gave of their time. I should hasten to point out that no one at the company was allowed to review my articles or this book prior to publication. I am equally grateful to the dozens of people outside the phone company who also willingly put aside time to contribute their views. For an understanding of AT&T's history, I was helped immeasurably by John Brooks's excellent book *Telephone*. As always, I am thankful to Bernice Kanner for her indulgence.

I brought no strong bias to the subject (I initially knew little more about the company than that my phone generally worked well), and I left with none. Along the way, I found many aspects of AT&T amusing, and some things frightening. I very much believe that checks and balances on the biggest of corporations are vital, that it is inadequate to rely strictly on the supposed "good intentions" of corporate chieftains, and although evidence of malfeasance at AT&T is not extensive, there is little question how much power it wields. I feel more comfortable knowing that the phone business has been opened up to competitors who will help in policing AT&T. For the most part, though, I have tried to show the company as it exists rather than attempt to suggest what should be made of it. The more I learned about the extraordinary universe that is AT&T, the more cautious I became about summing it up.

Preface to the 1982 Edition

January 8, 1982, will go down as an unforgettable day in the history of the telephone company. In an electrifying and shocking move, AT&T settled the seven-year-old government antitrust suit leveled against it by agreeing to a partial dismantlement of its system. Under the terms, Ma Bell will shear off within eighteen months its cluster of operating companies that provide local service, such as New York Telephone, Michigan Bell, Pacific Telephone, etc. It will keep Western Electric, its manufacturing arm; Bell Laboratories, its research unit; and its abundant long-distance operations. What's more, it will be free to leap into whatever new businesses it cares to (fast foods, perhaps, or maybe dry cleaning?) without the inhibitory shackles of legislators and regulators. Also, the antitrust settlement specifies that AT&T will hold on to certain businesses that traditionally have been the province of the local companies— the actual rental or sale of phones in customer homes, the Phone-Center stores, the mightily profitable Yellow Pages (the financially less appetizing White Pages will stay with the operating companies). Even stripped of its local appendages, then, AT&T will still, in many respects, be the world's largest company.

By agreeing to the breakup, the phone company has turned its back on its past. For more than a century, AT&T's basic mission has been to furnish P.O.T. (plain old telephone service) to anyone who wanted it at a price just about anyone could afford. Now it will be getting out of P.O.T. Tired of being chained down, it figured that it was wisest to dump its most heavily regulated, slowest growing, least profitable businesses (what a number of observers have dubbed the "railroads of the future") in exchange for a clear path to the high technology opportunities it recently has trained its eye on.

As this edition went to press, a mind-boggling jumble of questions remained unanswered. It was not clear what tinkering regulators and legislators might do. AT&T was still laboriously formulating its game plan for carrying out the breakup. It was not yet known whether there would be one gigantic local company. Or twenty. Or five. Would everyone now get two phone bills instead of one? Would several repairmen be crawling through one's house when the phone breaks?

Early expectations were that local phone rates would shoot up once Mother Bell was no longer around to subsidize them. The rural farmer, it was said, might no longer find room in his budget even to keep a phone. Fears abounded that service would steadily atrophy. Years are expected to elapse before all the ramifications of the settlement become clear.

The one thing that was clear was that the AT&T of tomorrow will be profoundly different from the formidable gray-haired old lady we have known for a century. As one long-time student of the phone company phrased it, this is good-bye to Ma Bell and hello to Go-Go Bell.

The Biggest Company on Earth

Sixteen Million
Dollars a Day

First I went to take a look at it from the corporate home. This is where—ultimately, unmistakably—the nation's phone system is run. Bounded by Broadway, Fulton, Church, and Dey Streets, just a brisk stroll from Wall Street, the bluff building at 195 Broadway was set down on the block in such a way that it looked vaguely like an immense mocha layer cake. Twenty-eight layers. Already, a sense of gigantism, of glandular excess. The massive columned ground-floor portico brought to mind the mood of an Egyptian temple, until you squinted catercorner across the street at the compression of fast-food plastic and sober discount shops (Music World, Taft Electronics, Tinkerers' Paradise). Above the entrance protruded ornamental panels that symbolized the four elements of Fire, Water, Air, and Earth. An American flag neighbored by a Bell System flag flapped in the breeze. In the right-hand corner of the building, behind glass, perched a regal window clock, ticking steadily since 1929, reputed to be one of the world's most accurate timepieces, never wavering more than five-hundredths of a second. Atop the roof roosted one of the area's more improbable points of interest, a sixteen-ton winged bronze hero—the "Spirit of Communications"—which is the telephone company's symbol. In a feat of practicality that one would come to expect from the phone company, the thunderbolts it held up to the sky were not only symbolic but also functioned as lightning rods. At eight in the morning, a swell of phone workers was already parading through the blustery air, all these people converging, like the rays of a diamond, toward the big revolving doors, above which were really tiny black letters totally out of character with

the nature of the occupant: AMERICAN TELEPHONE AND TELE-
GRAPH BUILDING.

Inside the headquarters, there was a palpable feeling of great
size and great hush, of great sums of money being made and great
sums being spent. Acres of exquisite marble flooring stretched in
all directions. The muted lighting fell from big, brutish chande-
liers. Huge plants bloomed here and there. A somnolent, not
especially chic-looking place, like a courthouse or a government
office building, or the King of Siam's convention hall. Several
banks of coin telephones stood unused. Centrally situated was a
check-in desk for all visitors, where two drowsy-looking reception-
ists were engaged in earnest conversation. Watchdog security
guards patrolled the elevators, none of which whooshed directly to
the top. Occasional men and women bustled by. Woe betide the
straggler. Shreds of early morning talk: "We've got that important
meeting at nine, right, Bob?" "Roger." "Don't be late. Last time, I
was late and caught hell on wheels." "Roger." "How about that
speech yesterday? Should have been delivered at a cemetery."
"Did you see that dog they hired in accounting? She has to be a
whirlwind typist." "Do you know that for a fact?" "Well, I'd bet on
it." "Okay, here we go, another day making the telephones work."

Lumbering through the maze of relatively bare, unprettified
corridors in the catacomblike recesses of the building, I discovered
surprisingly spare and modest offices, less daunting than one
might find in the headquarters of a corporation a tenth as large.
Fluorescent tubes gleaming in the ceiling (flocks of them were
turned out, part of an energy-conservation program). Walls
covered with an array of artwork of various periods, regularly
rotated from one facility to another. Rabbit warrens of ordinary
metal desks, files spilling onto the floor. Signs of a company in
violent, headlong expansion. Attire bordered on the starchy side.
Lots of white shirts on the men, sober dresses on the women.
Placatory smiles. People seemed to be working with a sense of
considerable urgency. The hallways boasted stately drinking
fountains whose spouts were buttressed by small turbaned Orien-
tal maidens. The hallways were uncarpeted, except on the lofty
twenty-sixth floor where the top brass—including Charles (Charlie) Brown, the dexterous, stolid chairman—was sequestered. To
ever get that high for a privileged peek, a visitor needed to clear a
guard downstairs in the lobby, then another posted on the
twenty-sixth floor. "Welcome to Fort Knox," telephone people like

to greet visitors. As I strolled through the company offices, I paused to chat briefly with Frank Hutson, Jr., the corporate secretary, a warmly engaging and gracious man whose benign smile suggested that when he was a small boy he dreamed of being able to make all the phone calls he wanted free, and that the dream had come true. Hutson was a small, straight, Yale-schooled lawyer, and there was nothing he would rather talk about than the phone company. He said, "People think we're stuffy, aloof, all that. We're not. We're down-to-earth, and most of all we want to provide the best phone service at the cheapest possible cost." It was a motto I was to hear again and again. "Yeah," Hutson concluded, "we just want to help the people to talk."

This being phone country, the burr of the instruments and the banter carried over them were particularly conspicuous. There were thirty-three hundred phones in the building. Touch-Tones mostly. Phone company business (or nonbusiness) gets conducted predominantly on the telephone. A kinky-haired young woman on one floor was hugging one of them and blathering, "Now, does it come in a double album, or just a single album?" and not far off I overheard a stout man saying, "We'll have to discuss it. Lunch tomorrow?" In the sitting room just shy of the chairman's office there was a comfy couch, a wooden coffee table, and a stylish side table with a phone reposing on it. I wondered how many visitors sitting impatiently there awaiting the signal that the chairman would now see them thought it might be faster if they simply phoned from there.

Telephones are its trade, but the most conspicuous thing about the American Telephone and Telegraph Company is its size. It is, in fact, the biggest company on earth. AT&T runs off the edge of the imagination, with its bigness, its surprises, its imprint on anything and everything. With such vastness, most other companies are a mere dot, a minim. There is more of AT&T than anything else, a very great deal of it being people. No one, outside of the federal government, employs more human beings. Everyone seems to work for it, and 1,030,000 people actually do. Of these, there are 7,452 Smiths, 5,880 Johnsons, 3,934 Williamses, 3,660 Browns (one of them the chairman), and 3,547 Joneses. Someone once took time off from serious matters to calculate that if not for the arrival of automatic switching systems, the phone company would by now have to employ just about everyone alive simply to work the switchboards. As it is, if a skimpy 5 percent of its workers called in sick, the bedridden would equal the entire labor force of an average-sized city.

It is the wealthiest company. Its assets count up to an eye-popping $114 billion. That is a great deal of money in any man's language. That's more than the combined assets of General Motors, Ford, General Electric, Chrysler, and IBM, and more than the gross national product of all but some twenty countries. A particularly dear asset is a jumble of wire and cable long enough to stretch to the sun and back three times. The company makes a potful of money: a whopping $6 billion enters its bottomless belly every year. That is $16 million a day, $11,000 a minute. The company takes in revenues of a seductive $45 billion, shy of those realized by Exxon, General Motors, and Mobil—but who is to complain? (Actually, to AT&T folks, being anything but first in a category is almost a violation of the natural order of the universe.) The unrivaled 750 million shares of its common stock fill the safe deposit boxes of almost 3 million people, a raggle-taggle gang of investors that is more than twice as large as has plowed savings and hopes into any other company. Many of them (the preponderance own fewer than 100 shares) are decidedly untutored in the arcane nuances of high finance, but are flush with confidence that the nation's largest company will prosper as long as the nation itself does.

People on the subject of the phone company are something special. I guess I have spoken with several hundred people about AT&T, and I have been continually amazed by how many individuals harbor powerful feelings about it, one way or the other. People marvel at its gee-whiz technology, and they tell it to go fly a kite. But no one seems reluctant to air their views about the phone company. Here is a sampling of some of the things people have said to me (in person and on the phone)—ordinary customers, big businessmen, government officials, and phone company workers themselves.

"They are the worst company there is. I mean that. I think they're as corrupt as they come. Nobody is worse. I'm not kidding. The phone company is the absolute pits."

"I think they do a hell of a good job. Our phone system is the envy of the world, that's for sure. There are so many things today that are bad, it's refreshing to see something that is good."

"I have tremendous respect for the phone people. They've got a thankless job. I tell you, my phone always works."

"My phone never works. I haven't noticed anybody hightailing it over here to fix it. They are a monster that should be put in a cage and the key thrown away."

"You have to put up with them. Without a phone, you might as well be dead."

"I hate 'em! Hate 'em! Hate 'em! Hate 'em! My phone bills are just absurd. The government ought to run the phones, if you ask me. That's my opinion, the government ought to run the phones."

"Big is bad. I've said it all my life. Big is bad."

"I'm a free enterprise man, though I have to admit that even as a monopoly the phone company has been pretty damn good. I marvel at their ingenuity."

"Show me somebody who can do a better job. I haven't got any candidates. Who else is going to make the phones work? I admire them. I like phone people."

"Anybody could do a better job. I could do a better job."

"All they're interested in is money. If you look closely into the eyes of a phone worker, you begin to see dollar signs."

"It's a no-win situation. You give excellent service, and the rates are too high. You offer low rates, and the service is lousy. People have a need to complain. People want something for nothing. I believe the phone company does what is humanly possible. I also realize that that is not enough to suit many people. Too many people believe in the superhuman."

"That AT&T has one smooth mouth. If it weren't in the phone business, I'm sure it could do well selling soap or snake oil."

Spreading across all fifty states, the AT&T kingdom is actually a stew of various ingredients. The largest chunk of the empire is Western Electric, the sprawling manufacturing and supply branch that punctiliously churns out everything from strands of copper wire (enough each year to wrap around the world twenty-three hundred times) to telephones (15 million a year) to exotic telecommunications equipment. Then there is Long Lines, the manager of the long-distance network that tends conversations between states and across seas and international borders. There is brain-rich Bell Laboratories, innovator of the system's equipment, where the work of dreams is carried on; the personnel there have worked on just about everything, military or civilian, that people use to talk through, and it is hard to imagine any sort of communications device that would draw from them more than a glance. Finally, AT&T has complete or partial ownership in twenty-three operating companies scattered throughout the country that actually provide telephone service, most of them big enough themselves to rank among the nation's fifty largest utilities. Their names are etched in the consciousness of every person who pays a phone bill, so familiar they run like fountains all day in the mind. I repeat them here: New England Telephone and Telegraph; Southern New England Telephone; New York Telephone; New Jersey Bell Telephone; Bell Telephone Company of Pennsylvania; Diamond State Telephone; Chesapeake and Potomac Telephone Company of Maryland; Chesapeake and Potomac Telephone Company (D.C.); Chesapeake and Potomac Telephone Company of Virginia; Chesapeake and Potomac Telephone Company of West Virginia; Southern Bell Telephone and Telegraph; South Central Bell Telephone; Ohio Bell Telephone; Cincinnati Bell; Michigan Bell Telephone; Indiana Bell Telephone; Wisconsin Telephone Company; Illinois Bell Telephone; Northwestern Bell Telephone; Southwestern Bell Telephone; Mountain State Telephone and Telegraph; Pacific Northwest Bell Telephone; Pacific Telephone and Telegraph. The minuscule Diamond State, which serves only Delaware, is the smallest in the chain, the mammoth Southwestern Bell the largest (hotly pursued by Pacific Telephone). Through the lines of these companies ripple 180 billion conversations a year, 18 billion long distance calls, 300 million overseas, and the rest local.

As such things go, AT&T is a very old institution. It was spawned, of course, by Alexander Graham Bell's momentous invention of the telephone in 1876, at a time when the nation was a lonely and loosely-knit entity. The company's predecessor was the Bell Telephone Company, formed on July 8, 1877, with Bell a shareholder and the company's "electrician." He was paid $3,000 a year, and did not complain. After patenting the invention, Bell handed over his rights and business affairs to his principal financial backer and father-in-law, Gardiner Hubbard of Boston. Hubbard was the man who craftily cooked up the Bell Company's cornerstone policy of leasing—not selling—telephones. Most solid citizens of the day, however, looked on the telephone with half-lidded eyes—as a toy or some creation of witchcraft. Promotional money was hard to drum up. In the fall of 1876 or thereabouts, Hubbard grew strapped for cash and despondent over telephony's future and thus offered to sell all of the Bell patents to the Western Union Telegraph Company for $100,000, which in retrospect would have been the steal of a century. Western's president reportedly laughed in his face. Subsequently, Hubbard managed to scrape together the necessary cash to keep the Bell Telephone Company going.

In 1878, Hubbard hired Theodore Vail as general manager. Vail had been a telegraph operator and station agent for the Union Pacific Railroad, but his ambition led him to come to preside over the federal Railways Mail Service in Washington. Providing phone service was an assignment that, in these less complicated times, called for an engineer and a laborer. Now difficulties began to thicken to a point near desperation, and the business required scientific and diplomatic talents undreamed of before. Having second thoughts, Western Union came galloping into the telephone business. It had bought the telephone patents that Elisha Gray had filed only hours after Alexander Graham Bell had submitted his. What's more, Western Union had signed up the services of none other than Thomas Edison. His carbon-sensitized telephone transmitter was quite a bit better than Bell's. But the spunky Vail battled Western Union, then fifteen times the size of Bell, to a standstill. When Western Union, bleeding badly, tried to establish an agency in Massachusetts, Vail boldly sued for infringement of patents. In a settlement struck in 1879, Western Union acknowledged the validity of Bell's patents and agreed to keep out of the phone business. Bell purchased all of Western Union's telephones and exchanges and also agreed to steer clear of the telegraph field in territories occupied by Western Union.

In 1880, the grand design for the Bell System began to crystallize, with the American Bell Telephone Company organized to serve as the parent company of the system. Then, two years later, Vail bought control of the Western Electric Company so that he would always be assured of a ready supply of standardized equipment. In 1885, the company was completed by the incorporation, with Theodore Vail as president, of the American Telephone and Telegraph Company. It was chartered for the purpose of building and operating long lines connecting the city exchanges throughout the United States, Canada, and Mexico, and also with the rest of the world as that became desirable. All of one hundred years ago, Theodore Vail completed, in all its basic ingredients and most of its details, the model of a modern corporation that is today's AT&T.

Clouds appeared. Competitors were beginning to phalanx upon the phone business, and the intervenors seemed to be multiplying even more rapidly than the number of phones at large. When the Bell patents expired in 1893 and 1894, a tidal rise of independent telephone companies began to organize around the country, many in cities where there was already a Bell exchange. By 1907, about half the phones belonged to independent companies. Various interests—including that old nemesis, Western Union—were attempting to acquire these companies and assemble them into a huge rival system. Vail was having none of that. Raising money by the bushelful, he bought and merged into the Bell System as many independents as he could. He told the American public that AT&T was committed to stamping out dual telephone service. Too costly and not efficient. In 1908, he loosed a national advertising campaign revolving around the theme of "One System, One Policy, Universal Service." Two years after that, he managed to wrest effective control of Western Union and had himself elected president. He envisioned AT&T with both telephone and telegraph service. But the Justice Department punctured the dream when it threatened to throw an antitrust suit against AT&T in 1913. In December of that year, AT&T agreed to dispose of Western Union stock and relinquish the telegraph business. It also agreed not to purchase any more independent telephone companies except in deals approved by the Interstate Commerce Commission. Since that time, AT&T and the independents have lived in relative harmony. AT&T has expanded very little geographically, and its penetration of the telephone business in the United States has held fairly steady at about 85 percent. AT&T now owns and operates roughly 138 million phones (some 25,000 of them in the Pentagon, the largest single phone network in the world; the monthly bill averages $725,000). About 30 million phones, in half the American land area, including good-sized cities like Tampa, Florida, and Rochester, New York, as well as the entire states of Alaska and Hawaii, belong to sixteen hundred independents. Some of the smaller ones have such homey names as Farmer's Mutual Cooperative Telephone Company, the Yell County Telephone Company, the William Butts Telephone Company, and my personal favorite, the Silver Beehive Telephone Company.

The largest of this species is General Telephone and Electronics, serving about 15 million phones. Both AT&T and the independents are regulated in their practices by the federal government and the states, and they are interconnected with each other so that users of independent phones have no trouble getting hold of a Bell customer.

In a country indissolubly wedded to free enterprise, AT&T stands as a corporate enigma, being a regulated monopoly and the only major phone company in the world not owned and run by a national government. It is like some culture in a Petri dish about which scientists cannot agree whether it is harmful or beneficial. What is clear, though, is that AT&T's grip on the domestic phone market is not what it once was. Diminishing over the years ever so slowly, it has more recently taken visible leaps downward as administrative and judicial rulings have allowed a bevy of competitors to chisel away at its empire. The preoccupation of AT&T's top officers has shifted from the jolting service problems that plagued the system in the early 1970s, and that seem to have been permanently eradicated, to fending off competing companies. But the enterprise that its customers and shareholders refer to as "the phone company," or simply "Ma Bell," has already weathered a procession of roily events—suits, scandals, fires, financial headaches, earthquakes, strikes, wars, depression—to grow from a frail infant into an awesome giant. The impact of its product has gone from dew to downpour.

Its tasks are burdensome, and the Bell System is heavy with sixty-five hundred different job descriptions. The payroll works out to a staggering $21 billion a year. The average pay is $20,388, which could be to a handsomely paid cable splicer or a first-level supervisor. The lowest salary is $7,020 a year (an office clerk). The highest is $588,187 a year with bonuses (the chairman). The company is implanted deep in the nation's psyche, because AT&T employees manage to get fairly chummy with customers. Indeed, the company figures that it has far more contact with them than any other business. On an average day, it has calculated, it has 33 million brushes with customers, on the phone or in person, often prompted by one problem or another. ("No, I did not make any calls to Arkansas." "Yes, the phone is out. Without doubt, my phone is dead.")

Besides supplying home and business phone service, the Bell System superintends some 1.4 million pay phones. They are found in stores, on street corners, in subways, but also on Metroliner trains, stashed inside the Statue of Liberty, and rocking on some Coast Guard boats. Nothing is out of the question. A number of coin phones have been installed in forests to oblige talkative hunters. The decision on when to collect the coins from the phones (usually when about $72 piles up inside) is made by computer. In most cases it costs a dime to make a local call, though until recently it was a nickel in Louisiana and it's a quarter in Florida. Despite the relatively modest amount of money to be found in pay phones, they have long been a popular mark for criminals. Since it can take an embarrassingly long time to jimmy open and empty out a pay phone, coin robbers often take the whole phone with them, if they can. Ecologists once cleared out a Detroit municipal pond and discovered 168 coin phones buried in the debris. Some pay phone receivers rest on their hooks for months. At the other extreme, the phone near the ticket counter in the bowels of the Greyhound Bus Terminal on Chicago's Randolph Street is snatched up an average of 270 times a day. It's the busiest pay phone in the nation. Have to call the doctor? Go anywhere else.

AT&T's range strays some distance beyond phones. It is a major publisher. Each year, it turns out some 120 million copies of telephone directories (four hundred thousand tons of paper). The Bell System has to keep cranking out directories since about a quarter of all listings change each year. The print in them is a specially designed Bell Centennial, which recently replaced Bell Gothic. Bell Gothic has been used by eye doctors to test vision. The biggest directory in the country is Houston's. It has 2,899 pages and 939,640 listings, 8,350 of which are Smith. The smallest directory is one printed for Farley, Missouri. It has 3 pages and 282 listings, four of them Smith.

Not only does Ma Bell attend to real numbers, but also "dummy" numbers. When a telephone number is dialed or asked for in a movie or play, on the radio or TV, or in a short story or novel, chances are it's been furnished by the phone company from its supply of unworkable combinations. This wasn't always the case. The use of real telephone numbers in plays, novels, and the like was making people miserable almost from the day the telephone was invented. A cartoonist once made use of his home number in a drawing published in a national magazine. In the first two hours after the fatal issue hit the stands, the cartoonist's wife was obliged to answer the phone 106 times. It was hard on her, and she finally hurled the telephone from its cradle and went to bed. A TV skit once suggested that if you dialed the letters of the word "penguin," you'd hear a penguin squawk. Viewers dialed. No bird, just annoyed people. The phone company came to grips with the real number problem in 1938, when complaints from subscribers whose numbers had been used for such purposes began to reach alarming proportions. It started issuing, on request, numbers that linemen and repairmen use in testing phones, temporarily unassigned numbers, and unworkable combinations of numbers. All such test numbers give a busy signal. The phone company hands out something like a hundred dummy numbers a year from its assortment of electronic improbabilities. A telephone man and an Actors Equity lawyer once spent a couple of weeks sifting through telephone numbers before they found a musical phone number for Judy Holliday, star of "Bells are Ringing." (The number they picked was PLaza oh double-oh double-three.) Some movie companies have been using the same dummy number for years and have grown terribly sentimental about it; Universal Pictures wouldn't dream of giving up TRafalgar 7–5098.

Other things. The Bell System owns a grand total of 24,000 buildings (and rents space in another thousand). No company owns more. They range from glassy modern to brick elderly, from tiny microwave stations of 500 square feet squatting lonesomely on hillsides to the spanking new Southern Bell headquarters in Atlanta of close to 2 million square feet. And what downtown is complete without the familiar phone company building nestled in a prominent location? The Bell System splurges more on construction than any other company (something on the order of $15 billion a year), a good piece of the money going for a hundred or so new buildings ever-expanding the network.

The system is replete with a fleet of 177,000 motor vehicles, the biggest in private hands. It includes vans, station wagons, passenger cars, jeeps, vast brutes that lug cable around, trucks with cherry pickers, and scooters. A substantial number of employees ride bicycles around plants; some of them scurry about on tremendous tricycles. Bell owns or leases 17 planes, leases helicopters, and rents horses to get equipment into hard-to-reach areas. It pours away $160 million a year to maintain and replace vehicles (it buys about 20,000 a year, favoring no particular make) and keeps 4,000 garages in which to house and repair the fleet.

Still other things. AT&T has a navy of sorts: Long Lines owns a giant vessel that buries cable undersea to carry calls to foreign lands; New York Telephone keeps a boat to sink cable in metropolitan waters; Pacific Telephone has a barge to drop cable into bays. New York Telephone owns Empire City Subway, which digs up streets so cable can be put down. The system has a railroad. It's called the Manufacturers Junction Railway, and it chugs along 10½ miles of track in and around Western Electric's Hawthorne Works in Chicago, where telecommunications products are made.

For its annual meeting each spring, AT&T stuffs into the mails more invitations than go out for any event held on a regular basis. Frank Hutson is responsible for all the inviting. One might imagine he gets more frazzled than any party host worried about how many will show up, but his expectations are modest. As it turns out, AT&T gets more no-shows than any host could be expected to live down. Owing to indifference and problems of geography (it's a long haul from, say, Wyoming to New York for just one day), a healthy turnout is three thousand people. It was noticeably higher prior to 1970, when AT&T momentously ceased serving a free box lunch.

The phone company has swollen to its current vastness by always paying gallant attention to small things—little economies, little efficiencies, little people. As a result, whatever its continued unslakable expansion, its own workers have maintained a kind of implied boasting that takes the form of breezily dismissing the size. "Sure, the size of this place is as real as daybreak," one Bell System person told me. "But so what. Actually, when you've worked here awhile, you look at things differently. You don't smack your head every day and say, 'Good God, is this place big! How in the hell did it get so big?' I mean, sometimes you even think it's small."

2

Who Is Hello?

Every day, millions of telephones ring millions and millions of times. Nobody is obliged to answer them, but everyone does. Unthinkingly, people are willing to interrupt the delights of a pleasing supper, to spoil a delectable bath, to break the suspense of a TV soap opera, all to rush blithely to answer, their fantasies fed by the numberless possibilities waiting at the other end. The spell the phone casts is irresistible to almost all. Statistically, the United States is epitomized by three great homogenizing forces: television, the automobile, and the telephone. More than they are drivers or lookers, though, Americans are talkers. Some 95 percent of all American families, whatever their race, geographical location, financial standing, or educational attainment, have the opportunity to snatch up phones in their homes and call people— and, if they should all elect to avail themselves of the opportunity at the same time, to create clogged circuits of fantastic proportions. Only a smidgeon more than 28 percent of households have any kind of washing machine. Yet 30 percent of them boast two or more phones. There are twelve cities in the country that have more phones than people: Washington, D.C.; Southfield, Michigan; Columbus, Ohio; Evanston, Illinois; Richardson, Texas; Skokie, Illinois; Springfield, Illinois; Sunnyvale, San Francisco, Palo Alto, Newport Beach, and Fullerton, California. Every time a new city joins this select group, AT&T's public relations department issues a release congratulating itself on its latest conquest. Much to the phone company's consternation, however, there are still slightly more domiciles minus phones than without TV.

The telephone, despite its polymorphous character, has been largely snubbed by scholars and popular-culture pundits as a subject for sociological study. Precious little literature has grown up around its impact. Marketing and research types at AT&T, however, love nothing better than to take a crack at explaining the effect of their company's product. A veteran planning and research man at the phone company, his demeanor friendly and accommodating, talked one day about the use of the phone: "By now, of course, nobody even thinks about using the phone. It's a habit. People have told me that sometimes they were barely conscious that they were using the phone. It's almost an extension of the body. Alvin Toffler once remarked that the telephone is far more deeply wired into our lives than television, and indeed it is. My view of the phone is that it sort of acts as a social glue for the expanding population. No matter how far away you move, acquaintances are never more than a convenient phone call away. There's no doubt that the phone has hurt letter-writing. The number of telephone calls per person per year is something like three times as great as the number of first class and airmail letters per person, and telephone calls are growing about twice as fast as letter-writing is growing. The phone, though, isn't really replacing travel—not yet, at least. The number of phone calls and the number of air miles flown have increased at about the same rate, and the number of car miles traveled has gone up at about half that rate. It's amazing to think how much our lives are affected by the phone. You could look on it almost as a sort of societal insurance. Who knows how many lives have been saved, or how many injuries prevented, by a simple phone call? All of Wall Street operates on oral contracts struck over the phone. All these millions of dollars changing hands because of a few terse telephone commands. Something like 95 percent of Bell's internal business is conducted over the phone. Airlines couldn't operate without phones. Commodity markets would fold. Credit card systems probably couldn't function without the telephone to assure the validity of cards. Bookie operations are built around phones. Call girls took their name from the telephone. Even families on welfare are allowed phones—for safety purposes and to call prospective employers for jobs. What was once a luxury is in every sense a necessity. President Johnson was a real phone maven. He pioneered the car phone as a status symbol, and he was one of the earliest users of the call director. He became so attached to the phone that he created 'executive override,' a system that enabled him to talk to whomever he wanted whether or not they were already talking to someone else. People don't feel entirely comfortable in a new home until that phone is put in. As we all know, one of the standard terror scenes in a thriller movie is when the culprit stealthily cuts the phone line with a knife. Everybody gulps. By my reckoning, Ingrid Bergman and Cary Grant in *Notorious* hold the distinction of indulging in the longest telephone kiss in history. It just goes on and on until you're squirming in your seat and absolutely dying for it to end."

The research man talked about answering the phone: "It's always interested me that people answer the phone in different manners. Alexander Graham Bell would scoop it up and say, 'Ahoy,' a ship's greeting. In England, people answer and give the number being called. In Germany, they say, 'I'm listening,' which is what you'd expect them to be doing, I would think. Back in the 1940s, you know, the phone company mounted a campaign to get people to stop saying 'Hello' when they answered the phone, since we think this is superfluous and totally uninformative. We wanted them to answer with their name. Then you know right away whether you've got the person you wanted. We sent out a ton of blotters that were inscribed: Who is Hello? Unfortunately, the campaign didn't work so well, though in business it's pretty common to answer with your name. You'll notice that if you call anybody in the phone company, that's how they answer. One of the nice things about the phone is that it's totally democratic. You don't have any idea who's calling until you pick it up. Everyone is equal, at least until he starts speaking. Sometimes, matter of fact, the phone caller has some more rights than the person in the flesh. Recently, I went to Bloomingdale's for a bottle of perfume for my wife. There was a line of fifteen people at the perfume counter. I was in kind of a cranky mood and didn't really want to wait around just to find out if they even carried the scent I was interested in. So I walked outside, found a phone, and dialed Bloomingdale's and asked for the perfume department. I got right through and was told they had the scent. They said they'd have it ready for me, and I said I would be over in a few minutes."

Then the AT&T man talked about fear of phoning: "For senior citizens, in general, we've found that the telephone is something of an intrusion. One of our studies showed that the sound of the phone bell was most commonly an unpleasant experience for older people, since they tended to associate a phone call with bad news, often of somebody dying. On the other hand, the same ringing sound has a stimulating effect for people in early middle age or younger, since it promises them relief from boredom. Therapists have encountered certain personality types who can't at all cope with the phone. They literally fear making a call. I assume there aren't all that many of this type, but I understand that a treatment has been worked up. For instance, with a male patient, he might be instructed to call up the therapist and, assuming she's female, request a date. The woman will be totally receptive at first. In succeeding calls, however, she plays harder and harder to get. If the patient hangs in there, he presumably conquers his phone problems."

Some glimmerings about just how the phone gets used can be gleaned from phone company market studies—numerous and never-ending pastiches of who calls when and how much and to whom. The United States is now considered "full," saturated with phones, all kitchen walls and night tables reserved—roughly 1.7 phones per home. The trend away from the nuclear family to singles living alone has contributed to the development of slightly fewer phones per household but higher usage. Some 5 percent of households still have no phones at all—there are many reasons why: the inhabitants are cheap, they're senile, they really like to be left alone—but no amount of marketing persuasion will do anything for them. They are not phone inclined. One of the astounding facts to be culled from AT&T snooping is that phone usage grows at a rate that almost defies analysis. One would not expect particularly rapid telephone growth once a nation had reached the saturation point, as the United States has. Yet telephone usage continues to climb at a breakneck pace, much faster than the rate of population growth. It has been theorized that telephone usage might grow by the square of population growth, since every new person would create two new telephone conversations, but that doesn't work either. Telephone usage grows faster than that, at roughly 8 percent a year.

A Bell Labs statistician explained something of the growth model for phone usage: "Three main factors actually come into play: the size of the population, its demographics, and its mobility. Mobility is related to a very important variable called 'community of interest.' People are clearly going to be communicating with people with whom they share a certain interest. So people who move from one community to another leave behind interests that they are going to keep in touch with. They will call people in their new community as well as their old one. So the population can be entirely stable, but if it moves around, phone usage will rise."

According to evidence the phone company has collected, the average family spends approximately a half-hour a day on the phone. It makes and receives a total of 32 calls a week, just under 5 a day. A smallish amount more are outgoing than incoming. Roughly 4 in every 100 calls are long distance (which the phone company, in its studies, defines as further than 100 miles away). AT&T has found that there is quite a sizable body of people in the country who practically never make any long-distance calls, a contingent that, according to the phone company's latest figures, comprises around 40 percent of the population. Some of these people, it is speculated, are worried about long-distance charges. However, a good portion of them, the company found, certainly had the income and education profile that would have suggested a long-distance caller. All that AT&T was able to conclude was that a lot of people either have no relatives or friends in towns other than their own, or else they have relatives and friends in other towns but they don't particularly care to talk to them, at least not on the phone. Marketing people refer to these persons as "detached communicators."

Overall, however, phone company studies have found that somewhere between 40 percent and 50 percent of calls originating from a particular household are made within only a 2-mile radius. In one study of an urban area, about a fifth of all residential calls went to the same receiving number. The next four most frequently called numbers accounted for nearly 40 percent of all calls. "What we can only conclude," one marketing person told me, "is that a lot of people seem to keep a fairly restricted phone acquaintance."

Household banter on the telephone fluctuates tremendously according to the size and life cycle of the family. Young families make an average of thirty-six calls a week. Older families make a lot more calls (forty-eight a week). Single households get on the phone the least of all (about twenty times a week). However, the last group makes the highest percentage of long-distance calls and the windiest calls. The heaviest talkers of all (according to the findings of several studies) are the households with teenage children that recently came to roost in a new neighborhood in the same metropolitan area. Presumably they will be calling new neighbors as well as old ones, and will be less deterred by long-distance charges than the family that uproots itself and settles far away. Forgetting about income and transiency, the most significant single factor determining how many calls a household will place is the number of people in the family who are old enough to use the phone. Few people can be ruled out anymore. The telephone company has always made a habit out of blanketing grade schools with goodwill ambassadors who can run filmstrips and demonstrate how to use the phone. Thus kids become a consequential element of the phone crowd as early as five years old. Few five-year-olds are scared to pick up a ringing phone today and see who's calling (in fact, many kids seem to answer the phone by outright demanding, "Who is it?"). A seven- or eight-year-old often routinely places his own calls. They tend to be to the point: "Hank, come on over." "Okay." "See ya." "Yeah."

Next to the sheer number of people, the most important factor influencing the quantity of calls is a woman on the premises between the ages of nineteen and sixty-four. Women are the preeminent talkers, in jokes as well as in reality. Of the thirty-two calls a week that the average family makes and receives, the score is nineteen for the female and only ten for the male (put down three for the kids). However, Bell marketing people have found that in lower-middle-class families the man tends to act as a gatekeeper on the wife's phone usage. That doesn't happen in the higher economic classes. The second most important boost to telephone originations is the presence of a man over sixty-five who is not the head of the household. Then comes the presence of a girl between the ages of thirteen and eighteen, then a girl or boy under ten (both genders apparently are gabby at this age). When the head of the household is past fifty-five, the number of calls tumbles fairly rapidly. The length of time per call tapers off even more rapidly. (It is an odd footnote that researchers have noticed that people, when asked how many calls they make each day, invariably guess too high. The reason is that people generally don't distinguish between outgoing and incoming calls, but merely bunch them all together. Rate awareness studies find that people also significantly overestimate what a call costs, perhaps because long distance rates have come down over long periods of time.)

More information: the most puzzling statistic to many people who care about phone marketing is that usage doesn't seem to go up with the number of phones. "We simply have found no correlation between the number of phones and usage," an AT&T marketing man told me. "In other words, the household with three phones is not necessarily generating more calls than the household with one. In marketing, there is no one who doesn't have the gut feeling that more phones produce more calls. But we don't have any uncontestable evidence to that effect."

About seven out of ten calls, market research shows, are social calls. Another 12 percent are service calls, 10 percent are connected to one's job, 5 percent have to do with community service, and 3 percent are either unspecified or not completed.

Who you are seems to have a definite bearing on how long you take with each call. Overall, the average duration of a call works out to slightly more than 7 minutes for the young couple, young family, older family, and older couple household. In contrast, calls in young single and older single households are significantly more windy—lasting 10.2 minutes and 9.2 minutes respectively. Female heads-of-households and other adult females, it should come as no surprise, spend more time on the phone than anyone else, clocking slightly less than 3 hours a week of phone calls. The phone company has even gone to the trouble of arriving at how many words people fit in during their conversations. One of its projects found out that a slow speaker will average 450 words in a 3-minute call, while a speedy fellow will squeeze in a full 750, and therefore acquire a far better bargain. Were the phone company able somehow to convince everyone to slow their speech by one-half, its revenues would climb wildly.

A smattering of calls drag on for more than twenty minutes. Who's making them? Talkative teenagers yakking away. Engineers with data-sets at home who are conversing with computers, seeking remedies to their thorny problems. Babies are on some of the lines. Parents cunningly arrange to call a neighbor they are to visit, then leave the receiver off the hook beside the card table so that they can keep tabs on what's happening in the nursery while they slap down the canasta cards.

People don't make calls in an entirely random fashion as the day passes. The network is most heavily used on specific days —namely, holidays—and during certain portions of the day. Volume drifts up on rainy days. The heavier the storms, the heavier the calling. Calls from business phones peak at about eleven in the morning, then diminish to only around half of that volume between noon and one in the afternoon, then ascend nearly as high as the morning peak about three. Suburban studies point out that residential calling hits its highest point between three-thirty and four-thirty in the afternoon, this being the time when school kids are released from class and get on the phone to set up their evening plans. Households headed by somebody over sixty-five generally do most of their talking in the morning, when they are otherwise unoccupied.

Calls seem to drag on longer once the sun sets, and the later it gets, the longer the calls seem to last; after ten-thirty, for instance, conversations average nearly eight minutes. Presumably people feel lonelier in the evenings and reach for the phone and some audio companionship. Also, during the day many calls are abrupt, functional exercises—to see if the hardware store carries Liquid Plumber, to find out if Sadie's coming over for tea—whereas in the evening it's time to settle in and really hear what's doing with relatives and friends.

On February 27, 1975, the Great Phone Fire ravaged a key switching center of the New York Telephone Company and knocked out 170,000 phones in a 300-block area of Manhattan. For twenty-three days, twelve exchanges—an AL, three GRs, three ORs, a CA, an SP, an LE, a YU and one 260—were silent, disrupting the communications of some 90,000 Ma Bell subscribers. The phone blackout provided a ripe opportunity for phone company researchers to see how people behave minus phones, and so, immediately after New York Tel restored service, a gang of investigators phoned 600 randomly picked phone numbers and (after discarding business phones, disconnected telephones, no answers, and the obstinately uncooperative) amassed responses from 190 people on questions such as how much phoning they did, how they felt about using the telephone, whether they missed their phone, and what other forms of communications they relied on during the blackout period. Did they visit more? Did they send telegrams? Did they become hermits? Did they go berserk?

Half the sample replied that they made and received three to five calls a day. They said they perceived the phone as a necessity of daily living. Curiously, they looked on it as indispensable enough that hardly any of them increased their use of other communications means during the blackout. Nearly half said that, to get in touch with others, they used the emergency street phones the telephone company had provided, and a third said they made calls from work, regardless of what their bosses might have said about that. Only 10 percent reported writing more letters, and less than 2 percent said they had sent telegrams. Four out of five respondents confessed to missing the phone. The majority agreed that they felt either "isolated" or "uneasy." Life became more "frustrating" for more than half of them. The majority said they were "more in control of things" once phone service was restored. In short, nothing but the telephone would do. There was no alternative.

Despite the evidence, and despite the protestations of the phone company, there are still those 5 percent of households that don't have phones. While 5 percent of anything doesn't sound like much, it represents 2.8 million households. Little is known about these people. The most curious, it would seem, are those who choose to go phoneless not because of lack of money or lack of anybody to call, but who simply detest phones.

I met a young woman in her mid-twenties who was working as a waitress in a tawdry coffee shop while her acting career found its momentum. She had no phone. She had never had a phone since fleeing her parents' home several years previously. She was not flush, but she could have found the room in her budget to put in a phone. Why, then, no phone?

"I reject phones," she explained. "You get calls that wake you up. You get calls from cranks and nuts. You get calls from people who want to sell you something. You get calls from drips who you don't want to see. Yuk! It really bugs me that people make so much of the phone. If you get tons of calls, you're Miss Popularity. If you don't get calls, you're a deadbeat. Frankly, that just tees me off. If you're at your place all day and no calls come in, you start to get depressed. Why doesn't anyone call? Aren't I somebody? I don't have that worry. Nobody can, in fact, call. I am unwilling to complicate my life by having a phone. I'd rather deal with my life in a more natural way."

How did she arrange to see people? I asked.

"I'll tell you, I do a lot of what many people in big cities think is not only kooky but socially reprehensible. I just show up at apartments of people I want to see. And I get in touch with people on my lunch hour. I use pay phones when I have to. And I drop people notes. Nobody drops people notes. I do."

What about the protection a phone affords? What if an emergency comes up?

"It ain't happened yet."

3

When You See Red, Get Yourself Moving

It was 9:00 A.M. The East Coast was at work. Phones were jangling. Orange and red squares were dancing up and down the board. "Hello, Granny, this is Ed." "Tom, I'm gonna need that report right away, this afternoon at the latest." "Mom, please, Mom." Meantime, the West Coast was asleep. Snores, heavy breathing. It was 6:00 A.M. there. No squares were flipping. Phones sat peacefully in their cradles. The Midwest was beginning to shuffle along to work. Conversation was minimal. Just a trickle of calls, one orange square.

"You want to know what's happening, you just peek at that board," one of the supervisors was saying. He was a tall, offhand man with the direct bearing and firm jaw of an officer in the Marines. He was stroking his firm jaw. "Those squares are telling you the telephonic pulse of the nation. See the orange and red squares? Those are people hitting the phones."

It would not be at all clear what was happening here if you were walking in cold on the scene. The eyes of a visitor appear almost bedazzled after a brief encounter with the board. This was the Network Operating Center, in Bedminster, New Jersey, one of the denser jungles in the topography of communications. This was where the Long Lines Department managed all of the nation's long-distance calling between states and to foreign lands. By any reckoning, it was the busiest communications center on earth. The network operating room was a large, open space located in the low (so low, in fact, that it was almost underground) Long Lines headquarters that stretched out beside leafy woods in a tranquil area an hour and a half from New York. From the adjoining highway, the entire building was invisible. People were coming and going, speaking in terse sentences. The place seemed rather public, as if it were a depot. A caravan of fifth-graders from a nearby school gawked downward from an elevated observation deck. The atmosphere around the center suggested a scientific frontier. For some, the watching could become almost an addiction.

The focus of attention was a gargantuan board mounted on the main wall, split up into twelve columns. Names of cities ran down the columns. The board resembled the kind used in railway stations for the listing of incoming trains. In this case, however, the cities stood for primary switching stations within the sprawling telephone network. Beside the station names were colored flaps (known in the blue haze of phone company terminology as bi-states) triggered by computers. When heavy traffic swarms through a high-usage route, an orange flap clacks into place. When a final switching system is choked with calls, a red flap pops up. That's cause for alarm (but never panic). If more calls pour in, they aren't going to get anywhere. Customers will hear a very rapid busy signal, which will continue until the lines open up as callers drop off or, better yet, the phone company watchers do something.

"Yes, when those red babies go," one of the men in the room said, "when those red babies go, we hustle."

The phone system is vaguely mysterious. Many billions of dollars, the imaginative resources of thousands of scientists and engineers, and assiduous manufacture by hundreds of thousands of workers have gone into it. It takes nothing more than a few seconds delay in dial tone to stoke the ire of many customers, who may begin to wonder why the government hasn't taken over the phones already, but the wonder is that problems don't rage unchecked through the phone network. The things that take place in the simplest of calls—to the nice lady across the street—are gallimaufric. Any attempt to explain the full mechanics of the phone system in engineering terms is next to impossible, for one would be obliged to rewrite a set of extracts from technical manuals, but in crude summary it works something like this.

Taking the phone off the hook lets you into the network. This disengages a spring that closes a circuit. In a less complicated era, a light simply flickered on before an operator sitting at a switchboard. In would go a plug. On would come a voice. "Hello, number please." As the number of phones swelled, this way of doing business wasn't going to do. (Old ways, though, die hard. The last manual office in the Bell System was sent to the switchboard graveyard only in March 1978. It had cheerily operated on Catalina, a tiny island floating off the Southern California shore. People there had phone numbers like 3, 129, and 46. The phone book was the size of a steno pad. Many of the residents were awfully fond of the old system, and they complained to the hilt when it was displaced. For those who remember that far back, there was nothing to compare to the local operator —somebody named Millie or Winnie—who would place every call, disgorging all the neighborhood gossip in the process.) With phone demand rapidly escalating, the phone company was lucky that a wily Kansas City undertaker named Almon B. Strowger concluded in 1889 that sloppy operators were misdirecting many of his incoming calls, losing him precious bodies. He needed all the bodies he could get. He would fix that. He invented an automatic dialing system. The nucleus of his conception was that the closing of the circuit could not only flip a switch but also work a motor. The motor was the key, because it, in turn, could move an electrical contact point to a host of different positions that would thereby connect with one of a slew of wires. As Strowger worked things out, the first three turns of the dial, or steps, would automatically connect the caller to the central office for the subscriber whose number was being called. Then the subsequent four would get the caller directly to the recipient of the call. (With push-button phones, acoustical tones at varying pitches trigger the switching gear.)

Wire is the string with which the whole phone system is sewn together. There's wire everywhere in the phone network. Torrents of wire: diving into sewers, fanning out to terminals on tremendous steel frames, poking out of the wall beside your bedroom night table. When AT&T studies its need for new wire, it figures in terms of b.c.f.—billion conductor feet. To handle new capacity and replace worn-out strands, the phone company needs four hundred such lengths—each enough wire to span the distance to the moon—every year. The line that runs to your home phone is, in fact, nothing more than a "cable pair" of wires twirled together. It snakes out from the phone on your kitchen wall, out beneath the street, usually for miles, to a central office. (Unlike local calling, most long distance calls of more than a few hundred miles, after initially traveling through wire to the local office, are flung between microwave towers, bizarre-looking things crowned with antennas like great horns that repose on hills every few miles in all directions throughout the country. Some overseas calling is done by satellite relay, the balance by giant submarine cables. One of the more wondrous inventions of the phone company is the TASI system [Time Assignment Speech Interpolation], created for use on the very costly transatlantic cable, which vastly increases call capacity by managing to sandwich additional conversations into the pauses that take place in other calls. One drawback of submarine cable is that hooks dropped by sea trawlers sometimes rip up cable. Long Lines periodically deposits T-shirts and leaflets on trawlers that remind the crews to beware of phone equipment.)

Once it winds into the central office, the wire is curled around a steel frame and attached to bulky chemical storage batteries. As it happens, the phone system still works, as it did a century ago, on a low-voltage direct current. (That is why the phones rang during the big power blackouts in New York in 1965 and 1977, and everybody thought how terrific the phone company was.) As you speak into the mouthpiece of your phone, the sound waves from your voice are transformed into electrical waves that bounce off a diaphragm (a circular wafer of thin aluminum that vibrates against a chamber stuffed with hundreds of grains of carbon). The waves move through the carbon chamber and out through the switching gear to the party called. Along the way, your voice undergoes some stunning changes: in many instances, it's actually broken up into small digital bits and added to a common voice line transporting other bits from other conversations. The bits of different voices all travel at the same speed so that, unlike cars on a freeway, they can't bash into each other. Once your voice arrives at the party called, the receiver converts the electrical impulses back into sound waves, and the person hears whatever it is you called to say. In the United States, connections like this can be made among more than 150 million telephones hooked in through about 10 million billion possible connections. To get two voices speaking to one another, however, takes a switching unit.

To return to Strowger's step-by-step switching system. This

continues to connect a certain number of phones in the Bell System, but it's slow and necessitates a sizable amount of maintenance. The panel system hit the scene in 1914 (and is still in limited use). With this approach, so-called common controls zip up and down metal frames bearing the wires coming from customers' homes. By touching a set of wires, these controls complete a call, and then, when the call is done, move on to other calls. Moving controls, however, weren't nirvana, and they were improved upon by a Swedish invention known as the crossbar system, which was imported into America in 1926. The No. 5 Crossbar, the ultimate in this system, remains the most common installation in the telephone system. The way the crossbar is designed, wires for incoming calls are strung on the horizontal part of a giant frame and wires for outgoing calls on the vertical. Magnetically driven switches complete calls by closing shut across a set of vertical and a set of horizontal wires.

Meanwhile, in an attempt to serve the burgeoning growth of the telephone industry, and to solve some of its consequent economic problems, Bell Labs people began to tinker with the idea of an electronic switching system—no mechanical parts at all. Designing the ESS turned out to be one of the hardest things human beings have ever tried to do. All of a dozen years of intense work were required. Equipped with the ability to offer all sorts of snazzy services (like conference calls to several numbers at once), ESS machinery began to come into use with an installation in the improbable locale of Succasunna, New Jersey, in 1965. A third of all local offices are now ESS; by 1990, as much as 90 percent ESS is expected.

I examined one of the giant ESS systems at a Midwestern Bell installation and, with the aid of a veritable army of phone company technicians, was able to get something just beyond a feeble understanding of its intricate, not quite indescribable workings. The office, lighted by overhead fluorescent bulbs, was filled with computers, tape reels making intermittent jerky starts and stops, and rows of storage and retrieval discs that whirled at high speed. It is difficult to imagine what an ESS can do until one is told what it can do, and then it is still difficult. For instance, what looks like scarcely more than a bland forest of tall gray steel cabinets can take care of as many as 550,000 calls an hour without getting tired. Associated with ESS is a flock of bizarre numbers. ESS performs in mere millionths of a second (referred to as microseconds) the same switching operations that standard electromechanical units take thousandths of a second to perform (called milliseconds). Certainly the scant fractions of time saved may not seem terribly useful to the ordinary individual, who has never done anything much in a single microsecond, but not so to ESS. In the five to ten seconds that it takes the typical person to dial a telephone number, an ESS can handily polish off millions of chores. "If you want me to put a perspective on this kind of speed," one of the Bell technicians calmly pointed out, "then just mull over the fact that these babies get millions of jobs done in a microsecond, and then consider that there are more microseconds in a minute than minutes in a century."

Within the dark confines of an ESS, a central control unit plugs away, dishing out orders that come to it in the form of electrical pulses. The unit is itself controlled by a permanent memory, a sort of electronic textbook crammed with instructions on how to complete a telephone call. Rather than being recorded on pages, however, these instructions are stored on magnetic discs in the form of millions of bits. (Bits are coded dots that are basically yes-or-no responses to prestated questions. The bits are read off the discs and translated into electrical pulses by magnetic heads vaguely similar to what are found in tape recorders.) Also within the ESS are so-called temporary memories. These record the condition of phone lines and dial pulses by "reading" and "writing" electrical resistance.

So much for ESS's innards. As for its performance, when ESS is working, high-speed scanners gaze at as many as twenty thousand telephone lines every one hundred milliseconds to check whether they are on or off. In effect, the scanners are asking: does anyone want to make a call? When somebody does wish to and snatches up his receiver from its cradle, a scanner instantly senses the presence of voltage and reports it to control. Control quickly consults with the temporary memory, which relates the fact that a mere fraction of a second ago the phone was doing nothing. Aha, control gets the idea that the customer wants to call someone. Next, a series of orders go out. The switching network is told to send the customer a dial tone. Space is set aside in the temporary memory to register the digits of the phone number about to be dialed. Control discerns from the permanent memory the customer's number and what kind of line—either party, coin, or private

—he is using. After the human laggard sitting in his office manages to get his mind and finger working together well enough to begin dialing (by which time the ESS will have disposed of numerous additional operations), control dashes back and forth between memories, asking the temporary one for the digits it has recorded and the permanent memory for a translation of the digits into orders. Once control has determined that there is a line free to send the call out on, it orders outpulsing to begin. Outpulsing is simply the sending out of the number that Laggard wants to call. Once outpulsing is finished, control orders a ringing connection to the number being phoned and a ring-back tone to the customer making the call. Many people think that the ringing they hear is in fact the ringing of the other person's phone in his living room. Not at all. Then, as soon as the called party grabs the receiver (possibly hurtling out of the bathtub to do so), the ESS office instantly connects the two lines. With a local call, all of the activity between the conclusion of dialing and the first ring takes place in just a couple of seconds. To assure the phone company that it gets paid for its service, the temporary memory records the precise time that the called party answers and the time that he hangs up. This information is recorded on a magnetic tape which is shipped off to a computing center that figures out the rate for the call; it then gives the data to your local billing department. When you're done with your call, if you forget and leave the phone off the hook for more than a few seconds, the line is connected to a howling noise (known as a "permanent signal") that tells you to put that phone back where it belongs so somebody else can call you.

Calling long distance, as might be expected, takes a trifle longer. What happens is that the call trundles through a hierarchy of switching offices, like a football being handed off to a succession of players. There are five levels: in telephone terminology, they are the local office, the toll office, the primary office, the sectional office, and, at the top of the heap, the regional office. At present, there are roughly 18,000 local offices, 1,400 toll, 265 primary, 75 sectional, and 12 regional. The movement from office to office is not killingly slow. You can place a call completely across the country and have the phone at the far end ringing within several seconds in most instances.

No two central offices are altogether alike. They are tailored, to the extent that they can be, to the community they serve. To figure out what capacity an office should be designed for, engineers pick several busy hours in the busy season for that area and look at numbers of calls and lengths of calls (arrived at by traffic studies), factor in a certain amount of blocking (blocking occurs when calls can't get through), and then design capacity for that load. "It's a bit like figuring out how many ladies' rooms to have in an office building. You take a look at the peak traffic and figure out how long the ladies will sit in there and then you work it out," is how one engineer explained it to me. Traffic is measured in "erlings." An erling means that a line is busy for an hour. "If I picked up the phone and talked to my wife for an hour, which you better believe I wouldn't ever do, I would generate one erling of traffic," an engineering vice president explained. A suburban line would typically generate a tenth of an erling during a busy hour; a business office would register two- and three-tenths of an erling.

Offices are basically designed so that anywhere from 10 to 20 percent of the subscribers served by a given central office can pick up the phone at the same time and make a telephone call. Most of the time, that is plenty of capacity. During unusual circumstances, though, callers will occasionally find themselves blocked. They are notified of this either through a busy signal that blips at twice the speed of a normal busy signal (known as reorder), a recorded announcement trumpeting the fact, or when all the recorded announcements or reorders are in use, your line will just go dead (a condition described in telephone circles as "high and dry"). Blockage is rare on a local call, and the entire long-distance network is engineered for a 1 percent blockage rate, meaning that 1 out of 100 calls won't get through at the busiest hour, which is ten to eleven o'clock in the morning on weekdays. When too many calls congest a system and there is blockage, the calls are handled chronologically as they come in, except for certain priority numbers—doled out to the likes of the mayor, the police station, the fire house, and hospitals—that get first attention.

Very well. In recent years, the most advanced ESS systems have worked in conjunction with a technology known as CCIS —Common Channel Interoffice Signaling. Rather than carry a voice together with information on the call's origin and destination on only one line, the switching system splits up the data. Since 30 percent of calls are not completed (busy or nobody home), a trunk line has to be put into use only after the CCIS line reports that there's no busy signal at the other end. This allows more capacity to be handled on the expensive long-distance trunks.

Because an ESS must keep on completing those calls no matter what if there is not to be a revolution, it has been designed to keep a close watch on itself. It is able to do this because an ESS, like Siamese twins, comes stocked with two of everything. It's got two central control units, two permanent memories, and so on. The two controls use every spare microsecond to give each other a thorough audit. Every switching problem gets solved by both units, and then when one of them makes a goof, the central control units sort of argue back and forth with each other until one of them persuades the other that it is the dumbo. "These are sane machines," a technician explained to me, "and the one that erred will not be ashamed to acknowledge that it was wrong." Click. Off goes the faulty control unit. Its twin promptly takes up the entire burden of providing telephone service, and simultaneously combs through the diseased partner to try to figure out what happened. (On exceptionally rare occasions, it is possible for both twins to break down concurrently.) Callers, meanwhile, have no idea that anything has gone awry; they can't tell which of the twins is taking care of them, or whether one is having a nervous breakdown. Once the healthy unit has figured out the ailment, it prints out the diagnosis in funny code on a teletypewriter. Then since the ESS cannot do the rest alone, that all-but-outmoded contraption, a human being, appears to do the dirty work of fixing the unit.

From the office to the observation deck to the network board itself, I wandered around among the Bedminster crew, was offered and accepted coffee, and squinted with imaginary experience up and down the board, where the colored squares had, if anything, increased. Every twelve seconds, all phone circuits are automatically sampled and the flaps change to represent the new conditions. Orange flaps appeared in Eau Claire, Iowa; Atlanta, Georgia; Waukesha, Wisconsin; Camden, New Jersey.

The crew at the time numbered seven. The daily watch begins, in full strength, at eight in the morning, and goes on till around five in the evening. The board is manned by someone at all times, but the sentries tend to thin out with the lengthening of the day. No matter the magnitude of the crew, august computers are keeping close watch themselves at all times. "A good rule of thumb," a Long Lines man said to me, "is that people tend not to place a great many calls in the dead of the night."

What's happening is this: if you make a long-distance call —Uncle Norton in Buffalo wants to chat a bit with his niece Olive in Portland—and the first-choice route on the network is clogged with calls, then the call is automatically shunted along other routes. Once the final channel of the hierarchy (the regional switching center) is reached, however, network managers have to do something or calls won't go through.

Robert Madden, one of the network supervisors, was peering fixedly at the board. His eyes darted up and down the columns. He is a big man, with big gestures, disheveled hair, a weathered face, and frequent smiles. Walking away from the board, Madden fell into a ruminative mood, smiled crookedly, and said, "The way the system works is the engineers design the telephone circuits based on averages. Bell doesn't provide enough service for the busiest hour on the busiest day. That would be nutty. It provides enough for the average volume. We take care of the surges, the unexpected, the bizarre. We take care of the wacky. Basically, we step in when things get hairy."

When that happens, network people can manually divert calls along less occupied circuits. This is called, in the parlance of telephony, a TORC—traffic overload reroute control—and is accomplished by calling whichever of the twelve regional switching centers are involved and telling their managers to push some buttons. The idea is to take advantage of time zones. Early morning calls heading from Chicago to Atlanta can be whisked to San Bernardino (where circuits would be empty) and then onward to peach country.

Sample conversation:

"San Bernardino here."

"San Bernardino, take Atlanta."

"Will do. Good day."

Callers, incidentally, won't have the foggiest notion what's going on with their call. Telephone signals bolt across the country at 150,000 miles a second. At that clip, who cares about a 3,000-mile detour? Matters get particularly frenzied in Bedminster every Christmas and Mother's Day (Father's Day, though, is okay). Everyone's chattering away ("Well, Merry Christmas, Sam," and "Now, have a super day, Mom"), and network people are shooting calls all over the place. On Mother's Day, the champion calling day of the year, blockage on calls may bob up to 20 percent for brief periods. Every now and then, network managers witness an unforgettable spectacle. Their eyes swim with calculations.

When a massive earthquake rocked Southern California in 1971, the network board lit up like a tote board after the daily double. ("We were really going smoking rockets then," Madden said.) If a hot TV movie is playing, the board will tell you when there's a commercial break as viewers make a blaze of calls to friends to see what's cooking. One of the worst days in American telephony was April 13, 1945, when the radio reported that Franklin Roosevelt had died, and just about everybody in the country reached for his phone. The slaying of John Kennedy unloosed almost as much calling.

Bob Madden said, "One of the worst problems that we ever had was the New York fire, when that central office burned down. We spent six weeks rerouting calls. Some calls going from New Jersey to Long Island had to be hauled all the way to the West Coast and back to be completed. At one juncture, we had a hundred and sixteen reroutes in effect simultaneously. Weather's always a worry. For instance, a tornado tore up a trailer camp in Orlando the other day. That lit up the Florida circuits like Broadway after dark. We constantly monitor weather reports from the wire services, and we keep the TV news on to see what's doing. When Elvis Presley died, a lot of entrepreneurs, as you know, saw a chance to clean up by selling these Elvis products. A number of them advertised their wares on TV with area code 800 numbers to call. We had to do a lot of rerouting to handle those calls. But it was a short-lived difficulty, like a crack of thunder —here and gone. On winter Sunday mornings, we have a surge of calls from the Northeast to Florida. I don't know why. My theory is that the Sunday paper is full of travel ads for sunny Florida. You see snow outside, and so you pick up the phone and call Florida.

"The funny thing is we don't have any more messages on Christmas than today. Yet most of the board isn't lit up now and on Christmas it's blinking like crazy. How can that be? The thing is, the average conversation then is double what it is today. To-day, the average conversation is six or seven minutes. On Christmas, the average call is twelve or fourteen minutes. We've fought Christmas a long time now. Yeah, we've fought that beast for a lot of years. We know what to do by now."

Noontime. The East Coast was stepping out for lunch. The West Coast was opening its mail. Orange and red flaps were popping on and off like popcorn cooking on a stove. Sacramento flicked orange. Fort Worth went red. Computer terminals aid the managers quite a lot. One flashes alternate routes to choose from at reroute time. Another feeds detailed information on how lines are faring. Most of the time, however, the supervisors simply sit and squint at the board, watching calls flit across the country.

"Is there a technique?" I asked one of the men.

"Just look," he said. "Run your eye over the board in one quick skim. What we're looking for is not hard to see. You just sit and sort of gaze at the board, that's all."

He leaned back against his desk in a slouched and nonchalant position. "Yes, you just have to look. When you see red, get yourself moving."

Dallas–Wayne was red now. The Hazeltine 2000 video display terminal showed six suggestions for a reroute. When calls are particularly heavy, there may be only one possibility. The computer also keeps track of what reroutes have already been performed. Right now, nine were in effect.

"Hello, Dallas?"

"Yeah, this is Dallas."

"Dallas, take Wayne."

"Okay, thank you."

To the left of the domestic board was a smaller display that reported on international and overseas calls. These average 350,000 a day. To the right was a tremendous map of the United States (something a failing geography student might dream up), across which wound a forest of lines representing the nation's phone circuits. When blinking lights appear, that means there's trouble with a cable or a microwave station. (Construction crews have a nasty habit of drilling through phone cables.) Two electronic blackboards hung on the wall, on which unusual circumstances are posted. The international board reported that service between the United States and Lagos, Nigeria, was knocked out for an hour and fifteen minutes. The cause was still being investigated.

"Probably something to do with pirates," someone muttered.

Long Lines is a peculiar entity. It is the only operating arm of AT&T that is a department rather than a separate company. Its head, a spunky man named Robert Kleinert, carries the title of president. Calls handled by the department bring AT&T something in excess of $15 billion a year, an amount that would make Long Lines one of the twenty-five biggest companies in the country. All told, Long Lines employs some 35,000 people in 647 cities (including Show Low, Arizona; Jackie Jones, New York; and Zelienople, Pennsylvania). They do things like care for microwave stations, monitor satellites, operate test centers for private line business systems, and look after the transmission of radio and TV signals. Long Lines has quite a few account supervisors, including one man with a single customer—the President of the United States. One of Long Lines's fastest-growing offerings is its WATS lines, allowing businesses flat-rate long-distance service. Everybody has periodic brushes with WATS when they dial an 800 number to get a hotel reservation or to book a flight to Tahiti.

Long Lines branches out widely from call-watchdogging to actually placing calls to far-flung lands. Only about a quarter of overseas calls are now handled by direct distance dialing, so Long Lines retains six overseas operating rooms scattered around the country where operators connect people across oceans. The biggest center is in a shopworn brick building at 32 Avenue of the Americas, in a run-down commercial district of Manhattan. A phalanx of 850 operators works on two floors there. They sit shoulder to shoulder, plugging cords into the jacks of old-fashioned switchboards—Des Moines to Athens, Hartford to San Juan, Wheeling to Beirut. Overseas people have to worry not only about Mother's Day and Christmas but also about the arrival of Nowrouz, an Iranian holiday that causes calls to Iran to triple.

Since early on in the phone's development, there has been an irresistible tendency on the part of certain ordinary citizens to put through calls to famous and powerful international figures to whom they wished to express their ideas. One of the oddest exemplars of this phenomenon was Abe Pickens, an oil company president in Cleveland, Ohio, who at various times in the 1930s intrigued Long Lines overseas operators by placing, and sometimes completing, long-distance calls to Hitler, Franco, Mussolini, Neville Chamberlain, Emperor Hirohito, and other world leaders, at a cost to him that he once estimated at roughly $10,000. He would make his calls at two-thirty or three in the morning, since he figured that the best time to get diplomats on the phone was about ten o'clock their time. The day he spoke to Hitler, early in 1939, he was connected with the German Führer and said, "Hello, A. Hitler, this is A. Pickens of Cleveland, Ohio, U.S.A. Can you talk to me only a few minutes before hanging up? I have an average American mind, I was wounded in France with the A.E.F., and I'm interested in peace. What would you think of a general election in Spain to settle the war?" Hitler, unable to speak or understand a word of English, switched Pickens to an aide, who wouldn't commit himself one way or the other on the proposal.

"Yeah, we sure get our share of wacky calls," one of the overseas operators at the Manhattan center said to me. "There are periodic calls to the Pope, for instance. We place them. We're obligated to place any call a customer asks us to. However, the Pope tends not to be in. I haven't heard his voice yet."

Chances of success on an overseas call are not the best. Only about half of the calls handled, I was told, manage to get through. With the rest, there's no answer or circuits are blocked. Because of the limited circuits to some countries, calls must be reserved days, or even weeks, in advance. On this particular afternoon, a blackboard reported that there was a two-day wait to get in touch with someone in Bolivia, four days to reach Libya, only a day to call Egypt, and thirteen days to phone Ghana. Yemen and Tunisia, however, were available right away. Calls that don't get through produce no revenue for the phone company and are known among the operators as "air and water calls."

Back in the Network Operating Center. The stage set for the evening spate of calling. Night was settling in. The East was quiet, the West and Midwest were jumping. Up went an orange square. Too much chat between Dallas and St. Louis.

A short, talkative man consulted his watch and said, "See how the calls have migrated from one side of the board all the way to the other. Happens like that every day. Very predictable. People make calls when they're awake. People don't make calls when they're asleep."

"You have always been renowned for your penetrating insights," a beefy man said.

There was a moment of silence.

A red square now snapped into place. Eyes up. Far too many people were yammering between Denver and San Bernardino.

The network supervisor, studious in appearance, got on the phone. He brought his mouth close to it in an approximation of a conspiratorial whisper.

"Pittsburgh here," came a voice over a small speaker.

"Hey, Pittsburgh, you want to take that Denver to San Bernardino?"

"Have I got a choice?"

"Either take it or I'll route those calls to your home phone."

"I'll take them. Good day."

4

The Boss Man

At 195 Broadway, in the labyrinthine fastness of the AT&T headquarters, the twenty-sixth floor is the top rung of the corporate ladder. The contours of this landscape are obscure to the thousands of operators and linemen who people the phone company. Here, gloomy corridors wind past muted metal door frames inset with frosted glass panes that are carefully lettered: C. L. Brown, chairman of the board; W. M. Ellinghaus, president; W. M. Cashel, Jr., vice chairman; J. E. Olson, vice chairman, and so forth. Beyond the doors sprawl roomy suites of offices, done up in warm shades of relentless good taste. These ultimate trappings of top AT&T executives—featuring broad secretarial warrens with fine wooden desks, nicely appointed sitting rooms, an occasional fireplace, and silver luncheon service—have barely changed since 1916, when builders pounded the final nails into the AT&T palace. Tradition is almost as strong among the tenants of the suites; for AT&T is ruled by officers whose effectiveness is rarely disputed, though whose style outsiders may find odd and even exasperating. One longtime observer, reflecting on how AT&T is managed, has said, "It's a kind of anarchy. It's so big I'm not sure it's really run by anybody. It just goes on."

One unorthodox aspect of the organization is that in some respects it is autocratic—the top echelon of AT&T calls all the important shots—and in others it is democratic—most daily business is thrashed out at the grass roots, down in the scattered regional operating companies. A truly illustrative chart, some AT&T people think, would have to be three-dimensional. There is a striking resemblance between the Bell System structure and that of the U.S. government. The local telephone companies are somewhat like states, each equipped with its own state government. Then AT&T, like the federal government, acts to bind them all together into some kind of sanity. At corporate headquarters, like the elected leaders in Washington, AT&T's officers, guided by task forces and committees galore, are fabled to be stern taskmasters who tend to be reflective and lumbering. When AT&T takes up a question, it doesn't just discuss it, it pulverizes it. In coming to decisions, officers often seem to move arteriosclerotically (six executives, one of them a medical director, once exhausted four hours contemplating the design, colors, and wording of some Blood Bank posters).

It is apparent, almost beyond quibbling, that a company that has never truly been gnawed by economic insecurity and has defeated every calamity that has befallen it must have crafty men in its executive suites, and corporate commentators have generally cast only the mildest of aspersions on the ability of Bell management. Critics do natter about the ferocity of management use of its brute power to stymie competition. The officers are cautious, sometimes to a fault. All of them are decidedly percentage players, not chance takers. "When you get to be the size of AT&T," an executive at a competing phone company told me, "you don't decide destiny by a quick game of cards."

The top management at AT&T, like a gallon of whisky, can be split into fifths. There's the chairman, the Office of the Chairman, the Executive Policy Committee, the Cabinet, and the Board of Directors. The most important person at AT&T—the spider, as it were, in the center of the whole inexplicable web—is the chairman. Some phone company people describe him fondly as their "boss man."

The way to Room 2628, the chairman's suite: a bulbous desk, a receptionist dressed in a style just one step ahead of matronly, a floor covered in carpet of the sort that makes for easy walking, a quaint waiting room with a chocolate brown phone conveniently on the table next to the couch. Reading material on a coffee table: the *Wall Street Journal*, the *New York Times*, *Fortune*, *Newsweek*, *Time*, *Book Digest*. Around to the right of the secretary's desk: this was the working room of Brown's suite. His desk—a big wooden one—set catercorner to the walls. Behind it a thin table on which a Picturephone reposed. A colossal flop when AT&T tried it on consumers, the Picturephone is used by Brown to chat with fellow AT&T officers and with the presidents of the operating companies. Again to the right to the inner office, where visitors are taken and offered great soft orange chairs and coffee. On the walls: a rug from Iran, a painting from Egypt. A 20-foot-long pike that looks vaguely like a harpoon. Line gangs once used it to raise telephone poles into position. It was presented to Brown when he left Illinois Bell to come to AT&T. A photograph of the University of Virginia, Brown's alma mater; an aerial view of the battleship U.S.S. *Mississippi*, aboard which Brown served. And a golden samurai helmet, a memento from the Nippon Company of Japan. And books on the bookshelves: *The Autobiography of Benjamin Franklin, Middle West Country, The Gulag Archipelago, Bartlett's Familiar Quotations, The Prints of Rockwell Kent.* And Brown himself.

Brown stands 5-foot-10, is a spare, intense, handsome man with penetrating eyes, a finely chiseled nose, a determined chin, and a striking profile somewhat on the order of the Presidential busts carved on the Mount Rushmore National Memorial, in South Dakota. His suits are sober. He has an anxious, sometimes tormented, often sweet expression. He also has a jaunty, self-aware humor. Besides being polite, serious, and naturally withdrawn, he is remarkably modest for someone holding down the biggest job in corporate America. Patient, conscientious, orderly, persistent, deliberate, courtly, and stubborn, he has a delicately spun nicety of manner.

Brown seems more powerful in his office than out, since he is so visible in it. You can tell he is very tough underneath. He looks delicate, his voice is subdued, but people do what he says. In his office, Brown acts like a magnate. He slips on his jacket before he summons anyone in.

Sunk into a chair in the inner office, one shoe propped up on top of the coffee table (protected, Brown made sure, by a sheet of cardboard), the chairman put one hand on his knee and tapped his fingers. He looked across the room abstractedly, then spoke about his leading concerns as head of the phone company (and here I am condensing his remarks somewhat): "I think it's important that the company continue on the positive trajectory that it's been on for some time, both in terms of service and financial aspects. That's always an important goal. Over and beyond that, we've been faced with a host of unresolved issues down in Washington, where there is considerable debate over what should be competitive and what should be monopoly. So we have a blurring of the ground rules. We've got to see if we can resolve those ground rules so we know what we can do and what we can't do. One of the things that has happened is we have competition in both terminal equipment and long-distance transmission, but the exact rules under which competition will work are still being thrashed out. It's a long process. One of my jobs is to husband the company through all this, to make sure that AT&T, so to speak, doesn't get ambushed. We have the best telephone system in the world by almost everybody's standards, and it didn't get that way through having a fat monopoly that didn't pay attention to the customers' rights and the customers' needs. So I think there's a lot to be said for regulated monopoly, and it just so happens to have worked in this country. There's an enormous pressing now in this country for deregulation. That's all right. This company can take care of itself under a deregulated situation. I'm not concerned about that, except that it ought not to be done abruptly and there ought to be some thought as to why there was a monopoly in the first place and how, if it's so bad, how come it works so well. Whatever happens, though, we are not faced with a choice of freezing in the snow with Angus MacDonald [a legendary Long Liner who patrolled the New York to Boston phone lines during the blizzard of 1888, and whose portrait graced early phone company advertisements] or becoming an army of hustlers. We will continue to be the Bell System with our traditional goal of providing a channel that will transport any kind of information from anyplace to anywhere."

The chairman triggers conflicting emotions among the troops, as he liked to refer to the employees of the Bell System, and he attracts no dearth of comment anytime his name enters the conversation.

"He's the main man. I stick by everything he says. I support him whole hog, and then some."

"He's very hard on his people. He cracks the whip. And he has a short fuse."

"He has the service idea. His attitude is that people should be willing to move from one post to another. They should do what they're told. He inspires both fear and respect. This is true of any strong man."

"Instead of being preoccupied with the process, he is preoccupied with the idea. I've never heard him discuss reasons why things can't be done."

"I don't get to see him much. But when I do, he makes everybody feel as if they're important. He knows that a few people don't row this company. Everybody pulls an oar."

"I'm not sure he's what he's cracked up to be. It's possible he just lucked into the job."

Brown's colleagues at AT&T have come to regard him as being "the tough, silent one." As one associate characterizes him, "He's something like a bomb. He just sits there quietly, then all of a sudden—boom! Something momentous comes out of him."

Another high-management type who knows Brown fairly well told me, "There's nothing he can't do. He understands the dynamics of business life. He gets things done. Running this company is one big job. Charlie rose to it like a bird. He stumbled occasionally, and he walked in with his jaw now and then, but each time he got stronger and better. There's never been much wasted motion or wasted words with him. He always moves through a meeting with a minimum of words. Mr. Economy, we call him. There's just no dallying around. He will cut to the problem right away. What's wrong here? What is the issue? One thing about him in his style of management, he never did like big meetings. He didn't see them as productive. Some managers like to bring in everyone, including the janitor. He prefers to deal with as few people as needed.

"There's one thing I always like to remember about him," this associate of Brown's said. "When we had a strike at Illinois Bell—a pretty bad one—in the late 1960s, he was the chief operating officer there. The craftspeople were out for several months. On the weekends, Charlie would get his work clothes on and grab some tools and start repairing phones. One weekend, he got this call from the country club he belonged to. Their phones were out. Without batting an eyelash, he went out there and fixed those phones. Believe me, he got some real ribbing for that."

Of what cloth was cut the man who holds corporate America's top post? Brown was not an overnight success. He was born in Richmond, Virginia, in 1921. When I asked him about his early years, he knitted his brow and said, "I think I had a conventional, stable, middle-class childhood. The years during the Depression weren't at all very easy ones for anybody, but I can't rightly say I was in any poverty. We lived in an assortment of rented apartments and houses until into the 1930s, when my family first bought a house. In most respects, I guess you could say I had a fairly uneventful early life. But my family gave me a stable spring-board." Telephone blood ran thick in the Brown household. His mother, prior to her marriage, worked the cord boards as a telephone operator. Though his father began his career as a college mathematics instructor, the phone company seized his interest and he abandoned numbers to hook up with Long Lines, where he settled in as a district traffic manager. Before he was done, he had put in thirty-seven years inside the telephone company orbit. "An atmosphere about the phone company was caught by me," Brown said. "An atmosphere that here was a good place to work, a place that set high goals, a place that employed people who were good people. But I was never consciously shoved in the direction of phone work by my parents. Neither pestered me, 'Go, go, go work for the phone company.'"

In high school, Brown toiled several summers as a lifeguard, then in his final summer before college he took a job with Long Lines laying and splicing cable. He learned to shinny up telephone poles and descend into manholes. He was wonderfully easy to please. "I enjoyed it tremendously. It was my first time away from home. I was living in hotels with a crew of people who were hard manual workers, with people who had substantial responsibility. I still, though, didn't think much about what I would ultimately do when I got out of school." Brown enrolled at the University of Virginia and pursued an electrical engineering curriculum. "I was interested in logical thinking and problem solving." He was a B student in school. To earn part of his tuition, he served as a dormitory counselor and as a professor's assistant. During his first year at Virginia, he played basketball, and he made the baseball team all four years. In his senior term, he began to suffer inordinate difficulties hitting curve balls. Perplexed, he consulted an optometrist, who reported that Brown had a most peculiar eye condition. His left eye saw long and his right eye saw short. "I can't hit any curve balls," he has said, "but I don't have any trouble reading with one eye and seeing trucks with the other." After graduating, Brown's thoughts turned to the World War at hand, and he enlisted in the Navy to pursue a radio career. His eye condition might have dashed his plans, but when he was adminis-tered an eye test and told to switch eyes, he used the same eye and changed hands instead. The bored yeoman giving the test never noticed.

After he was discharged from the Navy, Brown cast about in

a variety of vague directions, including a beguilement for a while with an electrical equipment manufacturer, and then with the airlines (it sensibly occurred to him that the airline industry would mushroom after the war), but he finally chose to go to work for the Bell System. "It just looked to me like a good place to start. It was a close decision. I was not at all sure that I was going to stay. I merely decided I would give it a whirl."

His first responsibility was as an equipment maintenance person in the Long Lines' Hartford office, where his duties consisted of testing lines and machinery used in long-distance transmission of calls. After a six-month stint, he was transferred to New York, where he engaged in equipment engineering. When I asked him what aspirations he had then, he replied, "I certainly expected to climb in the business, but I didn't really worry that much about it. The person who's looking around to see where he or she is going next, that's wrong. The person who'll tolerate the job he or she has because it won't last long, that's wrong, too. I found out early in my work that if I enjoyed myself on the job, the next step would take care of itself. I went into every job on the basis that that was where I was going to be, and I had better do it well."

The way things operate at the phone company, AT&T officers are made, not born. Aspirants must battle their way through a tangle of companies and myriad jobs in the system, and the handful who get to the apogee typically have never cashed a paycheck from any other company. As one AT&T person confided to me, "The management system here is much the same as the Army's. You start at the absolute bottom, digging ditches if need be, and slowly—ever so slowly—worm your way to the top. By the time you get there, boy, you're an Army man through and through."

Brown followed the gradualism pattern to the tee. Never sitting behind any one desk for more than a couple of years, he scuttled through a cascade of twenty-three different job assignments in the next quarter of a century. They went like this: equipment maintenance man (Hartford), equipment engineer (New York), traffic equipment supervisor (New York), plant extension engineer (New York), systems planning engineer (New York), district plant superintendent (Birmingham), commercial manager (Atlanta), division plant superintendent (Philadelphia), assistant to the general manager (Cincinnati), area traffic manager (Cincinnati), area commercial manager (Kansas City), area sales manager (Kansas City), administrator, data communications training (Cooperstown), general manager—central area (Cincinnati), general manager—southeastern area (Atlanta), vice president and general manager of Illinois Bell (Chicago), vice president of Illinois Bell (Chicago), president of Illinois Bell (Chicago), executive vice president of AT&T (New York), chief financial officer of AT&T (New York), vice chairman of AT&T (New York), president of AT&T (New York), then, at last, the top of the totem pole, chairman in February 1979.

Somewhat dizzied from the endless progression, I asked Brown if he ever had turned down a transfer, or were his bags always packed.

"No, I never did," he said. "I always took the next move. I'm not saying it wasn't difficult. It often was. You leave old friends behind, you have to find new schools for the youngsters. But you surmount those kinds of things. I was certainly reluctant at times about transferring, particularly when I had to move after being in a house for ten days. This was back in 1963, when I had just come to Atlanta. There was a sudden retirement in Chicago that opened up a job that I was qualified for, and sure enough I was the one tapped. I was very distraught. I had lived in Atlanta previously and liked the city, liked the job I had there, what little taste I had gotten of it. I was disappointed and concerned. I considered turning the move down, but in the end I looked at what was probably best for the company and went ahead and took it."

As chairman, Brown does not affect a grand style. Mostly he pours his energies into his work. On a typical day, he is picked up by a company limousine at his Princeton, New Jersey, home (and returned there in the same manner in the evening), and he works during the hour and twenty-minute drive each way. A phone is in the car to allow for early morning business calls. Brown appears for work about eight and he is not gone until six in the evening.

To keep abreast of what's happening in the world, he scours the *New York Times* and the *Wall Street Journal* each morning. When he gets comfortable at his desk, he is confronted with a bulky news summary containing items that pertain to AT&T, culled by the public relations staff from several dozen papers and magazines. When he gets done digesting all that, he turns to a veritable blizzard of Bell System reports, both formal ones that are required on a rigid schedule from the operating companies and explanatory write-ups that are sent in on specific incidents, like the status of repair work following a flood. By the hundreds of thousands of words, reports and studies pour into Brown's office, onto his desk, and into his head. He has a highly retentive memory. He quickly fastens onto what is significant and does not readily forget it. He is somewhat less retentive about names. He has bothered to study a couple of memory books in the interest of keeping more names in his head, and found the tomes reasonably helpful. "Mostly I concluded that you remember what you want to remember."

When he is not devouring reports, he is meeting with people. His presence at meetings can be unnerving. He does not say much. But he listens. Few things escape his ears. An associate who has had occasion in his career to review closely Brown's style said to me, "One thing I've always noticed about him is that he is very intense and a keen listener, probably more so than anyone else I ever worked for. You invariably talked more than he did when you met with him. I never felt really uncomfortable with him, but you knew you had to be prepared. You could never wing it. He would ask a question that no one had thought to ask. And it would really bore in on the issue at hand."

I asked Brown to explain, in his view, the chairman's role in such a gargantuan enterprise.

"Well," he said, "the managing of the business is basically carried out in small units. We don't sit up here in New York anticipating everything and trying to carry out everything ourselves. The policy of giving reasonable freedom to a large number of people in handling their jobs is what keeps the service ethic high and customer contact there, and really establishes the reputation of the business. What is thought of us, what our basic image is, is largely determined by how we conduct ourselves in management. My feeling is that the leadership of the organization has to encourage freedom and responsibility for the smaller units. The whole comes together, and it seems to be a huge monolith, but the way it is controlled is by guidelines being issued from the top, and then the smaller units react accordingly. Otherwise, this business would be unmanageable. The first supervisor who sees something wrong in an equipment room does something about it. If the manager of an operating force sees that there are too few people on the board, that manager sets things right. The person knows what the goals are and what to do and so does it. Many people have a gross misconception about how this place is run. They think there are a bunch of peons doing what the signal from above suggests they do. That's not the way it works. I issue very few direct orders from here. I only issue orders on broad-scale matters affecting the whole system. Otherwise, we are formulating guidelines within which these smaller units operate. We're very concerned with the feelings of these people. We believe very deeply in letting the people down below know that they're wanted and that what they're doing is worthwhile. That's really the broad input of the direction from the top."

When I asked Brown to describe his management style, he threw a distracted glance toward the ceiling and said, "I think I have always had the characteristic in supervising a job of sampling the job—going down in a manhole with a splicer to see what his attitudes are, sitting down with a business office supervisor, or sitting in an operators' room and chatting with the chief operator to find out what difficulties are cropping up. Is speed of answering slipping? Is courtesy off? When I was president of Illinois Bell, I frequently paid sales calls with some of our salesmen. This was when the phone company was first getting into marketing in a really serious fashion. It served internal and external purposes. It showed my people how much emphasis I put on selling. And, in addition, it demonstrated to customers the importance we had placed on it. It helped me, as well, to understand what the needs were for these people. You obviously don't go into every manhole or sit down with every operator, particularly when you have the responsibilities I have, but I feel you can do a fair amount of sampling for yourself. People are the important thing in this business."

Oddly enough, the chairman is not stupendously well-known in public circles, a fact that can be partly attributed to his temperament, though by the yardstick of motion picture stars and million-dollar athletes, the main man at the biggest company in the world has always dwelled in comparative obscurity. Search out a dozen people at random from a sidewalk crowd and ask them to produce his name; the chances are good that there would be hemming and hawing and none would be able to do it. The position itself is just not tremendously exportable to Mr. Typical Individual. The overwhelming anonymity of the job was baldly demonstrated by Brown's immediate predecessor, the highly visible and gregarious John deButts. Affronted that, on his assuming the chairmanship in 1972, the news media and the public at large more or less discharged an enormous yawn, deButts resolved to take action. Reviewing the results in a speech some years later, he said: "It bothered me, because I do not think that my business—or business at large—is well served by the notion that its leadership is comprised of faceless and virtually interchangeable executives rather than men and women of flesh and blood and purpose. So I resolved to do something about it—to make sure, if nothing else, that AT&T would not lack for a visible spokesman. Accordingly, over the next two years, I made something like a hundred and fifty speeches, granted every news media interview requested of me, and generally did my best to convince whoever might care that people—not machines—run the telephone company. So what happened? Along came a survey by the Roper organization designed to test public recognition of a variety of public figures ranging from Henry Kissinger to Bette Midler. What the survey showed was that two percent of the American people recognized John deButts as a corporate executive, six percent as a cabinet officer, three percent as a labor leader, and one percent as an astronaut! Undaunted by that blow to my self-esteem, I pressed ahead. I made a hundred more speeches, appeared on 'Face the Nation' and the 'Today Show,' was featured in *People* magazine —and even got sued by the Department of Justice. Since that time there's been another Roper Survey. Nobody any longer recognizes me as an astronaut. Instead, one out of a hundred Americans apparently thinks I'm a TV journalist. But now, instead of two percent recognizing me as a business leader, one percent does."

Like his predecessors, Brown attempts to do what he can to make himself reasonably available to the public. He lists his own home phone number in the directory (as does the entire battalion of AT&T officers and presidents of the operating companies). Brown keeps six phones at home to take calls on—a white wall phone, a green wall phone, three green desk sets, and a white Trimline. He is a fussbudget and a stickler for detail. In his office, he always answers his own phone when it rings and he isn't tied up with someone, and he spares the time to survey the sacks of mail (four thousand letters a year) addressed to him by name or title. Although he doesn't personally draft responses, he makes a habit of approving and signing them, and he often fiddles with the wording. "I've always thought it important to get a feel for what people are thinking out there," he said about his mail habits. "Reading and answering the mail is purposeful. Besides, it's polite."

Letters to the chairman:

Dear Mr. Chairman:
Having received the report of your annual meeting, some comment was called for in regard to your statement on rates. Basically, I believe your return on investment is more than sufficient. If, as you say, some charges are lower than they should be in particular regions, is it not true that the converse must be true; that is, in some places certain service rates are more than adequate. Therefore, I wonder why the Bell System is not voluntarily reducing rates in specific cases before there is an order for refund.

Dear Mr. Chairman:
A recent *Washington Post* headlined an article to the effect that AT&T keeps an "enemies list."
It is hoped that you do keep such a list and maintain it up to date.
If you do so, you are to be commended for your vigilance.

(The chairman responded that the newspaper article "had no basis in fact, you may be sure.")

Dear Mr. Chairman:
I decided to invest in a 15¢ stamp and send you some thoughts from an AT&T stockholder and telephone consumer. I feel I can be somewhat objective for neither I—or any member of my family, friends, etc.—are employed by AT&T or any part of the AT&T system . . . .
I was stunned to read that AT&T may spend more than one billion dollars in the next five years in legal fees to defend against the government lawsuits. I personally believe that a reasonable person would have difficulty understanding these huge legal fees—when AT&T is already so heavily regulated. . . .
I suggest, if possible, AT&T organize its nonemployee stockholders—arm them with facts—and have them use their influence—if any—to stop the governmental attacks on AT&T . . . .

Dear Mr. Chairman:
As a Bell subscriber I have noticed one unusual thing about my telephone service. The more that long distance

rates are reduced, the higher my bill becomes. Now that the 60 percent discount rates are in effect 11:00 P.M. to 8:00 A.M., it is rare that I do not have at least one direct-dialed LD call on my bill.

It looks like this is a good thing for both of us. Each rate reduction causes us to use our phone more and this gives us wider service with more revenue to AT&T.

Dear Mr. Chairman:

I am all too wise to the fact that the phone company is trying to take over the world. Yes I am. You already have most of it, and if you're not stopped you'll get the rest. Well, you better stop. If you don't, I'll call the police. My brother is a policeman.

Two or three teachers used to write John deButts every year assailing his deplorable handwriting, which was exemplified to them by his spidery signature in the Annual Report. "How can I teach my students better penmanship if people like you write so miserably?" they would typically moan. DeButts also used to get calls several times a week from a pesky customer who would grouse that the phone company was deploying its satellites to ship messages to his brain. All this information bombarding him, he said, was really fouling up his life—how about quitting it? DeButts had a marked lack of success convincing the man otherwise.

Brown told me, "I suppose my mail containing complaints of various kinds—wrong billing, or your collection efforts are inappropriate, I'll pay my bill if you'll just get off my back—I suppose I get one or two of that kind a week from all across the country. When I pick up my office phone, I often get a customer or shareholder or an employee or ex-employee. Once every couple of weeks, I'd pick up a call like that. I get everything you might imagine. I wouldn't think that a stockholder or customer would take the trouble to call the chairman of AT&T with a friendly question, and the calls I get bear that out pretty well. They range from the completely irrational to the legitimate. A frequent call is from someone who wants to reach an unlisted number and can't understand why we won't give it to him. The most poignant one is when someone forgets his own unlisted number. I tell the person I don't know who he is and our policy is we just can't give it out."

Away from the often skittish pace of the office, Brown has a fondness for the quiet life. Extraordinarily protective of his privacy, he prefers to talk only in the sketchiest of terms about how he fills his evenings and weekends. If the conversation edges toward areas in which he feels ill at ease or unwilling to commit himself, defensive reflexes rise around him like an invisible cloak. His wife and his son, a surgeon in California, are no-trespassing zones. When pressed, Brown does disclose a passion for golf (he plays to an eleven handicap) and tennis, and he confesses that he polishes off about a book a week. "I'm interested in world history, and I also like some fiction. I have a bed table that's fairly well loaded." For vacations—he sets aside just three or four weeks a year—he more often than not repairs to a cottage he owns in Florida just north of Palm Beach. He regards himself as better than average at fixing things around the house, and he indulges in a good deal of walking, which he finds useful for mulling over problems. ("The joggers can have my admiration but not my company.") A fairly modest life, then, for someone who draws on the order of $12,000 a week in straight salary and various bonuses. (Going by the hefty standards of most of the behemoths of the corporate jungle, AT&T doesn't shower its officers with all that much in the way of perks. Brown has memberships in one country club and the tab for a pair of luncheon clubs picked up by the company, he gets a chauffeured limousine and access to a corporate jet, and his phone service is pretty much free. All Bell employees benefit from what's called "concession telephone service" that, depending on your rank, gets you a discount on your home phone. In general, Brown only pays for calls in the forty-eight contiguous states that add up to more than $35 a month, and all charges for calls beyond this area.)

Public relations being so all-important to the phone company, I asked Brown his perception of AT&T's image in the public eye.

He chuckled beatifically for a moment, and said, "I think people feel well served by the Bell System, as far as their telephone service is concerned. Our studies certainly show that they are quite satisfied with what they're getting for their telephone dollar. They have a high regard for Bell Labs and Western Electric and the telephone companies in their communities. At the same time, I have to say that anything as large as the Bell System gives people some concern, as does any large institution—governments, unions, other large companies. I suppose there is some nervousness about it. One thing I would hope is that the Ma Bell image of a maternal kind of outfit, a place where the chief operator always takes care of her girls and provides all the service, I would hope that that would go by the boards. The sooner the better, as far as I'm concerned. We have never been this Ma Bell organization. The name just happens to be convenient for headline writers. I would like to see our image become one of a high-technology outfit working in the forefront of solving business and residential communications problems. That is what we really are."

A $40-billion company is not a corner drugstore or a sidewalk newspaper concession. To make policy, Brown needs mounds of help, and thus delegation of major responsibilities is a management must. The three power people immediately beneath the chairman in the chain of command are William Ellinghaus, the earthy president, who busies himself with the day-to-day operations of the company; William Cashel, a vice chairman, who is in command of financial matters; and James Olson, another vice chairman who presides over rate-making, lobbying, and competition. Each of these men, like Brown, can be fairly certain of his security. At AT&T, officers never get fired or demoted, rarely is anyone elbowed into resignation, and a shake-up is something that happens somewhere else. In the often turbulent waters of the corporate world, AT&T is an island of serenity. The phone company's twenty-nine officers average more than twenty-five years with the company. Few of them are graduates of Ivy League colleges, a good deal of them hail from small towns, many of them with engineering backgrounds, and all combine unabashed dedication, a zealous sense of service, toughness, a competitive bent, sensitivity to criticism, and respect for proven rules. In certain ways, they are a breed apart. Above all, they view their job—helping the people to speak—as an almost priestly calling. "Oh, the officers are pretty normal when they start here," one longtime Bell manager who has seen a good many come and go told me. "But as the years go by, their heads become more and more Bell-shaped."

The company whose business is talk is managed, in large part, by talk. Phone company officers find themselves perpetually and inextricably huddled in a tapestry of meetings. More often than not, if you were to call one of them up, the response from his secretary would be something like, "Oh, yes, I'll have him get back to you as soon as he gets out of his meeting."

Under the chairman, the top governing entity is the Office of the Chairman, a fairly recent addition instituted by Brown. Its members include: the chairman, the president, the two vice chairmen, and the general counsel, a remarkably like-minded and tight-knit bunch of men. They get on best with their own kind, to the extent of lunching together with the rest of the officers most days in the twenty-second-floor executive dining room. "We discuss politics, families, golf, and maybe somebody's tennis elbow, but in the main we talk about business, which is what's foremost in our minds," reported one member of the inner club. During the morning of the first Thursday and third Friday of each month, members of the Office of the Chairman sit down in leather armchairs at 195 Broadway for a several-hour meeting. Generally, three or four subjects of the highest importance to the phone company are discussed. The intent is to provide counsel for Brown, who always makes the final decisions. If there is a dispute, Brown has the last word. "There are sometimes arguments," one Bell executive familiar with the meetings explained. "It would be ridiculous if the top officers agreed on everything. They all agree not to agree with anything unless they really and truly believe in it."

Beneath the Office of the Chairman is the Executive Policy Committee. During the afternoon of the first Tuesday and the morning of the third Thursday of every month, the EPC convenes either at 195 Broadway or at the phone company's ultra-modern Basking Ridge, New Jersey, building. Its members include: the two vice chairmen, the four executive vice presidents, the general counsel, the assistant to the chairman, and the vice president for planning, every bit as much a like-minded group of individuals. One by one, each man briefs the others on the latest developments in his particular specialty—marketing activities, spending plans, rate battles. The EPC seldom wastes time on detail or trivial topics, since AT&T middle managers are expected to have resolved most lesser problems before they get to the minds at the vice presidential level. "The EPC is a fairly modern development, dating back to about 1970," I was informed by Alvin von Auw, a lively, somewhat mischievous-looking vice president and assistant to the chairman (he has been described as being "the man who sits to the right of God," God, of course, being Brown, and someone else has called him "the back wall of the handball court"). "The EPC's role, strictly speaking, is not decision making. More precisely, it is to provide the chairman background and recommendations as to what his decisions should be. It is not conducted to the degree of votes or ballots being called for. The meetings could be best characterized as a mode of participatory planning. There is no ritual. They are all reasonably informal. They are very serious in topic, but the members know each other fairly well, of course, so there is no reference to 'my distinguished colleague' and that sort of stuff. Attendance is not mandatory, though it's hoped that attendance is complete. If you don't show up, you're not drummed out of the corps." On occasion, explicit decisions have emerged from the EPC. For instance, at a 1970 meeting, in the wake of the horrendous service failures that racked New York and other cities, the decision was made to set up a program of regularly dispatching Bell Labs scientists to work directly with the operating companies, so they could sniff out problems and solve them before they got out of hand. "The EPC's period of most intense activity is now behind it," von Auw told me. "It was called into being because of the rise of regulatory matters and competition and the need to make determinations of what the Bell System's position should be. But as the organization adjusted itself to the new climate, decisions came to be made at lower levels. There were times when I felt I was whiling away my life in the conference room. Now they let me out occasionally for air."

The management body that easily captures the honor of bearing the most illustrious name is the Cabinet. Its members include all the EPC people, the presidents of Western Electric and Bell Laboratories, and all eighteen AT&T vice presidents. Its meetings take place in a newish conference room at Basking Ridge on alternate Mondays. Von Auw explained its workings: "The cabinet basically functions as an interchange of information among the officers of AT&T and Bell Labs and Western. The chairman usually presides and sits at the head of the table. He generally goes around the room and asks each person if he has something to present to his colleagues. Sometimes nearly everybody does. Other times not. I have more recently been in charge of making sure that there is at least one substantial presentation that is scheduled in advance. This might concern new products or the status of regulatory proceedings or maybe legal proceedings or advertising plans. A meeting might last as little as three-quarters of an hour, or it might go from nine to noon." The very name of the body, being that it is customarily associated with a council that advises a government, has been the target of mild criticism. Von Auw says, "The name is vaguely uncomfortable, because it leaves us open to accusations of pretentiousness. From time to time, we have thoughts of another name, but none of them seems to take and we get dreadfully bored by the exercise and go on to things like running the company."

Final and absolute decision-making power is officially vested in the Board of Directors, but in practice, as at other companies, the functions of the board are often pro forma. It basically rubber-stamps what management has already decided to do. The board convenes on the third Wednesday of every month. It consists of eighteen members, almost all of them familiar faces in big business circles. Among them, just since 1972, are one woman, Catherine Cleary, the retired chairman of the First Wisconsin Trust Company, and one black man, Jerome Holland, the former ambassador to Sweden and a director of a throng of corporations (he has been known in some circles as a "professional director"). In 1980, Juanita Kreps, former Secretary of Commerce, became the second distaff member to sit on the AT&T board. Besides the meetings of the entire board, there are sundry committees of board members that visit every nook and cranny of the AT&T establishment, from regulation to executive pay.

The board room is the most stately chamber at 195 Broadway. You get to it through an entrance room dominated by a brooding painting of Alexander Graham Bell. The directors sit around an elongated oval table in high-backed dark brown leather chairs. On the wall are portraits of past AT&T chief executive officers. The chairman sits at the far end, on the window side. Directors have their names on plaques on the backs of their chairs. There is a speaker's lectern, and a screen behind some drapes to flash slides on.

In essence, a meeting goes like this:

Reports are delivered by officers on such pertinent matters as the state of phone revenues, bond offerings, inroads from competition, the quality of telephone service, and other subjects of keen interest. Directors generally find these reports exceedingly pleasing to their ears, since they are usually more favorable than the reports they heard last time around. Whatever topics require decisions—usually four or five per meeting—are mulled over and voted on. Votes are always unanimous. That is because any instance in which some members are unbending is simply dumped by the chairman. Some directors were once eager to modernize the old-fashioned AT&T stock certificate, which features a woman garbed in a long skirt that tumbles to her ankles, the kind of skirt that nobody wears anymore except to costume parties. Other board members rather liked the skirt because it showed that the company was a venerable institution. The matter never came to a vote. There are occasional moments of jocularity. One time, when board members were perusing a map of the United States that charted telephone growth, a director hailing from West Virginia noticed that his home state appeared nowhere on the map. He cleared his throat with a short cough and brought his displeasure to the attention of the board, which noted it and went on with its proceedings. At the following month's meeting, Charles Brown offered another map depicting phone growth. This time, West Virginia showed up as the size of the entire nation. The rest of the country came out about the dimensions of Delaware.

If any action is of hot interest to investors—like the dividend rate—a curious disclosure rite is rigorously followed. If the same dividend is voted, the company secretary (who isn't a board member, though he sits in on all directors' meetings) relays the news in code to an AT&T Treasury Department person planted outside the board room by pressing a button hidden in a drawer beneath the oval table. If the dividend rate is changed, as it often is, the new amount is scrawled on a slip of paper and the secretary quietly carries it to the treasury emissary. That individual then passes the news to a company public relations envoy, who grabs the phone and notifies the New York Stock Exchange, where AT&T shares are traded. He sits tight for about ten minutes to allow the exchange sufficient time to ready itself for any deluge of trading of AT&T that may be set off by the news (oftentimes the end result is so predictable that nothing out of the ordinary happens to the stock). He then gives the information to the wire services and sends out, by messenger or mail, releases to newspapers across the country. All of this is intended to lessen the odds of anyone improperly using inside information to make a killing in phone company stock.

Frank Hutson, the company secretary, says of board meetings, "They are all a good deal less detailed and a good deal less philosophic than the board meetings of most major companies, because so much nuts-and-bolts action is taken by the local operating company boards. We drift through discussions of fairly galactic matters, I suppose you might say, in a relatively sweeping manner."

The board, though, is far from the most distinguished body in the business world. One AT&T watcher, who has had the opportunity to study at close hand a great many boards, remarked to me, "I don't think you find the most dynamic people on it. They're good people, but not terribly aggressive people. Certainly it's not a patsy board, but it's not the kind that one would expect for a company of this stature. I would guess it has less influence on management than, say, an IBM board or a GM board. It's not the sort of board, for instance, that would tell Charlie Brown to go take a flying leap."

Board meetings, which start at ten-thirty and typically proceed without any rancor, usually wrap up between one and one-thirty, when the directors are eager to have their lunch. Good management, it is reasoned, doesn't come on empty stomachs.

5

Lightening the Drudgery
of the Mind

Murray Hill, New Jersey, is a small bucolic stretch of suburbia in central New Jersey, roughly 25 miles west of New York City. Its mostly affluent residents live in spacious homes with well-manicured front lawns and catch the Erie Lackawanna to their big-city jobs. There is a stone quarry, a colonial restaurant, Prudential and Allstate Insurance buildings. Also in Murray Hill there is enough brainpower to invent almost anything.

At the Lido Diner on Route 22, I stopped in and asked directions to the big building on Mountain Avenue. A blustery man who was hunched over his eggs at the counter gave them to me. I asked him what he knew of the place. "That?" he said. "That's where they make dreams come true."

Behind the counter, a waitress in a powder-blue uniform chimed in, "Yes, sir. That's where they work on dreams."

The yellow brick headquarters for the Bell Telephone Laboratories sat spread out high on a hilltop on two hundred acres of grassy fields and dense pine woods in the middle of this leafy suburb. There was a slightly precious air about it. One low complex of buildings dominated the grounds like a Pentagon of science. The main building was a stark and almost chilly affair, with a modernistic entranceway sporting a steeply pitched roof. Employees call the edifice "The Pyramid." Connected to it was a cluster of narrow buildings, two that ran twice the length of a football field. From one end of their corridors, it is impossible to see the wall at the other end. People were teeming through the doors. Their attire was of a noticeably more informal urban-Bohemian style than the dress at other phone company installations. Blue jeans here and there, some T-shirts. Many of the people were obviously not yet thirty. Virtually every bit of equipment in the telephone system can be traced inexorably back to this place.

For decades, almost beyond dispute, Bell Labs has been the premier industrial laboratory. One of its scientists told me, "From the outside, we sometimes are looked on as a bunch of absolute nuts who traipse around in bare feet and talk in crazy languages. The truth is we get some nifty work done here. I shudder to think what the phone system would be like without this place." Historically, Bell Labs is something of a paradox. Despite being the child of a lumbering monopoly, it has long piled up considerable evidence that attacks the classic capitalist belief that product improvement and technological advances spring solely from spirited competition in a free market. Even more, it has proved just how valuable investment in research can be to industry. A single development alone—the use of plastic cable sheathing to replace lead—has saved the telephone operating companies a comforting couple of billion dollars since World War II.

Bell Labs sprang into being in 1925 in a drab building at 463 West Street on the fringe of trendy Greenwich Village in New York. World War II military weapon demands prodded its growth from a fairly modest research outfit into a behemoth of invention, and the labs found it necessary to settle into roomier quarters in the suburbs in 1941. From the start, the labs' mission, as it likes to call it, was to further the art of communications. While it has been pursuing that mission, it has been chastized at times for being plodding and ponderous and for spending too much to get too little, but its stockpile of inventions has found remarkable application both inside and outside the realm of telephony. In 1926, the first synchronous-sound motion picture system, providing the basic technology for the modern art of film, was invented at the labs. A year later, Harold Black, just twenty-nine years old, got lost in thought as he chugged across the Hudson on one of his morning rides on the Staten Island ferry, and suddenly perceived the natural principle that was to prove basic to the understanding of the way muscle moves in living things and of telephone amplification: the principle of feedback. Black's negative-feedback amplifier made possible transcontinental multichannel telephone transmission, paved the way for high-fidelity recording, and was crucial to the emergence of computers and industrial control networks. The electrical-relay digital computer was first constructed at the labs in 1937.

In 1947, William Shockley, then an esteemed member of the Bell Labs staff, dashed off an informal note to some of his colleagues. It read: "I hope you can break away and come" to "an interesting demonstration." Those who broke away saw a fairly modest-looking type of crystal with some wire attached that could be made to perform many of the most critical functions of a vacuum tube amplifier without any of the auxiliary apparatus every vacuum tube requires. The crystal chip, in addition, could go on doing this forever without wearing out. This was the transistor, the most important invention in telephony since the telephone itself. It is the transistor that made possible the modern computer industry and allowed communication with man on the moon. For inventing the transistor, the 1956 Nobel Prize for Physics was awarded to Shockley, John Bardeen, and Walter Brattain, all of Bell Labs.

In 1958, Arthur Schawlow and Charles Townes published a paper on their research into a new way of generating light obtained from atoms induced to vibrate at a fixed frequency, in absolute unison, and traveling in a single direction, and thereby producing a visible beam of light of an intensity, concentration, and purity never before achieved. This was the wondrous laser. The limits of its use are still being explored, though it will certainly become the prime carrier of telephone communications in the future. The litany of Bell Labs developments is endless: coaxial cable transmission, microwave radio relay, direct distance dialing, electronic switching (the biggest and costliest of its projects). On less grandiose fronts, Bell Labs has managed to devise a typewriter that can operate by oral dictation, and it has figured out ways to keep squirrels from chewing up telephone wire. Its mathematicians have arrived at the most efficient manner of scheduling coffee breaks for phone operators. The word "bit" came into being at Bell Labs.

Altogether, Bell Labs maintains sixteen laboratory installations scattered in eight states, seven of them in New Jersey, as well as a facility on Kwajalein atoll in the Pacific Ocean. Nineteen thousand people work for Bell Labs, including more than two thousand who hold doctorates, the biggest concentration of doctorates anywhere. The duties of these wizards are to sit, think, read, and develop. In some cases, the only equipment they work with consists of a blackboard and some chalk. When the system works, they create new knowledge that in some way will benefit phone communications. The staff works on physical, chemical, biological, mathematical, psychological, and applied-science projects, which are budgeted at $1 billion a year. Broadly speaking, Bell Labs divvies its work up into three areas: research, which is work that it is hoped will be important to telecommunications; development, which is almost certainly important; and systems engineering, which is charged with systematically deciding what research and development projects ought to be explored and what ones could best be ignored. Down the years, nine Bell Labs scientists have been awarded the Nobel Prize. A prodigious nineteen thousand patents have been doled out to its scientists at a staggering clip of two per working day. One man there, Andrew Bobeck, co-inventor of bubble memory, has alone tucked 100 patents under his belt; he thinks it possible that he could some day acquire 200. Harry Nyquist, who retired from the labs in 1954, had nearly 150 patents to his credit. When an invention was needed to help solve a problem, a Bell Labs executive would summon Nyquist, in the way that a baseball manager might call for his ace reliever, and more or less say, "Harry, why don't you invent this." Most of the time, he did.

A human being, to enter the labs, has to sign in at a security desk. The arms crossed on the desk belonged to the security man. He was young and wore a blue uniform. He looked up slowly from a book. He was reading *Valley of the Dolls*. In a corner of the lobby was an exhibit area of Bell advances. A red digital readout disclosed just how the system was doing that day. Calls: 22,765,000. Bell telephones: 129,074,550. Circuit miles: 1,084,935,049. Investment: $82,677,340,600.

"Have a good day," the security man said, after he had been properly assured that I was cleared to go through. "You ought to see some real eye-poppers." He went back to *Valley of the Dolls*.

The chairman of Bell Labs is a lean, feisty, professorial man named William Baker. He is a physical chemist who, while a scientist laboring at the labs, discovered a new scientific polymer molecule called microgel, which proved to be highly useful during the World War II rubber crisis. For this, he received the Priestley Medal, the highest honor in American chemistry. Polymers are now the most widely used material in the telephone industry. Baker's view of the future of the labs is, "Do not underexpect." I dropped in on Baker in his office, where I found him aglow with enthusiasm, as if it were his first day on the job. His office was overflowing with books, dozens of books, stacked four deep in shelves around the room, many of them authored by men and women out inventing in the labs. Baker rhapsodized to me about the role of the telephone today. He said, "It appears that the telephone is the principal organizing element in the ordering of an information society. It appears that the switch telephone system is as big an element as anything in reducing the entropy and bringing order in the broad philosophical sense."

Baker said that, at the present time, his main tasks at hand were to develop still faster telephone switching systems (telephone researchers are perpetually interested in faster switching systems in the way that tennis players are forever obsessed with acquiring faster serves), higher-capacity transmission lines, tinier and tinier circuitry, and a method to run machines by vocal instructions. "We have managed very well to relieve a lot of the muscle drudgery," he said. "Now we need to lighten the drudgery of the mind."

Bell Labs, he went on, is somewhat alarmed by the mounds of information that people are being exposed to. "Since about 1945, the amount of information in the record has doubled every seven years," Baker explained (in capsule form). "Now, that imposes on society a huge burden, because people can't absorb information any faster than about forty bits a second. Our evidence is that people today can't absorb information any faster than Stone Age people. It has also been determined that a weekday copy of the *New York Times* has as much in it to read as the educated individual in sixteenth-century Europe absorbed during his lifetime. So you can see why fast telephone communication has become critical. We just have to depend on an interaction among our people that is much faster and much more selective than when people could grasp a bigger hunk of that information flood. In voice terms, there's not much that you can do. You can only talk so fast. You can do something with graphics, though. If we had a lot of Picturephones, a lot of video images around, you would certainly multiply the actual information flow by typically a hundred thousand times. A hat designer goes to a Picturephone and shows salesmen around the country his hats. If he had to just verbally tell them about the hats, it would take an hour. They can see them and understand them in a minute. We have all these ideas, you see. We are trying to squeeze every second of efficiency out of the telephone."

Bell Labs' president, a small impish man named Ian Ross, strolled in and plumped himself down in a chair. Baker talked on about the purpose of Bell Labs: "We are a facility, a laboratory for the Bell System. What we do is supposed to have some relationship to the system. Now, what the Bell System is about seems to be connected to every physical and social science we can think of. That takes a little working out, but that's the case. We never start out doing science and technology just for the sake of doing it, though that's been recommended from time to time. We always have a purpose in mind. However, the immediacy of application is not a constraint. The community of these buildings is that we're very aware of the functions of these systems. It's not that we just go ahead and produce a gadget or thing and then say to ourselves, 'Well, what can be done with it?' We're still mindful of where it can go in the system. Sometimes, it just takes a while before we figure out where it can go."

I wondered whether the labs was inhibited in its freedom to pursue new knowledge by being part of a huge industrial company, and Ross said it wasn't. When the labs wants to take up a new project, he explained, it pitches its "case" to AT&T for approval. A council of emissaries from AT&T, Western Electric, and Bell Labs then considers the matter and approves or rejects it. "Occasionally, we run into a wall," Ross said. A project is blocked because it is too costly or appears to be utterly impractical. Research projects that do not quickly justify their costs by improving telephone service drive up the expenditures of AT&T and eventually either erode the profits of the system or push up the cost of telephone service, if not both. The real telephone world, where consumers and regulators are constantly bickering about phone service costing the moon, is sometimes forgotten by the white-smocked scientists at Bell Labs.

Ross went on, slowly, "But it's not the case that we just sit here across the river and say, 'Let's look at what we can develop this week that will be interesting.' It can never happen that AT&T will say one day, 'Oh, my God, is that what they're doing!' They're in these projects from the start. We're in constant communication with them. Most of the decisions they hand us have to do with development projects. We wouldn't expect our owners to make judgments on pure research, and they don't second-guess us there. You can't look over the shoulder of a research person and say, 'Why are you turning that knob, because that doesn't look right to me.' We don't expect them to understand what we're doing, and if you don't understand what's going on, you should wait and see the results of turning the knob."

"They tend to be quite decent," Baker said. "It's as though the Department of Energy worked."

"You're being unkind," Ross said, through slightly pursed lips.

"I think it's an accurate summation," Baker insisted.

I had heard that one thing Bell Labs was looking into was DNA, which is the substance that transmits human genetic traits, and which seemed to me awfully far removed from telephones, and so I asked Baker about that. "Yes, we are exploring DNA," he shot back, "and you might say that whoever got into that isn't going to help the telephone one bit. Well, if you look at the storage of information and the transfer of information, one of the most impressive ways that that is done in nature is by molecules of that kind. The fact that there is coding there is of great interest to us. We do coding, too—digital coding on semiconductor chips. We're not quite ready to connect the wires onto the DNA molecules, but we're sure interested to see what they can teach us."

Though Bell Labs is more often praised than damned by the scientific community, it does occasionally find itself the recipient of scorn. It is frequently criticized by competing telecommunications companies for sitting on technology rather than hastening it out into the telephone system. One telecommunications consultant I spoke with, who shared an especially dismal view of the labs, told me, "There are times that I believe they are the greatest public relations machine since Josef Stalin. You ask Mr. Bell Labs what he has done for you, and he says, 'Well, I invented the transistor. Then there was the laser.' Yes, but what have you done lately? And he hems and haws and has a hard time answering that." That seems a bit extreme, though there is some evidence to support the contention that innovation has not been brought along as fast as it might have been, a problem that is without doubt better laid at the feet of AT&T. Its huge bureaucracy, and its belief in letting its operating companies figure out when best to bring in new equipment, makes it seem that the labs is sometimes lagging behind smaller companies. Baker gets infuriated over insinuations that the labs is not innovating fast enough. When I broached some of this criticism, he pushed his glasses a notch farther back on his nose and said, "If you can think of something that's not been done in the telecommunications industry that has been done in other industries, I'd like to hear about it. You sometimes get the comment that we put something in a telephone plant and just leave it there for forty years and that's all the innovation we do. Hogwash. This is just laughable. We have all these people here, flesh and blood, who are dedicated to getting that thing out of there. They feel all these forces breathing down their necks all the time. They don't forget that the word 'bit' originated here. They recognize that this phone system has got to get better. If there weren't any innovation, there would be an internal revolution here, and I would lead it."

I left Baker and Ross and went to take a tour of the laboratories. What were the makers of phones brooding over today? What was happening in the workshop of communications? What green fruits were swelling on its trees? Murray Hill was the country's first totally modular lab. All of its interior walls are moveable, and they are shuffled into new configurations on an average of once every seven years. Don't try to find where the transistor was born. That lab was long ago rearranged into something new. Tacked on the hallway bulletin boards were calendars of upcoming meetings, the subjects of which included "lattice gas model for the metal-electrolyte interface" and "molecular beam studies of the oxidation of CO on Ag(111) and Pt(a(111) × 100) surfaces." There were also notices for meetings of gardening clubs and wine tastings and chess clubs and chamber music groups. Animated conversations in French and German and Italian could be heard wafting from various rooms. Bell Labs scientists tend to fill up even their spare time with somewhat esoteric pursuits. One man, I learned, invested a good amount of his free time whipping up an electronic mouse that could thread its way through a maze better than a live one. It was duly entered in a competition at a national computer show, where it did not win. Another member of the staff whittled away his leisure hours attempting to synthesize the sound of the violin. He eventually succeeded. Even the casual conversations around the labs appear to be conducted at a fairly rarefied level. One scientist mentioned to me offhandedly while a table was being cleared in the cafeteria that the capacity of the human brain and the amount of information stored in the New York Public Library, in terms of bits, were roughly equal—ten to the twelfth power. "Should you choose to, then, you might put the library in your head," he said.

Down a confusion of hallways, development work was proceeding on laser chips. The size of dust particles, the chips are at the heart of a light-wave transmission system—one of the hottest areas in telecommunications. For decades, Bell Labs has invested a considerable chunk of its money making things smaller. (There is a probably apocryphal story told at the labs about the inventor of the first microtransistor accidentally inhaling it while showing it off to a colleague.) Light-wave work has its roots in a demonstration made by John Tyndall, at the Royal Society, more than a hundred years ago. He presented a container of water with a small hole carved out of its side. A downward curving burst of water gushed from it. Tyndall shone a strong light straight down into the water in the container. Light also emerged from the hole, but instead of shining straight down, it followed the jet of water, since it was trapped there by internal reflection. Hence, it was demonstrated that light can be imprisoned within a transparent medium that is optically denser than air.

Today, Bell Labs scientists are working hard on having light from laser beams transmitted around curves and over long distances through transparent glass fibers. Since the beams can be modulated so that their intensity or color changes to follow changing electrical signals, they can transmit a message. In the future, many telephone conversations are going to be transported in the form of laser beams along strings of molten fiber the thickness of human hair. It is a dream of a communications system. One laser is cemented to the tip of each fiber. The lasers flash on and off some 45 million times a second, spelling out a code like that used for blinker lights between ships at sea. A sheaf of 100 lasers, no thicker than a pencil, can send the entire contents of 200 standard-sized books in one second. An experimental light-wave transmission system has been in operation in downtown Chicago for several years now, and no major breakdowns have been reported. Part of the Atlanta phone lines was replaced with light-wave in early 1980, and considerable expansion beyond this is anticipated in the decade of the 1980s.

Being that they are so small, laser chips can be destroyed by an abundance of dust. Normal air contains an abundance of dust. So work goes on in what are known as "clean rooms." Filters root out enough dust so that there are fewer than a hundred particles with a diameter of more than one-half micron size per cubic foot of air in the immediate work space. (A cubic foot of normal air is clogged with something like several hundred thousand particles of dust.) To help out in the cleanliness process, workers have to don hospital-style robes. No food or drink is allowed in. So tiny are the chips that most of the work was going on beneath microscopes. "It's sort of like doing surgery on the head of a pin," one of the technicians told me. The work, he said, has been going well, inasmuch as laser chips when they were developed back in the late 1950s would "die" in a matter of minutes. It's projected that they can now live on for a million hours.

Late in 1978, Bell Labs announced that it had conceived a prototype of a prodigious new "light" phone that could be powered by light beams. It would be the final piece of a fully optical phone network. Pulses of light brought to the instrument were transformed into sufficient direct-current energy to set off the ringer. Sounds like small potatoes, but the ringing mechanism is the most power-thirsty element in the entire phone system. The fact that it has to be supplied with electricity is the principal reason why optical fiber had previously been thought practical only for links between phone company offices, and not right up to a subscriber's home. The light phone is still very much experimental and some years of development work, coupled with more years of slowly rewiring the phone network, stand in the way of its popularity.

James Flanagan, the red-haired head of the Acoustics Research Department, had a distant look in his eyes, as if he had just gazed into an intense fire. He was thinking about digital communications. His office was clean and well-lit. Digital communications, which is the way computers talk, is preferable to analog transmission, which is still the dominant method in the phone system, because signals can be flashed over long distances almost distortion-free. Flanagan and his compeers have been attempting to get computers to talk and people to be able to talk to computers.

He demonstrated for me a directory assistance system of Bell

Labs employees that has been undergoing testing for more than a year. By punching out the first five letters of an employee's last name and then his initials, a computer will fish out the number and recite it in computer-assembled speech. The expectation, Flanagan told me, is that all directory assistance might be accomplished this way in the future. "One of our mathematicians studied directories all over the country and determined that, in a given population, there aren't as many ambiguities as you might think," he said. "There's about a five percent overlap of the same spellings of the last name and similar first names. These would be the only cases where it would be necessary to get more information for the system to retrieve a number."

Flanagan's group was also diligently at work on a voice recognition system that would allow the possibility of a person getting cleared over the phone to take money out of his bank account without having to trot over to the bank or transfer a check. "One experimental system we have here has enjoyed a ninety-eight percent accuracy level," Flanagan said. "We think a level of ninety percent is very useful in many applications. This would be good for credit card checks, for instance. We take great pains in testing these systems. We have brought impersonators to the labs to give the system a real workout. We brought in some people who do radio voice-overs for commercials. They were asked to listen to tapes of voices and then try to fool the computer by impersonating them. And they could beat the machine at times, but the success rate was not as great as you might suspect. The computer was still about ninety-five percent accurate against the mimics."

Flanagan escorted me down the hall where an informal, rumpled technician was monkeying with the verification system. The man (tieless) explained, "Unlike fingerprints—your thumbprint is your thumbprint all the time and you can't change it—your voice is changeable. So we have to build in some tolerance for differences. You can't possibly say a sentence the exact same way twice. So we have to program the computer to compensate for variations."

The technician then proceeded to demonstrate the system for me. He picked up a phone and recited his code phrase into it: "We were away a year ago," a good phrase because it didn't include any nasal sounds, which tend to be tough sledding for the computer.

After a few moments reflection, the computer printed out on a video display terminal, "Your account has been cleared for charges."

The technician said, pleased, "As the message says, I can now do something with my bank account, maybe take some money out, if I have any."

Flanagan glanced at me, and said, "Well, you want to be an imposter and try to swipe some money?"

I said, "Sure."

Handed the phone, I said very deliberately, "We were away a year ago."

"Say, he's a pretty good mimic," Flanagan remarked.

The screen printed out: "Your account has been cleared for charges."

"I've just been wiped out," the technician moaned.

Slightly abashed by my success, he pointed out quickly that the voice tolerance of the computer apparently was much too lenient. He fiddled with the controls to tighten it, and I tried again and failed.

Flanagan whisked me over to another lab to check out a talking computer. Synthetic speech is an important research field for Bell Labs, because, among other things, talking computers could eventually replace operators (no wages, no coffee breaks). A technician gestured toward a computer whirring before me and said, "The computer has this vocabulary in it," and he patted a *Webster's Seventh New Collegiate Dictionary*. "The dictionary's got sixty thousand words in it, but we had to drop a few because of the pronunciation problems. Dictionaries are made for people, not machines. At least now they are."

The man batted out some commands on a control panel, and the computer said in a bland voice about a third as fast as normal speech, "Hello, I am a computer. I am happy to be able to talk with you today. I am at this very moment demonstrating speech synthesis. I hope that my performance will be satisfactory."

The technician typed out some more commands.

Computer: "I have a pretty good vocabulary, but my pronunciation isn't perfect."

"The reason it isn't perfect," the technician explained, "is because there are wide gaps in the knowledge of the way the English language is spoken. There's never been any need before for us to know this much about spoken language."

I asked whether the computer's voice could be altered to have an accent, thinking that might give the machine a touch more personality.

"Only slowly," Flanagan said. "You could make it have a more Southern accent. You could type in at some point the rules of a Midwestern accent. But we don't know what those rules are. Right now, we're striving hard just to produce a voice that sounds human at all. That computer is breaking its back just to do what it's doing."

The quietest room in the world was being used to test a microphone. Known as an anechoic chamber, the room had walls composed of 3-foot-thick fiberglass wedges that soaked up more than 99 percent of the sound that struck them. In terms of sound dispersion, that made the chamber as close as possible to the outdoors, while still being indoors. The work area consisted of wire netting suspended midway between the ceiling and floor. Everything being tested, in fact everything in the room, had to be clamped in place, because the entire floor trembled when someone sauntered across it. I had somewhat the feeling of a high-wire performer as I made my way toward the center of the room. "What this is is a free space," a young scientist named James West explained to me. "You can get a true measurement in here. No reflected sound."

West was working on a directional microphone that can minimize background noise and pick up a person's voice, even in a large room with other people talking. Called a unidirectional electret microphone, it looked vaguely like a hockey puck with spindles sticking out of it. It could find use in group conferences conducted by telephone. Several could be scattered around a table in New York, and several more around another in Chicago. When aimed in the direction of a speaker, even someone at the far end of a big conference table, the microphone would catch what he was saying and would reduce or eliminate sounds such as those made by shuffling papers and by air conditioners. "We're still very much in the research stage," West said, "but once we get this done, it will be quite a mike."

Not only is the anechoic chamber used to test microphones and speakers, but also to explore the way we hear. West said, "We did a recent experiment and proved that a person is very good at localizing sound in a horizontal plane, but not in a vertical plane.

You can find this out by just asking someone if he's ever located an airplane without looking for it. He usually can't."

After taking my leave of the quiet room, I had lunch with some Bell Labs executives in the company cafeteria—a noisy, unassuming place that boasted remarkably cheap prices—and my curiosity led me to ask a question that had been on my mind: What flops has the labs had? The truth is, the executives informed me in what seemed to be a wholly candid manner, Bell Labs has made a number of blunders. One flop was Picturephone, the much ballyhooed attempt to join a video display with the telephone. Though technically successful, its cost proved steeper than people cared to pay. Its use today is limited to conference calling and internal application around the Bell System. The brightly colored Princess phone, which was earmarked for bedroom use, was so dearly beloved by customers that they installed it throughout the house. The trouble was that the phone was so light that it kept sliding across desks and flopping onto the floor. The bottom had to be redesigned with a corrugated surface. "There are all sorts of things you just don't expect," one of the executives told me. "You don't expect phones to be wallpapered. They are. You have to design the phone cord so that babies can chew on it and not get poisoned. The cord has to be resistant to dog bites."

E signaling, the method by which the telephone machinery is notified of the number a customer is calling, must possess "talk-off properties" that prevent the machinery from being triggered by other background noises. Bell Labs undertook monumental testing to incorporate sufficient protection from anything and everything it could think of. Nonetheless, after the signaling technology left the labs and was put into operation, it was discovered that a small number of people and sounds disrupted the network. A woman in the Midwest complained to her local phone company that her calls were frequently disconnected in the middle of a conversation. Servicemen went out to the premises. Nothing. Bell Labs was consulted. It found that the woman possessed a highly peculiar laugh that would put out a sound similar to the signaling equipment. The network equipment, when it heard this tone, thought she had hung up. Also, there was a coin phone in Washington, D.C. Every time a car crossed the trip wire at a nearby gas station, conversation would be disconnected. The labs had to do some tricky redesign work on E signaling.

The biggest development effort in Bell Labs history was the perfection of an electronic switching system. Serious work began on it in the early 1950s, and it was predicted that field trials would start in 1959 and that the whole bill would amount to about $45 million. In the end, the development program consumed four thousand man-years of work and cost something on the order of $500 million. The first ESS office didn't go into actual operation until 1965. The huge underestimate of the work and cost has been rated by some communications people as the Labs' greatest single mistake.

The executives went on to tell me that Bell Labs experts find themselves in utterly bizarre situations at times. Some years ago, I was told, a New York man was standing on a ladder in his kitchen, just above a phone that was screwed into a cabinet. His wife bounded by, and the phone fell off the hook and whacked her on the head. She was dazed by the blow, though otherwise unharmed. However, she was miffed enough to take her husband to court for attacking her (the marriage hadn't been going so well). The man in turn sued the phone company for a poorly designed phone. A Bell Labs man was recruited to testify. Using angular measurements and whatnot, he demonstrated beyond any possible shadow of doubt that the phone couldn't have fallen off the hook without being bumped, whether by accident or intentionally. Nothing came of the suit.

"You also have these people who complain that they hear voices, that the telephone is talking to them when it's on the cradle," one of the executives said. "Bell Labs sends out people to try to convince them that there is no scientific way that voices can be heard when the phone is in the cradle."

"Do they succeed?" I asked.

"Not really," the man replied. "When someone believes that, they believe."

When the talk turns to what new frontiers Bell Labs is exploring, few departments are cited more frequently than the Human Factors Group, which is intent on finding practical applications for psychological research. It is based at the biggest labs installation in Holmdel, New Jersey, a huge, striking affair of glass and steel perched on the New Jersey coastal plain. A small pond outside the building is where the experiments leading to the discovery of radio astronomy were conducted. Human Factors consists of psychologists who, when they arrive at Bell Labs, do not necessarily know the foggiest thing about phones, other than how to use them. A fairly recent addition, for instance, held a patent on a new bit for a horse that operates on positive rather than negative reinforcement. Every time the horse bites down on the bit, some sugar is squirted into its mouth.

"One of the things we're very concerned about now is instructions," I was told by Charles Rubinstein, the cheery, self-assured head of the group. "We're introducing more and more complicated services. Can people understand the instructions? If they can't, what good are they? One of the problems customers have with some of the custom services—like call transferring—is flashing the switch hook. They don't know how long to hold down the hook to complete the action. One of our fellows just completed a study of what words we should use to explain this to people. 'Depress the switch hook momentarily' works very well. 'Depress the switch hook for half a second' comes out fairly well, though the half-a-second bit makes people feel a little pressed. Some operating companies use 'Depress the switch hook for a second,' which is actually the right interval, but people overestimate. We tested eight possibilities, and our recommendation is, 'Depress the switch hook momentarily.'"

Another researcher, I was told, recently completed a study of what people think the individual parts of the phone are called. The purpose was to decide which terms are best for instruction writing. The researcher expected fairly good agreement. There wasn't any. As many as twenty different names were offered for certain parts, particularly the switch hook. More investigation was planned; the researcher was thinking that drawings might be necessary with instructions.

Still another man was meddling with tones. "People are funny about tones," he said. "Many subscribers, for instance, don't know the difference between the trunk busy signal and the station busy signal. The trunk busy tone is faster, and means that circuits are busy. The slower station tone means the individual phone you're calling is tied up. The tone when the phone is ringing is interesting in that it happens at the same time the phone rings, and it has a fluttery quality to it. Most customers would say they think they hear the phone ringing. That gives them reassurance and keeps them happy. We've done some fundamental work—we have no data yet—to find out what meanings tones have for people. We ask people to describe tones—current and possible future tones—on a bipolar scale. We've got a new tone coming into the system that will tip people off that they are about to hear a recorded message. We don't want customers talking to machines and wondering why they don't respond."

"How will it sound?" I asked.

"Like a machine is about to talk to you," I was told.

The tone man went on to say, "The bell was patented by Thomas Watson soon after Bell invented the phone. It's just an inductive motor that drives a clapper between two bells. Now that bell has just about outlived its usefulness. It seems it's going to be replaced with a tone ringer, an electric circuit that produces a beeping sound. The ringer is better because it can produce a variety of sounds and tell you something about the nature of the call. It can tell you if a call is coming from inside the organization or outside. It would be possible to tell you if it's a long distance or local call. We did a project several years ago with a tone ringer, and I actually produced about two hundred different tones with it. Some of them sounded just dreadful. We tested about twenty of the sounds to see which ones were acceptable to people. A good ring shouldn't drive you crazy, but neither should it be too pleasant, or else you might not bother to answer the phone. People generally liked the existing bell as much as anything else, which I guess is to be expected, since they're sort of familiar with it."

Human Factors is also responsible for things like the idea of putting the numbers outside the dial wheel. And, since experiments demonstrated that people tend to dial more efficiently when they have a target for their fingers, the group introduced the dial with white dots painted inside each hole. The shape of the pushbuttons on the Touch-Tone phone was the handiwork of Human Factors. Thirty-eight variables in three categories were examined before the design was settled on. One category was the possible patterns in which the buttons ought to be arranged. Polling people at random, Human Factors received all manner of bizarre suggestions—a triangle, a half-moon, a cross—but they tested out poorly for speed, accuracy, and even how users felt about them. In the end, they chose the familiar three rows of three buttons, with one at the bottom for "O." Second, questions were asked about "force displacements." How far should the buttons project from the surface? How far should they move? How much force should one have to exert to get them moving? The third category covered the shape of the buttons and other miscellaneous factors. How big should the buttons be? Should they be concave or convex, matte-finished or glossy, rectangular or square?

When the labs was designing its Horizon phone system for small business users, it called on Human Factors to work up suitable features. Engineers gave a lot of consideration to having a special option that allowed you to put two people on hold at the same time. People, it turned out, didn't like that, since they found themselves putting people on hold when they didn't intend to. Human Factors recommended the conventional hold pattern. Slowly, the Bell System has begun to introduce coin phones in which there is no operator interaction, just recorded messages. Human Factors had to determine things like how much time to allow someone to drop his coins into the phone, and how much to have the machine say to the person before he got irritated that he was standing there listening to a machine.

After I left Human Factors, I spent some time with the Behavioral Sciences group, where a tremendous amount of research was going on having to do with learning. "There's an awful lot of education going on in the Bell System," one of the researchers told me. "Most of the people we employ undergo training of some sort. We probably spend just a little less than a large civilian university system spends on education. So that's a pretty good reason for wanting to find out everything we can about learning."

A young man with white bushy hair told me about some experiments he had been involved with. "People rarely learn anything on a single experience," he said. "There are anecdotal examples of particularly vivid things that happen to you and you remember them the rest of your life. But my view is that you rehearse these things over and over again by telling your mother and telling your friends. So we're trying to find out why it is that it takes several experiences to learn something. One summary of our work so far is that there are a lot of theories that do a good job on a lot of material, but no perfect theory. I'll tell you a pretty good theory. What happens when you encounter a fact is you store it in a storage device—like writing something on a card and throwing it into a bag. When you want to remember it, you reach into the bag and retrieve it. Now, if you only put it in once, your chances of finding it are slim. But if you put it in a lot of times, your chances are better. It is true by this theory that if you add a fact close together to the same fact, you will store it in the bag close together. If it's not added close together in time, then the records will be scattered through the memory device. By this theory, at any one time you can't search your entire memory. You can only search one small area. So if all the information pertains to one thing—all the facts have to do with one name, for instance—your chances are poorer of finding the name than if there are records on that fact scattered all over your memory device."

I nodded, and said the theory sounded interesting, but what did it have to do with the telephone business?

The man smiled and said right back, "Okay, what I'm going to do is tell you one far-flung way we've tried to apply this. That way is in remembering a telephone number. Most people say they try to remember a number by repeating it over and over again to themselves. That's an effective way to remember it for a very short time, but not effective, in fact essentially worthless, to lodge it in your memory. Research shows that to remember it best, you should recite it, wait a while, recite it again, wait a while, recite it again, and so forth. That, as you can see, is what this theory suggests."

"What's the advantage to the phone company of people remembering more numbers?" I asked.

"They won't have to look them up," the man said. "It will save people time. They will probably not dial as many wrong numbers. People might call numbers that they wouldn't have called because they couldn't remember them. It might cut down on directory assistance calling, which is a money loser for the system."

The bushy-haired man said that the group had also unearthed the fact that the best order for phone numbers for short-term memory is if the numbers were listed with the exchange first and the four digits last, and if you dialed it the reverse. Unfortunately, at the time that the researchers discovered this odd fact, it would have necessitated monumental costs to apply it, so it was just forgotten.

The Group Interaction Room was cluttered with scuffed-up chairs and tables. With everybody working eighty hours a week, there was not much time for cosmetics. Members of the Interpersonal Communications Research Department, one of the newest at Bell Labs, were struggling to find out how people deal with each other. The research head was a smiling, fast-talking man named Myron Wish. "I'm interested in understanding the different ways of communications," he said. "So far, this work is quite young, but we think that there are certain habits that are peculiar to face-to-face interaction and certain habits that are peculiar to the telephone, with some overlap. We did one study on the extent that the visual channel makes deception more detectable. Most people have a sort of intuitive feeling that you have to see a person to tell if he's lying, that the lie sort of oozes out of you. But what we found was that people were more effective in telling when someone was lying on the phone than face-to-face. Now I'll try to explain this another way. If a salesman wants to make a really good impression, he'll come and see you in person. He feels he can manage himself more. Part of the problem, considering our findings, may be that people may believe what they see more than would be warranted. This suggests that if I'm an interviewer and want to assess somebody I might do better to talk to him over the phone. We have found that sometimes people are more likely to give in to someone else on the phone. If you're having a discussion and you're concerned about losing face and if someone can't see your face, there's less to lose. The thing seems to be that people are less committed to what they say over the phone than what they say face-to-face. They hold things said face-to-face to be more binding. On the telephone, people are more likely to retreat from a position. It seems almost as if people are more likely to say what's convenient on the phone. I don't really know why. This finding, though, could have application in labor and management disputes. The two sides might do well to talk on the telephone first and work out their problems, then solidify things in person. We are also looking into how relaxed or tense people are in various modes of communication. People say they're more relaxed on the telephone than in any other mode. Part of it, I guess, is they're more free to doodle or put their feet up on the desk."

In another study, the voices of an assortment of people were recorded on tape and the tape fed into a computer that then manipulated the speed and pitch of each voice. Subjects were brought in to listen to the tapes and were then asked to decide what the personality traits of the voices were. As it turned out, fast-talking voices were discerned as belonging to intelligent people. Those with low-pitched voices and a normal rate of speed were considered to be the most honest. Low-pitched individuals were also discerned as being more persuasive and less nervous. What good is knowing this sort of information? I asked Wish. Well, he explained, with the telephone company going in for more and more recorded messages, it wouldn't hurt to know how subscribers perceive different voices and to work only with the voices that get the best ratings.

Work at the labs sometimes get unquestionably practical. For more than a dozen years, a team of Bell Labs engineers have been sporadically dabbling at the annoying problem of rodents and other animals that make a habit of chewing up telephone cable and wire. The telephone company exhausts something like $1 million a year mending damage by furry vandals. The engineers assigned to the task figured that the best way to solve the problem was to lock up some rodents and let them gnaw to their delight on various sorts of cable. Suspect species were detained in cages and outfitted with special transducers to measure the force of bites and print out the results on a strip printer. Gophers were found to inflict the most damage in the shortest time, with squirrels nearly as devastating. A single squirrel, if it has nothing else to do, can take forty-five thousand bites a week, some of them with a force of twenty-two thousand psi (pounds per square inch). Investigators discovered that rats shredded a good deal of cable as well, and that woodpeckers were the main cause of the tiny holes regularly found in roadside phone wires. Several different protective materials were studied, with tin-plated steel found to be the most cost-effective defense. The very latest product, I was informed, was a 10-foot-long, triangular snap-on squirrel guard fashioned from slippery, hard plastic that could be fitted directly over cable to repel squirrels forever.

At the Whippany, New Jersey, installation, an ocher-colored relic built initially as a temporary structure and never replaced, there is a building housing an energy systems lab; its purpose is to work up ways to save energy and to build efficient telephone buildings, extending the work of the labs from the tiniest integrated circuit on up to the buildings they go in. Some of the telephone buildings, of course, go up in California, which is earthquake country. So, sure enough, in a giant room in Whippany, there's a steel platform that is an earthquake simulator.

Telephone equipment is loaded on the platform, secured in the same fashion that it would be in a building, and an "earthquake" program is put through a minicomputer. It shakes the daylights out of the equipment. "This way we know whether our earthquake precautions are satisfactory," a man explained to me. "Naturally, along the way, we do shake apart some equipment here."

6

The Lint Requirement

One of the places where telephones are made is along Shadeland Avenue in a dank industrial corner of Indianapolis. Roads there are rubbled, pocked with chuckholes. Big trucks, graders, loaders produce the prevailing noise, the dancing fumes. The air is gritty from the brown smoke of buses. It is a good area for the traveler to put up. Motels are across the way from the plant—the Marriott, the Rodeway Inn. A row of fast-food emporiums is convenient. Dense groves of plastic stand on either side—flashing, whirling, flaky. Across the street, at any given time, are something like twenty-five thousand telephones, enough to suit the needs of a small town. Millions pour off the clacking manufacturing and assembly lines every year—Trimlines, Mickey Mouse phones, Snoopy phones, Centrex systems, phones for patios, phones for coal mines. "We make them every which way," a plant worker told me. "They all talk."

The hammering, humming Western Electric plant is so big that people drive golf carts and ride huge three-wheel bicycles (tricycles for giants) inside it, down long corridors and among the cascades. There is an incessant trill of bicycle bells. A Western Electric plant would be a good place to hide a stolen fleet of cars. When the phones are done here, they are carefully packed in cardboard boxes designed by Western Electric and trucked to Bell System operating companies, a telecommunications marketplace that outreaches belief. Installed, the phones are connected over Western Electric wire and cable (strung across telephone poles furnished by Western Electric) that then snake their way into central switching offices made by Western Electric. When the telephones wear out, they are routed to a Western Electric recycling operation, where they are converted into raw material that is trucked back to Western Electric plants to be reborn as still more Western Electric telephones.

In function, there is nothing quite like Western Electric in American business. It has just one owner, AT&T, and just one primary customer, AT&T. It's like TWA making its own DC-10s or A&P growing its own food. In 1979, Western reported revenues of about $11 billion and profits of $636 million, figures that were contained in an annual report prepared for but one shareholder, AT&T. It employs approximately one hundred and fifty-five thousand people, a full seventh of Ma Bell's overall work force, people who typically view the Bell System as a manufacturing company that happens to own a few operating divisions. Founded in Cleveland in 1869 as a one-room electrical equipment shop bearing the name Gray and Barton, Western Electric shortly afterward resettled in Chicago and blossomed as a haven for inventors. For instance, it manufactured the world's first commercial typewriter. Also: Thomas Edison's electric pen, precursor to the mimeograph machine. In 1881, the Bell people acquired a major interest in Western, and the following year its leitmotif in life became to manufacture Bell telephones and equipment. Before that, Western could easily have been confused with General Electric. It made vacuum cleaners and sewing machines and radios. The stylish house of the day might have included a Western Electric chandelier dangling in the dining room. Over the years, it has swelled to the point where it now embraces twenty major plants sprinkled around the country, from Kearny, New Jersey, to Denver to Atlanta. Only telecommunications products to be used in the Bell System are worked on at these plants nowadays—some fifty thousand kinds of equipment. In Columbus, Ohio, such things as billing data transmitters and common system recorded announcement frames and remote trunking arrangements are churned out. At Lee's Summit, Missouri, can be found thermistors and thick film devices and varistors. Meanwhile, at North Andover, Massachusetts, Western workers are consumed with N carrier systems and channel banks and echo suppressor terminals. The equipment looks as exotic as it sounds. At various junctures, Western has also served as an indispensable supplier to the U.S. government. It built much of the radar used by the U.S. armed forces in World War II. It constructed the Nike missile systems, the Sentinel and Safeguard antiballistic missile systems, and a good chunk of the communications and control equipment for the U.S. space program. It built and installed a coast-to-coast blast-resistant telephone cable, engineered to survive a nuclear attack short of a direct hit.

Whatever its commendable deeds, Western Electric has had considerable scorn heaped upon it because of its snug relationship with its owner, a relationship commonly known as one of "vertical integration." A multiplicity of critics, including many well up the rungs of the federal ladder, argue that if the Bell System owns its dominant supplier, then what is to prevent Western from charging big, fat prices that will then shove up telephone rates? Fluffing its feathers, Western Electric retorts that this isn't fair, that its average price went up a trifling 43 percent between 1950 and 1979, that the average price of Western equipment stands 18 percent beneath that of other telephone equipment manufacturers (though it concedes that technology has been steadily eroding the price gap, and may indeed wipe it out altogether). Still, Western's prices are basically internal bookkeeping entries determined by AT&T, and their underlying costs are not specifically broken out. Since Western is free of surveillance from regulatory bodies, unlike the regional operating companies, it has a pretty open hand to do what it pleases. Foes of Western—who would love to see the big manufacturer melt out of the way—grumble that it exaggerates, honing and bending the truth. They protest that they are systematically and unjustly kept from getting through the turnstiles to what is the biggest market for telecommunications goods on earth. A man over at ITT, which feels its equipment is better made and better priced than that of Western Electric, grumbled to me one day, "We've got better stuff, and yet practically none of it gets bought by Bell's operating companies. Western uses every trick in the book to get around buying from us. All we're asking for is a fair shot, and we don't get it." (Some time after the ITT man spoke with me, AT&T settled an antitrust suit filed by ITT, agreeing to buy as much as $2 billion worth of ITT products and services over a decade's time. Lawyers familiar with the suit told me that ITT seemed to have a powerful case, but then AT&T has often been willing to deal with these sorts of things outside the courtroom and to dole out especially generous settlements.)

The way Bell has set things up, all of the operating companies have contracts with Western Electric, under which the big manufacturer is obligated to make and supply all needed telecommunications equipment. The companies are technically free to buy products elsewhere, in which case they generally turn to a purchasing arm of Western that handles centralized buying. You might immediately wonder how Western can impartially evaluate products of companies that are, in effect, competitors. Western says it has no problem; after all, it only wants to provide the best phone service. Competitors say that is hogwash, that the operating companies are dragooned into buying Western's gear. The Federal Communications Commission itself has frowned on this matter and ordered Western to divorce itself from its purchasing function. But as these things typically evolve, several years have lapsed since the order, and a satisfactory arrangement is still being thrashed out.

The complaint about Western has been basic to the three dramatic shoot-outs between the federal government and AT&T. Threatened with federal antitrust action, AT&T entered into the Kingsbury Commitment of 1913, under which it reluctantly agreed not to dominate all forms of communications in the United States. A 1949 Justice Department antitrust suit sought to cut Western totally free from its AT&T moorings and slice it up into three separate companies that would pursue their own destinies. The Bell System's purchasers would then have been allocated among them via competitive bidding. It never happened. In 1956, the two sides sat down and signed a consent decree that did hardly any damage to the Bell System. The government's relief consisted principally of a requirement that AT&T license its patents, even though there was no real telephone equipment market in which competitors could exploit these patents. Also, under the terms, Western agreed to confine its talents to making telephone equipment for the Bell System, which was more than enough to keep it busy anyway.

The government didn't give up. In November 1974, persuaded that new technology and new FCC policies had made the consent decree obsolete, the Justice Department struck again with the biggest antitrust suit on record. Again, the suit asks that Western Electric be pried loose and broken into at least two companies, but it goes still further and requests that AT&T be ordered to dispose of some or all of Long Lines from some or all of the operating companies, and it raises the possibility of spinning off Bell Labs as well. AT&T, Western, and Bell Labs were named as defendants in the action, and all of the Bell operating companies were cited as co-conspirators. In sum, the suit provided that Ma Bell could be torn to pieces. Among other things, the big suit complained that AT&T had allegedly acted to prevent competing telecommunications firms from acquiring a foothold in the private-line business.

It has become convenient for journalists to picture the case as AT&T being on trial for its life, though in reality antitrust suits are hardly ever a fight to the death. Their tortuous deliberations plod on at such a languid rate that, to many, they seem a hopeless waste of time. The second biggest case on record, a similar Justice Department proceeding against IBM, entered its twelfth year in 1980, with resolution nowhere in sight. One private antitrust suit brought against AT&T by a tiny West Coast telephone company sputtered to a conclusion late in 1979—nineteen years after it was filed. AT&T won. The big government case has already taken six years without reaching the trial stage, and could still be going on in the 1990s, unless another consent decree is struck, something AT&T seems interested in discussing, though the Justice Department has remained intransigent. Though the suit continues to haunt AT&T like an unexpiated crime, the case may be unmanageable. For example, AT&T says that in order to satisfy the Justice Department's demands for pretrial discovery, it will have to sift through 7.2 billion pages of material and submit 1.2 billion pages to the government for copying. AT&T has sworn that it will fight this suit to the end, maintaining that fragmentation of its supply services would mean less efficient service and higher rates. At all events, telephone service would not stop if Western were removed from Ma Bell's arms. AT&T executives themselves have conceded that it is possible for the system to function without its precious manufacturer. However, most of the people I spoke with figure that AT&T is just too tough, and, one way or another, it will manage to cling to Western and once again escape the claws of the government.

The organization of Western's manufacturing business has resolutely acquired an elaborate superstructure; to the eye of the outsider, it appears that for every man in blue jeans there are five with briefcases. The office of the top man, Donald Procknow, is well up in a skyscraper at 222 Broadway, almost directly across the street from AT&T headquarters, with hallways painted in splashy modern design. Procknow has the appearance of a man who has spent his life buried deep in work. When I met him one day in his office, he was wearing a gray suit, a pastel-blue tie against a pastel-blue shirt, and black shoes. He had this to say about Western Electric: "We've just come off some very good years, and we are optimistic for the future. We have a good order input. Telephone companies are replacing older equipment with electronic equipment. That's business for us. But we are concerned, as everybody is, with raw material costs. We are the biggest user of copper, and copper costs are going up. So we expect more modest growth in the next few years than we have been used to. One of the things happening with our business is our products are typically smaller and more sophisticated than ever before, and hence our manufacturing processes are more mechanized. Not that long ago, a lot of our factory space was devoted to wiring components together. We had all these people wiring things together. Now the components and their interconnections are often manufactured as whole units. Integrated circuits are made with thousands of transistors on a single chip of silicon. The upshot of all this is that less floor space and fewer people are needed for each dollar of output."

I asked Procknow about all the criticism that has been leveled at Western Electric.

"We are used to it by now," he said firmly. "It seems that the bigger you get, the more criticized you are. But we think these allegations are groundless. They make no sense at all. Criticism is something you learn to live with in industry, I guess in life."

"What would happen if Western was to be split off from AT&T?" I asked.

Procknow is not one to show emotion—his manner is flat and factual—but when he heard this question, he clutched the arm of his sofa, and his eyes blazed. "You know, this notion has been thrown around and thrown around for so long, and I just find it totally impossible to comprehend. Part of the reason for the superb phone system we have is the fact that the Bell System has been able to operate as one big unit. It just wouldn't work anywhere as well in any other fashion. This idea of splitting us off just because it's nice to have smaller companies is a lot of garbage. It doesn't make sense. It's stupid. I am confident that people are going to come to their senses and recognize what a ridiculous proposition this is. We have to stay together. It's as simple as that."

Off in the factories, this clouded future was not much on people's minds. The plant engineer at Indianapolis, proud of his place of work, showed it off from top to bottom. The factory was an unpredictable pastiche of hand labor and modern technology. Everywhere there was a great stir—people moving around, machines clattering, odd sounds. There appeared to be a not uncheerful atmosphere of generally controlled confusion. The pace of work was not so demanding as to prevent conversations or the licking of ice cream pops. The plant engineer led the way down a corridor into a cramped space where molding was being done. Big machines were pressing and spitting out phone casings in a rainbow of colors—tan Trimline bases from one machine, rust-colored bases from another, chocolate brown handsets from a third. The engineer went over to where plungers were being inserted into bases, threads were being cut into handsets, holes were being punched for cords. All around the plant were what resembled miniature traffic lights. Green meant that the quality of the product pouring off the line, as determined by inspection people, was good. Yellow meant potential problems were festering. Red meant that the quality was out of control and production had to be halted. We went down some of the assembly lines. Lines and lines of dials being assembled. Largely by hand. Largely by women. Largely talking. ("I don't believe what Bill did last night. The nerve of him." . . . "And then what happened?") "When the women stop talking," the plant engineer said, "then we know we're in big trouble." A mildly unsettling part of touring the plant was that all of these phones were being manufactured, were plainly visible, but not one of them was ringing. Nobody was calling anybody.

The plant engineer took me over to an area where special categories of phones were being put together. There was the familiar red firebox phone, designed to be pilfer-proof, though, as one worker told me, nothing is truly pilfer-proof. A key is needed to get inside. One of the machine operators said that when he was a kid he used to believe that the secret to making phone calls was the possession of a key. There was a patio phone that was encased in a waterproof zinc enclosure. There was a phone inside of what looked like a blue lunch box. It was a portable set for temporary use, equipped with its own generator, to be used at disaster sites. Reporters also depend on it to cover the national political conventions, and it shows up, in some abundance, at the Indianapolis 500. Then there was the mine phone. It reposed inside a thick metal casing. Lifting it risked a hernia. The casing acts as a guard against triggering a mine explosion by the electrical current of the ringing. It is the most expensive phone made, carrying a price tag of roughly $500. Taped to one work station was a small photo of a newly born baby, underneath which was written: "AT&T is okay, but I'm investing my money in lollipops." Catching me staring at the amusing picture, my guide quickly removed it, tore it up, and threw the shreds away.

The material bought in greatest quantity for phone manufacture is plastic, but the most expensive material is gold. All contact areas in the phone are gold-plated, and gold gets used in the electric microphone. The Indianapolis plant makes a gold report every month to check that the precious metal isn't being wasted or stolen. Both things, I was informed, happen from time to time. In Kearny, New Jersey, one employee was stashing gold-plated anodes in his thermos bottle. When workers took their leave of the plant every day, they were required to open their lunch pails, but not their thermoses. Surveillance, however, tripped the gold thief up.

I was taken to the performance and reliability lab. "What we try to do here is destroy the product," the man in charge told me. "Outside we make the phones, and in here we try our best to wipe them out. If we can't wipe them out, I'd say nobody can." One machine was hanging up a dozen phones simultaneously. Half a million hang-ups were being simulated. That equates to roughly twenty years worth of calls, the design life of a Western Electric telephone. Next to this machine was another that was pressing down the buttons on Touch-Tone Trimlines to test the dial circuits. In an adjoining room was a big dust chamber. Phones were laid in the chamber and every twenty-four hours twenty years worth of dust accumulation was blasted on them. The dust was of two kinds—road dust for outdoor phones and household dust for indoor phones—for I was told that different dust has different effects. It was a wonder that nobody was sneezing.

Elsewhere, phones were being rung half a million times to test their ringers. There was an overwhelming temptation to answer. Then there was a steel temperature chamber. Phones were stuffed inside for two-week periods, during which, twice a day, the temperature would gradually climb from -40° to 140°, and back down again. Phones are supposed to work at those extremes. "It's important not to blow into a handset at forty below to check if it's working," a man explained. "I did that once and the moisture in my breath froze up the damn thing. At a hundred and forty above, you ought to be careful not to put the handset next to your ear. You might burn it off." Drop testing was being done by hand. Phone bases were being held 3 feet above the floor and released. Thunk. Handsets were being held 5 feet off the floor. Thunk. They rarely broke.

I stopped in to chat with the plant manager, whose name was George Welch. He was a ruddy, cheerful, stoutish man with crooked teeth. On display in his office was a sign that said, "No Amount of Planning Will Ever Replace Dumb Luck." Welch, slow of speech, candid, had come up the manufacturing ranks, right off the line himself. He used phrases like "dad-gum complicated" to describe his telephone plant. "As recently as 1955, we made eight million phones a year," he said to me. "They were all black and they were all rotary. They were all the same size. We were Henry Ford and his Model T. About 1956, we started making colored phones. That was the first change to come to the telephone. Today, a black rotary phone (it's known now as 'ebony') is practically a special set. We make about fifteen million phones a year now. They come in ten colors. Ivory, beige, and white are the most popular, and black is one of the least popular. The most popular model is the Trimline. We make about five million of them each year, compared to about four million of the traditional desk-type phone." At service centers, Welch said, Western Electric also reconditions some 32 million phones a year, more than double what it manufactures. It has received phones from slum areas that were inoperable because they were loaded with cockroaches. Fumigation fixed them.

The cable and wire plant in Atlanta is a new one. The world's biggest cable plant (1.8 million square feet of cable-making capability), it annually eclipses its own world's record for production of new cable. In 1978, the record got up to 115 billion conductor feet. As one Western person put it, "Yeah, they sure make a lot of spaghetti here." Copper from the big copper companies—Kennecott, Anaconda—comes to Atlanta wound on heavy steel rolls on the beds of trucks and railway cars. The copper is about as thick as your pinkie. It is fed through a series of machines, almost totally automated. The copper is drawn through eleven dies, until it reaches the thickness appropriate to carry phone conversations. Insulating pulp (made by Western in great vats) is wrapped around the copper, and the wire is then dried in ovens and spun onto reels—what looked like enormous thread spools from a giant's sewing kit. Geometry is important in cable. If you get two sets of wire too close together, you end up with "cross talk" (conversation scramble), so a pair of wires is twisted together in a machine fittingly called a twister. Then the pairs are combined into units that are drawn into cable. A cable contains anywhere from six pairs of wire (for rural applications) to more than thirty-five hundred (for dense metropolitan areas). The cable is fed onto reels, and a batch of workers—mostly women in the Atlanta plant—sit tediously sorting out the varicolored pairs and testing them with a beeper device. Finished cable is charged with gas to keep out moisture, and is then capped. "It's a artful process, making cable," one of the plant workers told me. "Some people make cable better than others; they have a feel for it."

Metronomically hydraulic arms move the reels, one at a time, around the plant. An operator flashes a green "X" onto the floor, as if he were a destroyer captain sighting an enemy submarine, and then down come the metal arms—clank—and away goes the spool. Each spool weighs around 8,000 pounds. The manipulator performs tasks no one but Superman could ever do directly. The operator of the big arms we were watching happened to be a hefty woman. "She's an interesting case," my guide said. "It seems her husband tried to get rid of her and poked five slugs into her. As you can see, she survived nicely. The marriage, of course, is gone." Once the reels are done, they are stored, on end, outdoors in a cable yard. I cruised through the yard. There were something like ten thousand reels sitting there, and they were secure in large part because no one could pick them up.

Although copper wire keeps spewing out of the Atlanta plant in profusion, the product, in fact, is ultimately doomed. The cable of the future will be glass fiber. At the Atlanta works, I was shown a prototype manufacturing line that was already churning out glass strands. People in the plant refer to it as "angel hair." Glass tubes were being drawn down by being heated at temperatures up to 2,000°C. The manufacturing process is slow and expensive at this point. A 1-kilometer cable can take as long as eight to ten hours to make. Speed is expected in time.

The most sophisticated electronic switching systems are made outside of Chicago in the tiny town of Lisle (population 12,000).

Snow was underfoot on the day I visited the facility, but virtually everyone had shown up at his work station. Western makes three basic types of ESS—one for rural use, one for small cities, and one for heavy-traffic metropolitan areas. The latter is known as the No. 4 ESS, and it is looked on as a contemporary demonstration of how far the telephone company can go to get what it wants or needs. It is made exclusively in Lisle, and is not an impulse buy. To purchase one, you need something like $20 million. "They're boring as hell to watch," a technician told me, as I stood watching one function. "There's no noise, only this slight hum. The old mechanical babies, boy, they were something. They would be clicking like crazy when connections were being made. You got excited watching them work. These marvels are dull, dull, dull. I wish I were making the old buggers." I roamed into an adjoining lab, where systems were being cooked by small electric heaters to 120° F., then put into service. This was to simulate an air conditioner failure. The systems didn't seem to mind the temperature.

In another building, a few blocks away, was a software center for switching, possibly the biggest software factory ever built. In it, computer programmers were toiling away at programs to make the electronic switching systems perform new magic. Most of the significant future changes that are likely to be incorporated into switching machines, Western Electric prognosticators believe, will fall within the realm of software. In one room, I was shown a newly developed program for 911 emergency call systems. When a call arrives at a 911 office, the program causes the name and address of the person placing the call to appear on a video display. The idea behind it is to aid the police when a distraught caller neglects, as so often happens, to provide a name and address when reporting a murder or burglary.

On the outskirts of Princeton, New Jersey, Western Electric owns a novel Engineering Research Center, a repository where several hundred scientists and technicians, 60 percent of them possessing doctorates, grapple with developing and improving telephone manufacturing processes. The center was created in 1958, when it became obvious to the telephone company that breakthroughs like the transistor were going to revolutionize telecommunications manufacturing methods and compel Western to cook up new ways of making its wares. The building is tomato bisque in color and briskly rectangular in lines. Planes of metal-framed windows are interrupted by planes of stone masonry. In sharp contrast to the earsplitting roar of Western's factories, the prevailing atmosphere is one of library calm.

In one lab, a researcher was working on ways of separating different types of scrap plastic insulation. Plastic has been routinely thrown away because hand sorting is the only effective means of separating it, and that takes too long. Researchers at the center determined that different plastics bounce at varying heights when dropped against sheets of metal. Hence, a tall contraption had been devised, down which the scrap plastic was dumped. Some of it would bounce over a little fence into one funnel, and the rest would drop into another funnel. In another lab, a technician was striving to get a better splice in a broken wire by making use of the intense heat generated by a small detonation. He showed me how the process worked. The bonding explosion went pop, like a bottle of champagne being opened. In a color lab, a device was being developed to sort phone mouthpieces by color. This would allow old phones to be repainted at service centers and put back into homes. The present system of sorting mouthpieces was too slow to suit Western Electric. With the machine in the lab, the caps come roaring down a conveyor, then drop before an optical scanner that determines the color and directs a lever to deposit it in the appropriate bin. The machine, I was told by the engineer demonstrating it, was capable of sorting seven thousand caps an hour.

Just next door to the engineering facility was the Corporate Education Center, Western Electric's "college." It stood back from the road amid vegetation that would have graced a fine suburban villa. There was a luxurious lawn punctuated by exotic-looking birches, evergreens, and other trees and shrubs, giving somewhat the effect of a mature Japanese garden. The college was complete with dormitories, eating facilities, computer labs, a film studio for making training films, and classrooms equipped with instant TV playback facilities so that students could gander with delight or alarm at their performances. There was also a library that contained no fiction. The center offered courses like "Analysis of No. 4 ESS Man-Machine Technique," "Security and Control in Data Processing Systems," "Thick Film Theory and Technology," and "Psychology in Industry and Creative Thinking." Around 250 students attend each week, almost all of them Western Electric employees and the rest hailing from elsewhere in the Bell System.

The teachers are Bell System men, supplemented by some 100 visiting professors who arrive for short stints from colleges. Most of the courses take a week, but there is a special class for uncommonly talented young hopefuls that runs for all of twenty-three weeks. Anybody planning to vault to president of Western Electric would be expected to take it. Although the vast majority of courses are deeply technical, there are a few offerings like sensitivity training, in which employees learn to be more appreciative of the feelings of their colleagues. To the delight of the students, there are no formal grades in any of the courses.

The residence hall, which is directly across the street, is reminiscent of a motel. There is a school bus that runs from the dormitory to the classroom building during inclement weather. Out back are tennis courts, some basketball hoops, and a paddle-ball court. The restaurant, when I looked in on it, served food several cuts above what I remembered from my undergrad days. "It's what we call a five-pound restaurant," a waiter told me. "You are expected to gain five pounds a week." Students are forbidden to bring their families along with them, however. They may patronize a bar (the only Bell System bar) that is open for an hour and forty-five minutes twice a day. "We give our students a heck of a lot of homework," I was told by the college manager. "So we can't very well have them boozing it up all night long. We let them drink just to loosen up a bit." At dinner, jackets and ties, or dresses, are expected of everybody. Students generally behave themselves. There have been no sit-ins or seizures of buildings at the college, I was told.

One of the services that Western Electric performs for the good of the other pieces of the Bell System is centralized purchasing of products—picking things up from suppliers in truckloads, then reselling the goods to the operating companies. The Purchasing and Transportation Division of Western Electric, which tends to all this consumption, is in a vast compound nestled in Greensboro, North Carolina. The boss is an expansive, white-haired man named Robert Kraay. About two thousand people work for him. He stands watch over the annual buying of more than $4.5 billion worth of products from forty-five thousand suppliers. He is sort of a super consumer.

"We buy the raw materials Western uses to make phones and other equipment," Kraay told me one morning over coffee. "Then we buy supplies for the companies. That means everything from office paper to operator chairs to flashlights to paper clips. Things like vehicles and furniture the companies usually take care of themselves. But we will get literally anything that is asked of us." Buying centrally, AT&T guarantees uniformity of standards. Also, by purchasing in big numbers (some examples: 200,000 tons of directory paper, 3,000 operator chairs, 200,000,000 paper clips, 3,000,000 ballpoint pens, 3,000,000,000 sheets of toilet tissue), Western can get lower prices than the individual operating companies could imagine in their wildest dreams. "Quality, though, is the big thing," Kraay said. "If there's a likely defect in one out of a thousand of a particular item, no big deal if you're buying ten of them. We may buy several billion."

Purchasing people test and set rigid standards for almost everything that is bought. More or less is not the way of AT&T. For instance, Western will not buy just any old paper towel. It has a lot of hands to be wiped, requiring about 500 million paper towels a year, and when you buy that much of something you tend to be fussy about what you get. An AT&T towel must be between 10 and 11 inches long. It must be between 7⅛ and 7⅜ inches wide. It must be at least .006 of an inch thick. It must totally absorb water within five seconds. There is even a lint requirement: no more than .6 milligrams of lint per towel. When towels are yanked from their holders, lint flutters off. "Too much lint on the floor," the AT&T regulations declare, "makes for a very unsightly restroom."

Most of the testing of products is performed at a facility in Springfield, New Jersey—a single-level, squat, unimpressive building set hard by Route 22. There are seventeen laboratories. On a snowy day not long ago, I paid a visit to the facility and took a tour of some of the labs.

In one room, a tall man with rampant sideburns was minding a bizarre-looking machine that was testing the steel device that affixes to a lineman's boot, enabling him to scale a telephone pole. The machine, which looked something like a small steam engine, simulated a 300-pound man shinnying up a pole. Not too many 300-pound men shinny up telephone poles (most of them, it seems, play linebacker for a football team), but AT&T takes no chances. The machine determines how many steps a lineman can attempt before his climber falls completely apart. The specification is half a million steps. The machine polishes that off in five days.

In another area, a contraption was putting ballpoint pens

through their paces. Ten pens were clamped in holders and a motor was furiously whirling them in circles. Paper unrolled under the pens. A medium-point pen must do 13,333 loops—a mile of writing—before expiring if it has hopes of finding its way into the hands of a Bell System employee. After the sheets of paper are filled (looking like a penmanship student's homework), secretaries use them as wrapping paper. Down the hall, in the shock and vibration lab, a transportation simulator was wobbling back and forth, rattling a telephone carton. It was simulating a truck lurching down a rough road, and thereby testing cartons of packaged products to make sure they could withstand things like trips through avalanches. In the paper testing lab, toilet tissue was really getting it. Machines were carefully determining how smooth it was. How strong it was. Its absorption, softness. Yes, even toilet tissue matters at AT&T. Why should it? "You haven't been to many train stations if you don't see why we have specifications for toilet tissue," a paper man explained to me. "We had a recent bidder offer us absolutely dirt cheap prices. They weren't so incredible once you looked at the absolutely miserable paper. Gaping holes all over. Not for our people."

Paper clips were being tested by hand. They were affixed to several sheets of paper, then yanked off to see if they bounced back into shape. If they didn't, that was bad. AT&T wants its clips to be used again and again. "Maybe this seems silly," a clip person confided. "But a great paper clip is a wonderful thing to behold."

As a whole, the Bell System has a thumping impact on its suppliers. For most of them, it is the biggest customer. Occasionally AT&T frets about other companies being mortally dependent on it. It could say it wants no more and, bam, a company could come to its knees. "We try to give suppliers advance warning of any change, any change at all," Bob Kraay explained to me. "We have about ten percent annual turnover. I know of no company that went out of business because they lost us, but naturally there have been instances of severe hardships."

What do the lucky suppliers think about having the world's biggest company as a customer?

The Noesting Pin Ticket Company, sole supplier of paper clips to Western Electric: "Well, we love them. They are a big chunk of our business. Losing them would be like losing a lung. You go on, but you don't like it."

The Warren Communications Company, a quarter of whose

rectifier business goes to Western: "They're tough as nails. They have, in effect, a resident inspector at our plant. Other companies, even giant ones, send in teams for spot checks once or twice a year. The Bell people are always checking. They seem to need to check, like other people need air to breathe."

The Waterbury Scroll-Pen Corporation, supplier of 1.5 million pens to Western: "Every year when our contract comes up for renewal, I start shaking like a fever has hit me. You don't want to lose them. I tell you, once you do business with them, you are qualified to do business with any company on earth. Because you have met the toughest customer."

One of the most important and most visible products that the system buys is telephone poles. Something in the neighborhood of a quarter of a million poles are bought each year, at a cost of between $75 and $100 apiece. Already, the phone company has 30 million poles holding up its cable. It is steadily cutting back on poles, though, since it is considerably cheaper to bury cable underground, assuming the terrain is not unduly rocky. At present, most poles that are being bought serve to replace old worn-out ones. The big headache with poles, I found out, is decay from fungi and termites. To do in these evils, the poles are coated with preservatives. Mostly, Western uses pentachloralphenol, but it continually tests new preservatives to see if it can possibly create a better pole. It owns two telephone pole test plots. One is in Chester, New Jersey, and the other in Bainbridge, Georgia. At the plots, telephone poles loom one beside the other, what appears to be the work of a telephone pole installer gone mad. Dummy phone lines droop between some of the poles to simulate actual loads.

Julian Ochrymowych, a thoughtful, practical person who is the company's resident expert on telephone poles, accompanied me on a visit to the Chester plot one afternoon to check out the poles. It was nippy out. The ground was icy. Bordering the plot were trees gnarled and bare. Someday those trees could end their lives as telephone poles. "Look there," Ochrymowych said to me. "There's a pole that's been standing for seventy years. Wonderful! We expect thirty-five years out of a pole. We don't mind, though, if one hangs around a little longer."

Nearby were some fiberglass poles. In quest of the perfect pole, AT&T has looked at fiberglass poles, laminated poles, and steel poles. All have proven too costly. Most poles, Ochrymowych explained, are 35 to 40 feet tall. Roughly 85 percent of them are fashioned from southern pine. Trees usually aren't considered poleworthy until they reach the age of forty or fifty. Old poles, he added, are generally given to charitable organizations, where they wind up their senior years as parking lot retainers, wall barriers, and playground toys. However, one row of old poles supplanted by buried cable had been simply left standing in Utah's Escalante Desert. There were eagles nesting in them.

"How about that?" Ochrymowych murmured as we moved through the pole yard. A gaping hole, big enough to stick your fist through, marred one of the poles. "That's woodpecker damage."

Each year, he went on to explain, woodpeckers sink their beaks into thousands of telephone poles. Pecking things wooden is instinctive with them, of course, and is not believed to reflect any hostility over phone rates. Woodpeckers have confused Western Electric plenty, Ochrymowych told me. Nothing seems to keep them away. Tin snakes have been nailed to poles to frighten them off. No good. A power company once tried painting poles red, green, yellow, and white in the hope that the birds would be so disgusted by the rotten taste that they would go hack up a log cabin instead. No good. "We have pretty much given up research on how to repel woodpeckers," Ochrymowych said, with a tinge of regret. "Basically we just pray a lot that they stick to trees."

On the Line

Conversation, bits and snatches of it, was bubbling through the room. About twenty-five operators (six of them male) filled the work space—standing, sitting at their stations, calling out instructions—all drivingly busy. It was going on eight o'clock on a savagely hot and sticky morning. The faces of those at the boards for some time flickered through a series of expressions —blankness, a wan grin, surprise, disgust, boredom. From time to time, the operators exchanged mocking glances or rolled their eyes to express comic disbelief, but mostly they just stared directly at their stations. Reservoirs of tact appeared to be in great supply. The men and women just coming on for the day's action, draining in a gulp their morning Styrofoam cups of coffee, plopped their headsets over their heads and plugged in. Numbers, charges, circuits were the stuff of working thought here.

"Operator, may I help you?"

"I'm sorry, the number you are calling is busy. Will you call back later?"

"Thank you."

"Operator, may I help you?"

"Just a minute please."

"Collect call for Arnie from Sherry. Will Arnie accept?"

"Go ahead."

"Operator, may I help you?"

"Card number."

"Central time is 8:47."

"Operator, may I help you?" (Punched out a credit card number.)

"No, I'm sorry, I'm not looking to adopt a kid."

Long-distance calls were being connected in a cavernous,

carpeted room on an upper floor of the Northwestern Bell Telephone headquarters, a huge twelve-story, block-wide structure on South 19th Street in downtown Omaha. I had made it out to Northwestern Bell to strike up an acquaintance with one of the operating companies. The operating company is the hub if not the heart of the phone company, literally carrying out its charter purpose and promise—to deliver phone service. Any operating company might have done, for they all work more or less alike. But in more ways than most of its kinsmen, Northwestern Bell seemed prototypical of the breed.

Few people realize why AT&T developed not as one massive operation, but as a jumble of subsidiaries. It had to do with money. When the phone company first sprang into being, it didn't have the wherewithal to establish phone service everywhere. A number of local companies formed, trading shares in themselves for the right to use the Bell patents. Even though AT&T later amassed the money to cement everything together, it saw that as undesirable. Having one huge company, it feared, might be psychologically disorienting to many customers, not to mention politicians. The Northwestern Telephone Exchange Company, incorporated in Minneapolis on December 10, 1878, was the first of a batch of companies that blossomed into Northwestern Bell. After a single year of operation, it had strung 301 miles of wire and installed 700 phones. Noisy circuits were a chronic problem. It was not until 1909 that Northwestern began to operate as a central company embracing the assorted local exchanges that had come into being. Its domain now spills into five states—Iowa, Minnesota, Nebraska, North Dakota, and South Dakota. It has about 5.25 million phones in service, roughly a third of them in the metropolitan area of Minneapolis and St. Paul. In the states in which it does business, close to 2 million phones are served by independent telephone companies. Northwestern subscribers make about 9 billion local and long-distance calls a year, or 1,320 calls per person. Numerically among the operating companies, Northwestern ranks tenth in net income, twelfth in revenues, twelfth in total number of phones, eleventh in plant investment, ninth in construction. It employs 28,000 people. Like the majority of the operating companies, it has just one shareholder, and that is AT&T. In money terms, each operating company turns over to its parent between 1.5 percent and 2.5 percent of its annual revenues under what is called "the license contract." In exchange, AT&T makes the telephonic equipment for the companies, operates the long-distance lines, furnishes central staff services, and tackles research and development. Besides this sum, each company pays AT&T cash dividends that help it to pay dividends to its own shareholders.

"No, this is not directory. Do you want me to connect you to directory?"

"Operator, may I help you?"

"I'm sorry, the number you're calling is busy. You want to call back a little later. I say the number you're calling is busy. You want to call back later."

"Collect call from Rosalie. Will you accept the call?"

"That will be forty-five cents for three minutes, please."

"I'm terribly sorry, but those are our rates."

Over the years, there have been about as many changes in the operator's job as there have been in women's fashions. It has been more than a hundred years since Emma Nutt plugged in and became the first woman operator for the Bell System. In the early days, there were relatively few long-distance calls and therefore only a smattering of full-time operators. They wore long dark skirts and white blouses, sat in high chairs to reach the switchboard above them, and lugged around heavy headsets. Not now. Everything is computerized. Since 1975, Northwestern operators have used what is known as a Traffic Service Position System (there is one cord board left in the Omaha telephone system that handles a few stray functions such as calls from mobile telephones). Each TSPS operator sits before her own sleek console. A narrow TV-style display automatically shows such needed information as the charge for a call. Before the TSPS's arrival, operators had to scribble down tolls on call slips, but these units house a memory unit to register billing data. The swifter pace at which the operators can work translates into savings of a few million dollars a year in Omaha alone. The office handles customers in a 50-mile radius (Waterloo, Fremont, Dodge, Bennington, Red Oak, Mo Valley). It is bombarded by about thirty thousand calls a day from people who for one reason or another dialed "O" for operator. Any one operator fields as many as seventy-five calls every half-hour.

"Okay, and what happens when you dial? Okay, deposit your dime and I'll dial it for you."

"I'm afraid the number is busy."

"No, I'm sorry, I can't hurry the call along."

"That's interesting that the person is the biggest talker on earth."

"No, I don't know any cake recipes."

Speed seemed to be the operational word. This was not a job for those who prefer not to deal with hortatory bosses or the pressures of time. Using a specially contrived machine, supervisors take measurements on a half-hour basis; two measurements per day per operator is the norm. The notoriously sluggish get watched even more closely. From these clockings is computed the operator's average work time (AWT), what equates to her (his) batting average. Numbers are capital law in this kingdom ("How was your latest AWT?"). Drawing from studies AT&T undertakes throughout the phone system, supervisors fix rigid objectives to shoot for, objectives for certain portions of the day as well as the entire day. Here, the day-long target was twenty-nine seconds. Objectives and actual times are chalked in on a king-sized blackboard at the very front of the room. There is no missing the board, just as ballplayers, much as they might wish to during a particularly dismal afternoon, can never evade the score posted on the scoreboard. Speed is the big thing, but operators are also scrupulously checked for accuracy and courtesy—sixty-two calls a month worth. As soon as a call flows in, a stopwatch is punched. The operator is supposed to answer—pleasantly—in three seconds. Answering pleasantly in three seconds is not always easy, as any number of customers will quickly testify. The operator is checked that the right fare is given, a credit card number is correctly taken down. She is rated as being "interested," "satisfactory," or "not interested." If she is "not interested" too much of the time, the phone company becomes not interested in her.

Done with her shift, Jan Corbett (trim, attractive, petite, a round face, long hair) unplugged her headset and straightened her disheveled hair. She has been on the phones for eight years, interested more often than not. "The volume of calls is just tremendous," she told me, undertaking to describe her calling. "The phones are always busy. You never have time to think. It's call after call after call. There are about seven or eight phrases you use and that's pretty much it. 'Operator, may I help you?' 'What number did you want?' 'Would you repeat that again?' 'I have a collect call for you from so-and-so, will you accept the charge?' 'That number is busy, can you try back later?' That's all you really say. The one part of you that gets worn out is your mouth. It may seem odd, but you get tired of talking. You're talking for hours without a break. Friends ask me after work how I feel, and I tell them I'm fine, except I've got a worn-out mouth."

Continuing, she said, "I try to be conscientious about handling calls quickly. Sometimes there's nothing you can do. Once, during a blizzard, customers had to wait fifty seconds to get a long-distance operator. Too many people were backing up the lines. The night Pope Paul died, there was a special program tracing the life of the Pope that replaced 'Star Trek' on television. By the hundreds, people called the TV station to complain. Waiting time soared to something like eighteen seconds. You can never tell what's going to hold up your calls.

"The job is pretty routine. Now and then, you have your oddballs. People call up and want to know why a street light is out. How should I know? The thing burned out, so it's out. How do you get someplace? I don't know. Once a lady was stuck in a phone booth and there were wild donkeys loose and she couldn't get out. This was in Arizona, where donkeys roam wild. I could hear them braying in the background. She wanted to know how to escape. I'm no expert on donkeys, that's for certain, but I advised her to flap the phone book at them and maybe they'd take off. I guess it worked. I didn't hear back from her."

"Okay, hon, you're not supposed to put your money in before you place the call."

"Collect call for Cheryl from Jean. Will she accept?"

"Collect call from Wendy. Will you accept the charge?"

"No, ma'am, I am not a recorded announcement. I am a real person."

Darlene Eledge was chewing gum as she was getting ready to start her shift. Short curly brown hair. Plain. Affable. "I used to work on a cord board. Your hands would fly back and forth. I liked that. Now you just talk. Talk. Talk. Talk. It's fast, but I like to help the people more. It wasn't quite as hectic when we were helping the people. It surprises me how some folks talk to you. The way some of the kids curse at you. I never know how to talk that way. You don't get many unusual calls. Occasionally, you get a person who wants to call the President collect. You have to put the call through. The White House operator always explains that policy is not to accept any collect calls. So much for that.

"The march of progress has sure made the operator's job less exciting than in the old days. It's less personal and it's less responsible. Back in the pre-dial days, when the operator was needed to make every phone call, she was a hero of sorts. She would have to seek out the doctor for a midnight medical emergency, round up volunteers to save a house on fire. She was a folk hero. It's a lot less romantic today. It's not as much fun, that's for sure. Customers don't understand sometimes why we get curt. We're not mechanical toys. We're people, even if all you hear are our voices. Operators are people and they have to get mad, too."

Inside a small, sheltered nook on the main floor of the Northwestern Bell headquarters, two women sat aslant in cubicles and listened to customers tell about breathers and kissers and whisperers and unrepeatable verbal onslaughts the details of which they were unwilling to divulge. The women wore a halo of omniscience. They remained bland and cool. They seemed understanding and entirely sympathetic. ("Yes, yes, we have them all the time. Isn't it awful. Where do these people come from?") This was the Annoyance Call Bureau.

Imy Schoneboom, a pert woman with wavy gray hair and large glasses, who seemed proper to the extent that she might faint dead away if she were ever the recipient of an obscene call, was in charge of the office. There were so many pieces of paper piled on her desk they could have been removed with a rake. Four hundred to five hundred complaints stream into the office every month. "During the summer and holiday period, you can count on the annoyance calls picking up steam," Schoneboom said to me in a low, halting voice. "Those are field days for the cranks. They just go wacko."

Crank calls take many forms. "Mrs. Porter," growls a man at the other end of the line. "I've been watching you. I know about your kids and when they get out of school. I'm coming to get them." That is a fairly extreme case. Often there is no sound at all, just an ominous click of disconnection when the phone is answered, this repeated again and again throughout a night. Sometimes the caller is a "breather," a person who breathes heavily into the phone until you hang up. Then there are moaners. There are callers who play musical instruments into the phone. In Omaha, there is at least one screamer, a man who calls at odd hours of the day or night, and when you answer, he screams at the top of his lungs and then quickly hangs up before you can scream back—as you are ready to do after a few times. Sometimes the caller, remaining anonymous, will argue at some length the issue that prompted his call. Naturally, there are the calls when the instigator will spew forth a barrage of denunciations and obscene remarks, until you are quaking.

Crank call stories traverse the system. One bureau remembers when a "Father Steiner" plagued the phone lines. He called thousands of women—as many as 135 in a twenty-four-hour period—asking if the person was Catholic. Eliciting an affirmative answer, he would casually explain that he had discovered the number lying on the switchboard of a local Catholic university. "The message says you've asked for a confession," he would go on. "This is Father Steiner and I'm ready to hear it." Oddly enough, many of the women went along with the ruse. The questions got increasingly personal and more and more pertained to sexual habits: "How many times have you had relations with your husband this week?" "Have you had relations with anyone else in this period?" The police eventually nailed Father Steiner. He turned out to be a twenty-five-year-old businessman, married, the father of two. He said he didn't know why he did it.

Several years ago, a Fairfield, Connecticut, woman groused to the police that she had borne the brunt of offensive phone calls from a particular man for some thirty years. She decided finally to file a complaint, she explained, because the language had lately surpassed her personal standards of decency. In St. Paul, Minnesota, there was the notorious "undergarment salesman," who would phone and ask for ladies' measurements, inducing them with a free pair of fine underwear. No one seems immune to telephone abuse. A Salina, Kansas, bank was swamped with lewd messages that were left by a husky low voice on the answering device set up to record calls on weekends.

Overall, AT&T claims that complaints about these abusive calls are few compared with other sorts of grievances. No one really knows how many such calls are made. Complaints lodged with the phone company or the police may not be the best index, for victims frequently don't report calls, believing it to be futile. In any case, the Bell System says it has noticed no significant rise in the number of reported incidents in recent years. Also, it reports that its records show no important regional variations in the level of grievances.

"With any legitimate complaint, we have a commitment to help the customer," Imy Schoneboom said. "If the calls don't seem to be all that serious, we offer scare tactics. For instance, we suggest the customer say, 'I have reported these calls to the phone company, and I have found out that they can be traced.' Taking the phone off the hook or wrapping it in a towel are basic ways to frustrate late-night callers. Or we suggest hanging up. That's really the best way to handle these crank callers. Just hang up on them. Cut them off." Blowing a shrill whistle into the phone has proven effective. One regular receiver of abusive calls used to keep a recording of dynamite exploding by her phone to play to callers. To avoid sex calls, women are advised to list themselves in the directory by initials. Police also sometimes recommend that people plagued by annoyance calls secure an unlisted number. The phone company isn't particularly big on that idea, since unlisted numbers cut down on business. It doesn't mind if subscribers resort to answering services to screen calls, though. Automatic devices are especially useful, because they offer the advantage of allowing the victim to listen in for clues to the identity of the caller. A New York electronics firm has developed a device that, when connected to a regular telephone, disguises the sound of a person's voice, the intent being to make a woman's voice sound like a man's in order to fend off obscene calls. The cost of the contraption, however, is $2,650, which would be abusive to many people's finances.

Should the problem linger, Schoneboom said, a trace will be put on the line. It is a time-consuming, laborious process that is at best just partly certain. The tracing equipment reveals only what line the call is coming in on, not the identity of the caller. Meantime, the customer is instructed to keep a log of the calls, jotting down their frequency, the time, the kind of voice, background noises, and anything else noticeable that could lead to an arrest. Finding the offending phone is not enough for court evidence, however. There must be proof of who made the call. The ideal way to establish this, naturally, would be to catch the crank caller in the act, yank the phone from his hand, and talk to the victim at the other end of the line. So it is easy to see why the police and the phone company want to know that they are working on something serious before they attempt to trace a phone call.

Deterrent interviews are conducted by the Annoyance Bureau, I was told, if it thinks it's on to somebody. Generally, these scare callers off. In rare instances, phones are disconnected. Schoneboom said, "One young teenager was calling people repeatedly and making kissing noises in the phone and saying, 'I love you.' He'd hang up, then call right back and repeat it. We caught him and talked to him three different times. He kept it up. He just wouldn't be swayed. The mother said to forget it, she couldn't control him. Finally, she asked us to disconnect the phone. So we took it out.

"A lot of times the caller is someone the victim knows, often a member of the family, and the calls are part of a personal feud. One suspect was a brother-in-law. Another time it was two women squabbling over one man. The girlfriend was calling the wife and harassing her. Once, a young boy was calling a whole array of numbers just for the fun of it. Most of the calls are children making harassing calls. There are a number of standard jokes. 'This is the telephone company testing. Will you step back three feet and whistle? Thank you. Now, three feet more. Thank you.' There are a lot of male obscene callers who pose as survey people who then start to ask some very personal questions. The hardest person to catch is the pervert who calls a lot of different people and doesn't repeat himself. Probably half the complaints involve people who simply call and hang up. A few are bomb threats or threats of bodily injury. 'I'm going to break your arm.' 'I'm going to break your back.' There was one guy who was ordering stuff by phone and having it delivered to people. He ordered pizza. Cakes. Real estate. Lumber. We finally caught him. There's a guy who calls up and identifies himself as a policeman. He gives his name as Bob Johnson and a badge number and precinct number. He says he'd like the customer's cooperation. She will receive an obscene call. He would like her to stay on the line while he attempts to trace it. He's been pulling this stunt for several years. We've worked with the police to try to figure out who it is. We must have had over a hundred complaints on him. The police have had another two or three hundred. But we don't have any idea who the nut is."

At the Northwestern Bell garage at 75th Street and Pacific Avenue, nine installation trucks were berthed. It was a rambling brick building set amid newly constructed condominiums, rolling hills, and lots of trees and bushes. Everywhere were puddles of grease. The garage foreman was a bearded, huge hulk of a man named William Harris. His office was tucked away in a corner of the garage. He was looking over a notice that had arrived from the district customer services manager, addressed to all supervisors: "With the occurrence of dog bites we seem to be having in our district I think it would be beneficial to review the attached 'Boomer Poster' with your people." The poster, in fact, was a cartoon strip depicting a garage foreman scolding an installer named Boomer. He says, "Boomer, you've been bitten by dogs four different times and you know why. The reason you got bit was because you didn't have the dog confined." The foreman reviews the four incidents, proving his point, until Boomer, sweat pouring down his brow, swears he will never start another job unless any dog is first tied up.

On a wall in the office was a sign that read: "We the unwilling led by the unqualified have been doing the unbelievable so long with so little we now attempt the impossible with nothing."

Thumbtacked to the bulletin board near the door leading to Harris's office were an assortment of charts. Scrupulous records are kept of crews' performances in a number of categories. How many additional phones and services each installer had sold. Gas usage. Accidents on the job. "Everything is very competitive," Harris explained to me. "It's awfully competitive between the companies, and super-competitive between the states. We all want to be Number One. We'll work our tails off to get there."

I went out on some calls with one of the men in the garage. His name was John Arends. He was a thin, stiff parchment roll of a man, twenty-six, with sandy-brown hair curling out in back and resting on his collar. He looked like the thousands of lifeguards who populate California's pools and beaches every summer. It was eight in the morning when we met. The hot and sticky air was perfectly still and seemed to amplify every sound. The temperature was due to climb into the nineties by mid-afternoon.

The phones for the day were strewn on the concrete behind Arends's truck. He scooped them up and stacked them neatly in the back. He was thorough and meticulous. He walked around the truck and checked the tires, tested the directional signals, the lights, the brakes, then he scrunched himself into the cab of the somewhat yeasty-smelling green and white truck, buckled his seat belt, switched on the ignition, and barreled out of the garage. The truck was a 1971 General Motors van with 48,000 miles on it. NORTHWESTERN BELL and the Bell System insignia (a small bell) were painted on the sides. We drove past rows of hamburger stands and shopping centers toward Arends's first appointment.

As he tooled along, Arends told me that about half of the customers in the area served by the garage had been wired with modular jacks that allow a phone to be plugged into the wall like a lamp. Thus customers could go and buy their phones from a PhoneCenter store and hook them up themselves. An installer was needed only to connect the wires from the central office—one way the phone company is saving on labor costs and speeding installation.

After a while, Arends said, "All apartments are about the same, but when you get a house, everything's different. Sometimes, people will have remodeled a house and pulled out the existing free wire. A lot of times, there are prewired outlets and people will want the phone on the other side of the room. You'll have to figure out a way to get there. It's like a puzzle. About the most unusual thing I can remember is when a pet monkey swiped my tools out of my pouch while I was working. I didn't realize he was sneaking up on me and was taking them until most of the tools were gone. It was a few hours before I found them stuffed under a chair."

We shuddered to a stop in front of a house at 62nd and Pine. Arends cut the engine and climbed out. It was a small, white, scruffy-looking house. The lawn badly needed to be mowed. Arends glanced at his order sheet and saw that it called for two phones—a white Touch-Tone wall phone and a beige desk phone. According to the slip, the wire was already in place for the wall phone. He strapped his tool pouch around his waist, unloaded the necessary equipment from the rear of the truck, and trundled up to the door.

A big, toothy, slovenly man wearing a Mobil cap greeted us. A powerful reek emanated from him.

"Telephone man," Arends said airily.

"Yeah, right, just come on in," the man said resignedly.

The house was in tumult. Obviously the family had just moved in. Boxes and boxes were stacked everywhere. The place was old and light came in at places other than the windows. A cat suddenly lurched through the mess and leapt onto the windowsill, where it began to purr.

First, Arends looked over the existing connection in the kitchen. Using a blue test set, which resembled a phone receiver without a base, he checked for a dial tone and found one. "I'm going to put a modular jack in here," he said. "Then the customer will have it easy in the future." He had trouble removing the previous jack from the wall. He cocked his arm and drove his fist into the wall with a punch that could have damaged a prizefighter. Some crud tumbled down. The jack slipped off. Arends put the new one on.

Done with that, he screwed the white phone to its base, plugged in the cord and handset, attached it to the wall. He dialed three digits that got him the central office, then punched the last four digits of the number. The phone rang. That's how installers check that phones are working. "Kids are always after me to get that number so they can ring the phone and drive their mothers insane," Arends said. "Of course, I never give it out. We protect it like a family secret."

Next, he dialed the three digits of another test number that reached a recording of the phone number. That certified that the number printed on the front of the phone was correct.

Finished in the kitchen, Arends clomped downstairs to the basement. The man in the Mobil cap was loading the washing machine. He dumped in some detergent. Perhaps he was a house husband?

"You having fun moving in?" Arends inquired.

"Trying to fix the place while you're moving in is something else," the man said hoarsely. "This place is a horror. It's a zoo."

Attentively, Arends ran some wire down to the basement, put in a jack behind a wall in a little alcove, then hooked up the beige desk phone. It was a stuffy, claustrophobic spot. A ridiculous place for a phone, it seemed to me. "You sure you want the phone here?" Arends said.

"That's the place," the man said.

Arends smiled tightly and whispered to me, "You do what the customer tells you to do. He wants the phone in the backyard, you put it there. He wants the phone on the roof, you put it there. The customer is always right, even if the customer is nuts."

Upstairs, the woman of the house was up. From the sounds emerging, it appeared that she was trying to salvage the kitchen.

"Well, I guess that does it," Arends said, scooping up his things. "Now are these the phones you wanted, or did you want the Trimline ones?"

"I couldn't care less what they look like," the man replied.

"Couldn't matter one whit to me how they look. Long as they work."

"Well, they ought to do that pretty well," Arends said.

When we got back to the truck, I asked Arends to tell me about his sales strategy. "I've done pretty good at selling," he said. "I sell something on close to fifty percent of my orders. The thing is, I don't try to pressure people into taking something they don't want. I just try to make people aware of what services we offer." Besides the amalgam of different models and colors, the company offered four special services in most of its territory: call waiting that enables you to keep a call on hold; call forwarding, whereby you can shuttle calls to another number; three-party calling, under which a third person can be added to a conversation; and speed calling, which lets you reach certain numbers by dialing just three digits.

"I usually ask about the Trimline," Arends went on. "Maybe a fifth of the people will take it. It's a nice feather in my cap, since it costs a dollar thirty a month more. I got the impression that this guy wouldn't have wanted it. He didn't seem so enthusiastic about the phone company calling, which is the way it goes sometimes. Maybe he got up on the wrong side of the bed or had a hot pepper for breakfast. I don't know. But I decided not to bother asking about our custom calling features. He seemed precisely the sort who would take the cheapest thing he could possibly get."

After a while, Arends explained that installation in the Omaha area was generally being done within two days, three at the outside. The basic charge was $5, plus $6 service order charge and $7 central office charge. "I heard that it costs five hundred and fifty dollars for an installation in Japan," he said. "I heard that it's a thousand dollars for a first installation in South America, and it's a two-year wait. So how can anybody complain about our charges and our wait."

I asked Arends about problems with animals.

"I had a Saint Bernard go after me once," he replied in a deadpan voice. "The owners assured me he was friendly, and all of a sudden he had me. I told them they had to chain him up. I was in the backyard, and the dog broke the chain and was on top of me again. I felt like a dog biscuit. I had a Doberman go after me another time. The owner said he was friendly, too. Besides dogs, we have to worry about hornets and wasps. We carry a wasp killer that freezes them. Wasps like to nest in terminal boxes. Sometimes

I have to crawl under a house to get at the wires. I once ran into a rat there. In manholes, you encounter salamanders and snakes. In the Dakotas, they have rattlesnake problems. They put worn-out tires around the base of the poles there to keep the high winds from blowing away the soil; snakes like to nest in the tires. Gophers like to eat underground cable. Squirrels eat aerial cable. Moose sometimes get their antlers stuck in cable. Mice in the winter will burrow underneath splice boxes and terminal boxes. Then, they start gnawing the insulation off the cable. We use a foam that fills up the bottom of the boxes. Once I got a rubber arrow in the back from a kid. I surrendered peacefully."

Bad weather has historically been a thorny difficulty in Northwestern's territory, and out of storms and floods have come moments of unusual courage. In March 1965, a blizzard that descended on Minnesota piled up drifts 15 to 20 feet deep. After the blizzard, floods devastated the territory for over a month. In Des Moines, flood waters weakened the old Sixth Avenue Bridge and sent most of it crumbling into the water. What remained didn't appear strong enough to support a man. Installer-repairman Jap Brown brought down his English pointer, Duke. He tied a fish line to the dog's collar. Brown then drove a circuitous route to the other side, whistled, and Duke trotted across. Plant men pulled successively larger cable across, until finally the heavy cable necessary to restore service to seven hundred phones was yanked across the waters. That same year, the capricious Mississippi carved out a new channel near Elk River, Minnesota, and washed out telephone lines. Again the problem was getting a cable across swirling waters. This time there was no bridge and no dog, and the water was obviously too dangerous for any sort of boat. Herb Miller, an amateur archer, reported to the scene. After knotting a fish line to an arrow, he took careful aim and shot the arrow into a tree 300 feet on the other side. Cable was then pulled across using the fish line.

Elsewhere in the country, other problems present themselves. Like crime. In New York City, guards from a private security agency ride along with installers who venture into high-crime sections of Manhattan and the Bronx. "Yeah, when I think about those guys riding with those armed guards," Arends said, "well, I don't worry as much about animals. I'll take the animals any day."

After several more calls, we drove down a quiet tree-lined street and pulled to a stop outside a stark, two-story apartment house, Hillcrest Oaks Apartments. ("One, two, three bedrooms. Professionally owned. Swimming pool.") Arends was running a bit behind schedule, so he picked up the pace. "The time pressure put on us has gotten greater over the years," he said. "The company really started demanding a lot from us when it began to ask for rate increases. So you hustle. At the end of the day, my arms sometimes feel as if they have gone eighteen innings each."

We went to apartment 107. A dog was yapping behind the door. A pale-looking, sloe-eyed woman wearing curlers answered Arends's knock. She had a soap opera on the tube. This was a PhoneCenter order. Arends only had to connect the line in the basement. The woman smiled as we entered, and Arends quickly went over and affixed a device to the phone that added a buzzing noise to the line so that he could readily identify it from the maze of lines in the basement. Down in the cellar, a dank, musty room, Arends found the line without any trouble and, using the color combination given him by the central office, hooked up the appropriate wires. He returned to the apartment and tested the phone. This time, however, he yanked out the cord momentarily after dialing the test number. Another phone rang. He plugged the new one back in. It rang.

"Is there another phone I'm supposed to pick up?" Arends asked the woman as he got ready to leave.

"Just this red one in the corner," she said. Nonchalantly, she pulled the phone out from beside the sofa, as if that were the most logical place in the world to keep a phone. Arends tucked it under his arm and took his leave.

On the way back to the truck, he said, "Pretty tricky how I found that other phone, huh? She probably was going to keep it. It wasn't on my order, but I thought I saw something out of the corner of my eye. That's one of the drawbacks of modular phones. People can easily plug them in anywhere. So they just steal their phones from previous apartments. We have to be detectives as well as installers."

Riding high in the elevator in the 19th Street headquarters, one finally reaches a lofty office with a huge window, and, peering out, obtains a splendid view of downtown Omaha. This is the hive of Jack MacAllister, president. Glasses. Short brown hair, plastered down. A blue striped suit, white shirt, red and blue tie. The airy office was paneled in light wood. The air conditioner was humming. Now in his early fifties, MacAllister assumed the top post at Northwestern Bell in late 1975, having spent his entire career with the company.

MacAllister seemed best equipped to answer the question of the exact nature of the relationship between an operating company and the parent company. Generally, I had been told, the relationship is pretty good, though there are times when things aren't going well at the operating company, or when AT&T takes a stand that the operating company doesn't much care for, and the relationship may become strained.

"It's really a case of the president has a lot of options," MacAllister said in answer to my question. "The fact is that AT&T does give an operating company president fairly good latitude in running the company. The contacts between the two are fairly infrequent, as a matter of fact. I presume that if your service program is very weak, or if you've seriously deviated from policy, there would be ample reason to talk to an operating company president. If not, there are more contacts on the staff level with people getting procedures explained to them than on the presidential level. Northwestern Bell has been fortunate during my tenure in not having serious problems. Our service has been fine and our operating results have been generally good. So our relationship with the New Yorkers is a pleasant one. I have heard that, at other companies, when things get a bit rocky, there can be fairly stern and uncompromising supervision from the parent. There are a half-dozen formal meetings between the operating company presidents and the AT&T officers every year, and I have less formal discussions periodically. But sometimes weeks go by during which I have no contacts with AT&T, either in person, by mail, or by telephone. I'm required to do a monthly report on service quality. I have generally not received much feedback, because we do fairly well. Once in a while, I get a brief handwritten note from the chairman. He will scribble, 'Nice job,' about something that he thinks is good. Another month, if something goes amiss, he may write, 'Jack—oops!'

"There are some areas in which tensions are likely to develop. For instance, labor relations. The companies have different arrangements with the unions, and if one union gets something the others want, people get ticked off. Management salaries also aren't uniform. Then there are the operating procedures. We pretty much all operate alike, but companies do decide to do some things their own way, which doesn't always please the people in New York. We at Northwestern have always put a great deal of emphasis on development of personnel. Accordingly, our officer group is generally younger than most other officer groups in other operating companies. The big thing ultimately, however, is what your earnings are like. If you bring in the bucks, AT&T leaves you be. If you're stumbling a little, it keeps a close watch. Pressure is always on us to improve our earnings—the same as would be true in any business—but we are never told to let up on service in order to beef up our profits. One other aspect of AT&T control is the fact that all of the operating company presidents are appointed by 195 Broadway."

MacAllister mentioned that total business in Northwestern's territory had been growing at around a 7 to 10 percent a year clip. "We don't seem to have the boom and bust situation that other areas have. Our business follows the growth of the Midwest's economy. We haven't had a Houston, nor have we had the disaster of a huge metropolitan area that loses business—like New York City. Our earnings had been fairly flat until a few years ago; then they started to grow at around fifteen percent a year. That should continue into the guessable future."

I asked MacAllister how he came to work for the phone company.

"I graduated from the University of Iowa, and I was interested in management," he replied. "I interviewed at several companies. I didn't know anyone at the telephone company, but I was intrigued by the opportunity, so when I received an offer from them I took it. In those days, the approach to hiring people from college was that they'd give you a craft job, and if you did well, they'd give you a job in management. If you didn't do well, then good-bye. I started off as an installer. I liked that, since I've worked outside with my hands all my life. Going to college, I wheeled cement and worked in a cannery, detassled corn, worked on a farm. My grandfather had a farm, and I worked for him. I helped my father build the house that he still lives in. I worked seven or eight months as an installer, and the one incident I still remember was when I was sent to take out a telephone for nonpayment of bills. I was promptly chased up a telephone pole by a couple of mean-looking dogs, not the kind you'd choose to mess with. The owner finally called them off and said he'd pay if I left the phone there. To make sure, I accompanied him all the way to the business office and looked on while he paid his bills.

"I became a service representative in the Des Moines business office next. I was an outside representative who took care of all problems that couldn't be handled by phone. For instance, if there was a disagreement between party mates on a party line, I'd be the one who had to try to iron out the problem. A good share of the work was plain old bill collecting. When we first put up our microwave tower in Des Moines, a customer wrote a long letter about the tower being the work of the Devil. The Bible was quoted at length. So I went out to see him, taking a Bible with me. The customer told me he had memorized the Bible. I told him I had a Bible with me, and he dared me to pick any page and he'd know it. Sure enough, he did know it. I recall we ended up having a very good discussion and we parted friends, but I don't truthfully remember if I convinced him that our microwave tower was a good thing."

Pausing to chuckle a moment, MacAllister continued, "From there, I swiftly moved along the ladder. I became a public office manager, then the manager of an office in Mason City, Iowa, then the unit manager in a business office in Des Moines, then I went to an area office as a personnel staff person, then to Rapid City, South Dakota, as district manager, then to Omaha as a commercial staff person in the corporate office, then a district manager in Omaha, then district plant manager, then general plant manager in Nebraska, then general commercial manager in Iowa, then I went to work for AT&T headquarters for two years, then I came back as secretary and treasurer, then chief executive officer for Iowa, then operating vice president, and finally president. As you can see, you hold a lot of titles if you make it to the top."

I was aware that every month AT&T publishes a thirty-page pamphlet officially known as the "Green Book," and unofficially dubbed the "Green Dragon" or "Green Hornet," that critically compares the performance of Bell's operating companies, one against the other, in an army of categories that range from the percentage of repair appointments not met to the number of fatalities on the job. I imagined that operating company presidents were exceedingly sensitive to how they were doing compared to their sister companies, and so I asked MacAllister how competitive he was with his compeers.

"Oh, sure, we're competitive," he said. "That's part of the game. It's friendly competition. I am always intrigued by how eager other company presidents are to share ideas that work with their colleagues. I think they all have a deep desire to make the Bell System better. I think most of the presidents are more competitive with themselves than they are with each other. The main thrust is, 'Are we really doing as well as we can?'"

One steaming day, I planed into Des Moines, then drove out to Urbandale, Iowa, on the outskirts of the city, where I visited the Iowa Training Center, one of two training facilities maintained by Northwestern Bell (the other one is in Minneapolis). The school was a new, buff-colored brick structure set on flat, arid land. Across the street at the Peppertree Motel (most rooms of which Northwestern rents to put up its students), a neon sign sizzled meretriciously in the warm sunlight. The roadside was edged with ragged grass and the inferior tarmac of turn-ins and parking lots. In the back of the training center, telephone poles marched at regular intervals, creosoted dark brown, their untapered trunks scarred by the crampons of student climbers. A smaller building stood close by the poles, containing midget 6-foot-high telephone poles for students to shinny up when the weather got nasty. Some days the temperature snaps to -20°F. in these parts. Snow spouts and whirls. Crazy winds tingle and blast.

I called on Jake Liebbe, the director of the center. He was a short, chunky man with a breezy manner and a cheerful, chipmunkish expression. He had both the bemused and amused look of someone who has spent his life teaching. On the shelves surrounding the office were copies of Bell System practices and course manuals, and on the desk in front of Liebbe were the galley proofs of a new course book. Liebbe was a whirlwind talker. He sat behind his desk and began to speak in short, energetic bursts.

"The phone business today is a complicated beast," he said. "When I first got into this business in 1946, a foreman asked me how long my legs were. I told him, and he threw me a set of climbing boots and said, 'Here, these ought to fit, go climb a pole.' Well, I hung onto that pole for dear life and got a job. I started off as a linesman, and I went through all the jobs to here, learning most by trial and error. Now, we do things a bit more civilized."

When Northwestern first set up its training center in 1947, there were 3 courses—basic electricity, installation, and toll instruction. Today, there are 438 courses touching every conceivable aspect of the phone business. Everyone who arrives at the center is first whisked through a basic employee training session that lasts two weeks. In this, they learn such basic things as how to hold a screwdriver and hammer, how to work from a ladder, how to drive a telephone truck (AT&T has its own standards for braking distances, looking far ahead, and so forth), how to administer first aid, and how to master the tricky and difficult art of climbing a telephone pole. About nine thousand students go through the courses in a given year. When a student first arrives, the odds are excellent that he knows no more about a telephone than how to make a call on it.

"It used to be that the people we got were farm boys," Liebbe said. "They knew how to do things with their hands. Now we get city boys who don't. They know how to watch television and drink beer. They don't even know how to take a brace and bit and bore through a piece of wood. When I look at the crop of new students we get sometimes, it just disgusts me." Liebbe threw up his hands and took a breath. Then he picked up the pace again. "We have a lower quality person than we had ten to twenty years ago. We get people who can't read or write. I'll give you a shining example of this. We had a new installation course that Bell of Pennsylvania drummed up. One of the problems with the course, they determined from a study of it, was lack of comprehension. So they designed the course with seven thousand slides. I wouldn't take the damn thing. What are the students going to do when they go out in the field and see words rather than pictures? It used to be you had to have a high school diploma to work for the phone company. No more. Courses used to be designed with tenth grade comprehension level. Now it's slipped to seventh grade. Maybe we'll soon hit kindergarten. You have to make things as simple as you possibly can. I really feel like we're talking baby talk sometimes. One of the problems today, I think, is that big business has not taken enough interest in public education. That's why people aren't prepared today. I've been on the soapbox on this for years. There are a lot of people who spend a lot of years getting educated who come out and have absolutely nothing to offer."

Donning hard hats and safety glasses, Liebbe and I sauntered out to the pole climbing area to see what was happening. Set up there was a videotape machine to film students while they were practicing on the poles. Afterward, the tapes would be run back and mistakes meticulously (and heatedly) pointed out. Something like a pro football camp—slow motion, stop action. Wooden chips were strewn about the ground. Poles have to be replaced almost weekly, they get chopped up so badly from the continuous climbing.

The act of climbing a pole is one of the most dangerous tasks any phone company worker does, a fact not lost on the instructors. "Yeah, this is where you can really get hurt," Liebbe said to me. It took little convincing. Indeed, there had been a number of fatalities from climbing poles. Something like 3 percent of the men and 30 percent of the women fail to ever master the art, generally because they aren't strong enough. The system tries to weed out probable failures before they even approach a pole. Applicants are run through three tests that they must pass before they can get a crack at climbing. Calipers are used to measure skin folds in the back of the upper arm, a measurement that indicates stamina. A balance test is administered. Then a cable with two handles on it and a dynamometer attached is used to measure strength. Only a few months ago, a woman was hovering at the 18-foot level, which is as high as the students progress to. She had been climbing for several hours. The instructor advised her to rest. She wanted to continue. Abruptly, she found herself much too fatigued to get her safety belt wrapped around the pole. Panicking, she started to scream hysterically. The instructor carefully shinnied up and stuck his hand behind her, which turned out to be a mistake. Feeling it, she let go and fell. Luckily, she suffered only a sprained arm and leg, but the sharp gaff on her climbing boot plowed through a man's hand at the bottom. He had been attempting to break her fall.

For a short, intoxicating spell, I watched some of the students going through their drills. All poles are slightly crooked, and so students are taught to go up the high side, so that they're leaning inward and can better retain their balance. A quarter-inch penetration of the climber gaff is critical. Toes should be turned away from the pole at all times. Heels should be close together. Knees should be directed away from the pole. Hands should be shoulder high. Heels of hands should be on the back quarters of the pole. Wrists should be away from the pole. Leading hand should be high. When you put your gaff into the pole, you shouldn't jab it, but strike it. Then you lock your knees and go up with your knees in a locked position, sort of as if you had artificial legs. Keep your butt out.

I looked on as one student practiced on a pole that sported boards cutting across it at the very top, where he was attaching a drop wire that connects to a house. The procedure is to first attach the line to the house, then you bring it over to the base of the pole and tie a rope to it. Using that, you pull the line up to the top of the pole, then climb after it and fix it in place. "Remember, always haul that line up from the ground, never from up above," an instructor was sternly telling the student, who appeared to be doing a pretty good job. It was an important lesson. Only a week ago, an installer decided to climb the pole first, then yank the drop line up by hand, which conserves time. A car caught the line as it was being dragged up, pulled the installer off the pole and killed him instantly. The man had been installing phones for twenty-seven years and should have known better.

Another student in the yard was stabbing a pole with what is called a "pike pole," though it looks like a javelin. The idea is to jostle the pole with the sharp blade on the end of the pike pole before you climb it to determine if it's rotten. "The thing is also handy to stave off irate customers," an instructor mentioned.

Kathy Sandstrom, a slender woman with short blond hair who was one of the teachers of the basic course, told me, "The biggest problem in climbing is fear of heights. You have to learn to trust your safety strap. We have people who absolutely turn white with fright." The last task the students have to accomplish is go to the top and hoist a weighted object. They practice balance by tossing basketballs and footballs from pole to pole. They have to circle the pole. They lug a 20-pound bucket up the pole on a rope, take it over their safety belt, then lower it slowly back to the ground.

A woman was climbing well to 8 feet. She strapped her belt around the pole, unstrapped it, and hooked it back around her, then headed down. A little nervous. She was moving slowly, very deliberately around the pole, like a lion stalking game. Sometimes, she would jab into the pole two or three times before she was satisfied that she was secure. As she came down, she looked like a marionette. "C'mon, lock your knees," the instructor yelled at her. "There you go. I know it's hard work. You got to keep at it to put those phones in."

On the Line · 119

Just as happy to be on the ground, I was conducted into a station installation room. Batches of pay phones were screwed onto one wall, all of them open so that their innards were showing. A pay phone is a surprisingly complicated piece of equipment. In another corner of the room were four dummy houses. Each had two walls to it. A small telephone pole stood outside. Students make use of the houses to run through all the steps involved in installing phones. The phones they put in actually work. Many lines run into the house for practice purposes. There are good pairs of wires and bad pairs.

One student was getting ready to take his final exam, which would last six hours. He had to cut a pair of wires at the access point, then run a drop wire from the house to the pole, install a protector, put in the actual phone, write up the order, then remove the phone. Installers have to have the makings of a salesman, a pitchman, so with the instructor posing as a customer, the student must succinctly explain what he did, see if any additional instruments are desired, ask about special custom calling features, and demonstrate how to use the phone directory. The dummy house being used had the address "210 Mulberry Street" painted in white on the outside. Students were expected to check the veracity of the addresses on their order slips. One time, a student put a phone into the wrong dummy house, losing him points. "We don't give away phones by putting them in the wrong houses," he was advised. The student who was taking his final seemed a trifle nervous, though very workmanlike and serious. Judging from the frequent nods of approval from the instructor, he appeared to be well on his way to becoming a Bell System installer.

Returning to Omaha, I made my way to the fringe of the city, where a level brick building in the Old Mill Shopping Center housed one of Omaha's two business offices. It was an airy room furnished in an inexpensive but clean-cut modern style that revealed a strong sense of order. The office served eighty-two thousand residential accounts. To cope with them, it maintained a staff of thirty-three service representatives, most of them women, and four supervisors presided over by a manager. "Service representative" is the highest nonmanagement job that exists in a Bell operating company. Each representative, arranged at a desk beside a microfiche file of customer records, handles a daunting thirty-five to forty calls a day, discussing bills, new installations, service complaints, and so forth. They are subjects of some discord, since reps periodically find themselves pilloried by regulatory commissions and consumer groups for conveniently neglecting to enlighten new customers about the most cost-efficient phone service they can sign up for, instead of trying to weasel as much business as they possibly can.

There is always a deluge of calls into business offices after a rate increase, people wondering why they are paying more. Monday is the worst day. People save up their problems from the weekend. Sometimes reps take as many as sixty-five calls apiece on Mondays. "Monday is holy hell," one of the reps told me. This was Monday afternoon. Several large status boards on the room's walls enabled the reps on duty to promise a customer a certain installation date. The lights on the boards showed that the earliest available date at the moment was Wednesday afternoon. Reference material kept at each desk supplied the answers to almost all of the questions that normally crop up. Experience helps with the rest.

Sandy Steffen is a tidy woman with an even gaze, the serene voice of a peacemaker. An irate woman had just phoned to complain that she had gotten a denial of service notice (meaning her phone was soon going to be taken out), even though she claimed she had paid her bill. Steffen's voice was as soft as sphagnum. From the expressions on her face, the customer's tone of voice was well off the scale of cordiality.

"Well, I'm sorry you feel that way about this, ma'am, because we don't send notices to you just to keep your deposit. . . . No, ma'am, we don't. . . . Well, ma'am, I really don't think every one of us in this office would give you a different name. . . . Well, ma'am, I'm not the same person. There are more than one of us in this office."

(This went on for about twenty more minutes. Through it all, Steffen somehow seemed to maintain her composure. I got the impression that she was used to being dressed down by customers, and momentarily wondered to myself what effect this had on her self-image.)

"Well, ma'am, I'm sure that you went to school, and I'm not saying that you don't know how to read your notices. . . . Yes, I'm sure that you can read. . . . No, I don't think you're a raving lunatic. . . . Well, that's wonderful. I'm glad that at your age you still don't need glasses. . . . I'm sorry you feel that way, ma'am."

Steffen took a moment to heave a large sigh of relief, then explained some of the workings of the business office. "Right after bills have been sent out, most of the calls have to do with bills," she said. "Somebody's got a call to South Africa, but they claim they never call there. During the first part of the month, we mostly take orders for new service. We get quite a few orders to change a listing, say from initials to a full name or vice versa, or to make a listing nonpublished. In the summer, we get a lot of requests for vacation service. That's where we temporarily disconnect the phone but keep the listing intact. Saves people some pennies."

Steffen said that the experienced reps are given fairly wide latitude in coping with unexpected problems. He or she may adjust a bill up to $25 without consulting a supervisor. A representative can also decide (within guidelines) whether to disconnect a customer for nonpayment or extend further credit. (Steffen said she disconnected phones four or five times a day, which seemed an amazing figure to me.) He or she may speak sharply to a rude or abusive customer (though reps say that they tend to control their tempers fairly well, since they usually grow immune to abusive customers after they have been on the job for some time), or may speak in endearments to a troubled one. The one hard and fast rule is never to keep a customer on hold for more than sixty seconds.

Above all else, service representatives are expected to soothe hotheaded customers and dispose of their problems before they molest the president of the company (who is bound by the Bell System protocol to personally reply to all grievances brought to his attention), or still worse, take their woes to the Nebraska Public Utility Commission. There is almost nothing worse, from a rep's standpoint, than to let a complaint leak outside the company.

Steffen, who had been a representative for four years, told me, "The job has changed a lot. It's gotten much more complex. There are so many more things you're responsible for. The rates and services and so forth. I like the job, though. It's a job where there's always something different. It's sufficiently complex that it's not something you can do by rote day in and day out. There are some days when you get nothing but complaints. Every time you pick up that damn phone, there's somebody on the other end hollering at you. But it can be a lot of fun to try to please the customer without giving away the company."

Like operator jobs, the position of service rep is subject to surveillance and constraints that must sometimes be utterly maddening to the employee. Supervisors in the office regularly listen to a couple dozen randomly selected calls. What's more, six service evaluators who operate from a remote station downtown and cover much of Northwestern's five-state area do nothing but check up on service reps. They sample a hundred calls for each office, every two weeks, following them to completion. That is, if a representative takes an order over the phone, the evaluator checks to make sure that that order is promptly processed. Every two weeks, the manager gets an evaluation sheet that lists any calls handled incorrectly. Waiting times are also calculated. This particular office had an accuracy objective of 98 percent. For the last several months, it had been hitting 99 percent, which might have partially explained the many cheerful faces I spotted. There is nothing in the Bell System to compare to beating the index goals.

Steffen took another call.

"Okay, now you want to reconnect the design phone and change the bell chime?"

"Okay, now my records show the phones are red."

"Now, my records show your phones are modular."

"Now, your chest phone is what kind?"

"All right, that's a nice phone."

"We'll set you up for Thursday. We'll set you up for, let's see, between one and five on Thursday. Thanks for calling."

I talked to another rep named John Sweeney. Long, shaggy hair. Coke-bottle glasses. Dressed in jeans and a short-sleeve shirt. Three and a half years on the job. He said, "Many calls are people saying they didn't make a call on their bill. It's a constant, constant complaint. When that happens, we automatically adjust the bill, taking the customer's word, then send the call in question to a Centralized Ticket Investigation office, if it was an operator-handled call. If it was dialed directly, we would check the listing and ask the party if they know that person. We have a name and address bureau. We call them with a phone number and they give us the name of the person if it's a listed number. If the customer says he doesn't know that person, then we know from our tests that the chance of error on a directly dialed call is less than one percent. We might, if the amount was enough, contact the other party and ask if they had received a call from the customer, though small amounts we just let go. I'll tell you, though, a lot of people try to get away with murder."

Sweeney explained that, like everywhere throughout the Bell System, Omaha had a persistent problem with people not paying their telephone bills. The entire city, he said, wrote off about $40,000 in uncollectible bills a month. Some money was subsequently retrieved through collection agencies that the phone company engaged as a last resort, but there was always a goodly amount that was never received.

At the end of a broad, 200-yard-long corridor of wall-to-wall carpeting in the 19th Street headquarters was the entrance to the Douglas Street Repair Center, charged with testing and repairing phones for about half of the businesses and residences in Omaha. "This is the mortuary side of the business," said Dale Erney, the thickset, talkative manager of the center. One tooth protruded from under his lip, which gave the impression that he was always grinning. The commodious room was atwitter with activity, people hugging phones and talking animatedly into them, others scrambling about for equipment records, still others talking to repairmen calling in for their next assignment.

Any subscriber who dialed 611 reached one of a bank of people huddled against a far wall. Adjacent to them were giant circular bins that contained line cards with the name, address, equipment, cable and pair information, terminal address, kind of service, and list of trouble in the last six months for every phone handled by the office. Erney showed me a few of the cards. "I get these out of sequence," he said, "and my ass has had it." The people fielding the calls fill out a trouble ticket for each complaint and stick it on a chute that transports it along a conveyor track. Testing technicians on the other side of the room scoop up the tickets. Using both voice and electrical test equipment, they test the line. Without even going to a customer's premises, they can at once tell if there's a short, a ground problem, foreign voltage on the line, or any of a host of other fairly straightforward problems. The test people usually call the customer as well, to pick up additional information. One deskman was occupied with a customer whose trouble was that although he could receive calls, he couldn't make them. After some electronic detective work, the deskman informed me that he had found the culprit: the wires were reversed. He called "Frame"—that is, the frame in the switching office to which the customer's phone was connected—and requested a reversal. He then asked the customer to try to dial him. He got him right off and airily reported that all was well.

Most calls, though, require a visit by a repairman. When that happens, the test person turns over the trouble cards to a dispatcher, who consults a magnetic map of the city on which he posts outstanding problems. Above the magnetic map was the sign: "Meet the appointments you can't change. Change the appointments you can't meet." A sign tacked over the dispatcher's desk read: "Come on in. Everything else has gone wrong."

"What does go wrong?" I asked Erney.

Six feet tall, he paced the room, tilted forward, jaws clamped. "Everything that can happen to a phone does," he answered. "Most complaints are for no dial tone, or they can't call out, or there's transmission noise on the line. One woman in our area breaks two or three Trimlines a month by beating up on her husband. Right now, her phone is disconnected for lack of payment. But she'll be back, I'll guarantee it. Kids set fire to phones. People dunk them in boiling water. They hurl them out windows. I heard of a guy who poured a martini down a receiver. Repair problems have been a little higher the last couple of years, mainly because we've been hit with such lousy weather. Prolonged bad weather gets basements wet that have wire or equipment housed in them. That shorts out lines. By far, most trouble is caused by normal wear and tear on equipment. Phones don't last forever, even though they last longer than ever. The phone gets used a lot more today than it ever has, so it breaks."

I went out for a period with one of the repairmen who worked on business accounts, a man named Rich Bingham. Thirty years old, he had curly, light brown hair. The lenses of his eyeglasses were small perfect circles rimmed in metal, and he wore brown corduroy pants and a striped short-sleeve shirt. For three years he had been a station repairman, and for a year and a half a PBX (private branch exchange) man. Here, there, he had seen a lot of dead phones.

"I like repair," he said as we drove off in his somewhat dilapidated truck. "It can be pretty strange work. You get it all in repair. Sometimes, you open a set and a mouse has chewed on the wire. You can drop a staple in a phone and short it out. I had that happen. What a bitch it was to find. On a switchboard, it's nothing for a person to spill coffee on the equipment and put it out of commission. A hard case of trouble to find is when the wire breaks but the insulation doesn't. You look at it and it's good. Only it's not good. You have to keep pulling the wire until it breaks off."

We stopped at the Northern Natural Gas Company, where a complaint had come about crossed lines on one of the phones. A receptionist directed us to the sick phone. A sour-looking man was at the desk, feet up, riffling through some papers.

"Hey, you better fix this," he said. "It's all screwed up." He picked up the phone and dialed a number. He handed the receiver to Bingham. "See that," he said. "Two people are on the line. I called Tulsa just before and two different people answered the phone there. I have here the most potent phone in the Midwest."

Bingham checked the line in the terminal room on the same floor, but the trouble was not there, so he headed down to the basement. Alas, the trouble was not in the lines in the basement, either. That meant the problem lay somewhere in the cable between the office building and the central office, and it would have to be searched for by the construction department. In the meantime, Bingham called the central office to get a different pair of wires to switch the problem phone to. "I just hope there's a spare set," he said. "If not, I'll have to go upstairs and tell that man that his service will be temporarily out of order until we can get someone here to fix the cable."

Bingham and the subscriber were in luck. An extra pair existed. Bingham connected the phone to the new set of wires, tried it out, then went up and informed the man that his problems should be over.

"Well, they better be," he said.

We moved east. White-painted, tin-roofed bungalows. Awnings shading the fronts of stores—prepared for heat and glare. Red earth. Sand roads. Houses on short stilts. Sloping verandas. Unpainted boards. Clustered sows behind a fence. An automobile wrapped in vines. Finally, KETV, local affiliate of Channel 7. Bad cords, the station had complained of. "I don't know exactly what that could be," Bingham said. "You never know what's up till you get there. Repairing phones is often like running in front of a speeding locomotive. You never know if you're going to get past the problem."

Humming tunelessly to himself, Bingham sashayed into the

lobby. A woman with a beehive hairdo sat slumped behind the reception desk, filing her nails. Looking up, she said, "Well, what do you know, the telephone company."

"Hey, don't give me that," Bingham said.

"I've been waiting and waiting," she said. "I called Friday. I called Monday. Now it's Wednesday."

"What can I say?" Bingham shrugged. "I just got the order ten minutes ago."

The problem, the woman explained, was that two cords on her cord board were not functioning. Unfortunately, Bingham wasn't familiar with the particular variety of board and decided it would be unwise for him to even attempt to repair the cords. He promised that another man with expertise would stop by tomorrow. The woman sighed and said that would be all right, then mentioned that there was also a phone on the third floor that didn't ring.

"I'll give that a look," Bingham said.

The phone was located in the traffic department. Three short, gnomish women were standing around a table languidly jabbering. The phone, a black rotary affair, not only didn't ring, it was altogether dead. Bingham disassembled it, revealing inside a neat, arresting work, and tested it with his test kit. The problem wasn't in the phone. Down in the basement, he discovered a wire that had snapped off. He swiftly attached it back where it belonged, and the phone at once came back to life.

"Well, that was simple enough," he said. "I could have been here five hours and not found a thing. You can't predict with repair. Some days are easy. Some days it's like you're looking for the Holy Grail. Some days I go home and I have nightmares all night long about broken phones. It surprises me at times when I pick up my home phone and it works. I'm so accustomed to picking up busted phones."

At the northwest hem of the city, in an area of industrial buildings interspersed with low frame houses, I made a final visit to one of the directory assistance offices. It was an antiseptic-looking room ingloriously lighted by fluorescent bulbs, the center of it cluttered with operators speaking into their stations. A knot of operators were talking in the corner, occasionally breaking into gusts of hilarity. The office employed 125 operators who worked in four shifts. They handled the entire state of Nebraska and the western portion of Iowa, a grand total of 120 towns. I sat down next to one of the more seasoned operators in the room. Her name was Shirley Goldsberry. She had short curly blond hair, with a platoon of freckles bivouacked on the crest of each cheek. A pink sweater was draped loosely over her shoulders. She seemed to be answering an unending stream of calls.

"Dr. Lambertz? That would be five-three-four, four-seven-four-one."

"You're welcome."

"The National Bank of Council Bluffs? Okay, that is three-two-two, three-four-five-six."

"Deborah Fischer?"

"I have a D. and a D.A., but no Deborah. Do you have an address?"

"Directory, may I help you please?"

"Weyerhauser Company is three-three-one, five-one-oh-oh."

Like the other operators, Shirley sat before a computerized system that was the most advanced in the Bell System. To obtain a listing, you punch the initial of the town (O for Omaha) and the first four letters of the last name of the party (for common names like Smith, a first name is needed as well). There are buttons for residential listings, business, and government. With this operation, calls are disposed of in about twenty-five seconds, an eight- or nine-second improvement over the former system, which used to call entire pages up from the phone book onto a microfiche screen.

"Directory."

"No, I have no William Dixon, not at that address. Let me check Bill."

"No, nothing at Bill, either."

"You're welcome."

"Yes, the number of the telephone company is area code four-oh-two, three-seven-one, four-six-oh-oh. There's no charge."

"Pizza Keg is two-three-six, four-five-one-one."

"Beaver City? Yes, the Hair Shop."

"I have Hair Shaft."

"The main number of the welfare office is four-four-four, seven thousand."

"Yes, Directory."

"Just a minute, please."

"I have a J., Stephen, and William, but no Michael."

"No, I don't know what's playing at the movies tonight."

There is no excessive camaraderie among the operators, chiefly because of the nature of the work—one talks to one's board. Still, the constant shift of personnel and position creates an informal atmosphere. Operators get up and walk around, always carrying their plugs and wires and wearing their headsets. As in an elementary school, everyone was reciting; the voices carry, but the words and the routine are identical. A steady chorus —constant, repetitious, chattery—contradicts the visual image of a quiet office. Here there is no clack-clack-clack of a typewriter or drone of Muzak to drown out a silence.

Shirley has been an operator for fifteen years, always in directory assistance. She started in 1949, stopped to have babies between 1953 and 1965, then returned to the boards. "Telephone work always intrigued me. Back when I first applied, there weren't such good opportunities for girls, and the phone company seemed the place to turn to." She started using cord boards. "Yes, 'pass the cord.' I liked it very much. I enjoyed manipulating those cords. Your hands were kept busy. The cords just fascinated me. There was one cord you plugged in that connected you long-distance with anywhere. That was something to me. We had directories hanging on hooks in front of us. It was much slower. Forty-five seconds or so to get a listing. It was easy as can be to make mistakes, and we made them by the barrels. You had to pass the cords as far as they would go. We could never let a cord stand or a supervisor would tap you on the shoulder. You had to take another operator's call if you had free cords. We used to have tubs of ice with fans blowing over them to cool us off, and I'll never forget the day that a supervisor stepped back and fell smack into one of the tubs. She wasn't hurt, but that sure perked up the day. You never got to look around. You just sat there like a little tin soldier. I like the new system, but it's not the cords. We're giving faster and better service, I guess, and some of the customers are very surprised how fast we give out the numbers. But it's not the cords."

"The number of Ship 'n Chip is four-five-one, nine-nine-one-one."

"Ed's Flowers is two-eight-two, four-oh-two-oh."

"What city, please?"

"Atlanta, Nebraska?"

"Atlanta, Florida, or Atlanta, Nebraska?"

"Atlanta, Nebraska?"

"You have the wrong area code, ma'am."

Continuing, Shirley said, "Most calls are for cab companies, the bus service, businesses, stores, hospitals. The first two weeks of school, most of the calls are for school numbers. That still puzzles me. A student can be in the fifth grade and his parents don't know the school listing. At Christmas, we get bombarded with calls for stores and Santa Claus. At Easter, we get some requests for the Easter Bunny, but we have no number. We say he's not listed. We get occasional calls for the Lone Ranger. We say he isn't listed, either. Kids call and ask if they can have the number for the manhole cover at Thirty-sixth and Dodge. I fell for that once. I thought it was a bar and went to look it up. Or a kid will call and say, 'Can I have the number for Grandma. She lives in the green house with the white fence around it.' Or, 'Can I have Joey's number? He walks home from school with me.' "

I asked her about the attitude of customers. She received my question as though she had been waiting a long time to unburden her mind to someone on that subject. In an animated voice, she told me, "I get the feeling that people are more unhappy, or at least more irritable today. The number of complaints has gone up. It used to bother me when I would go out of my way for a customer and he wouldn't even thank me. But if you let things get to you—and sometimes they really can—you might say something you're not supposed to.

"I think nine out of ten people who get angry at an operator, it's because they're mad at someone else and the operator just happens to be the first one they call to let off steam. I rarely get angry. My years of working at this have taught me not to snap back at people. One of the things I've been corrected for by my supervisor is trying to help a customer too much. I'm told that you have to do it fast. Fast, fast, fast. Too much has lost a personal touch that I'd like to give some of. But there's a lot of pressure to get things done fast."

I asked how operators have changed over the years.

She replied, "I think the attitudes have changed a great deal. I think there was a time when the employee was much more dedicated. Now they think that the company owes them. A lot of the young people don't want to be operators. They just want a foot in the door. They are a lot less courteous than they used to be. And they're not willing to bend as much. They won't search that extra five seconds for a listing. They are much less friendly. I've been called a stupid bitch by a customer. That's one of the milder things I've been addressed as. If that happens, you're supposed to turn the call over to your supervisor. The younger operators, though, feel this need to defend themselves. They snap back. They can really bark. Shoot off the steam. This job is a matter of give and take, but not that many operators want to give or take."

All directory assistance operators are trained to pick up names with alternate spellings. The older women know them by rote. "I'll check as many as four spellings," Shirley said. "We also know to check initials and nicknames. I'll go from Robert to R. to Bob to B. If someone asks me for a Helen Smith and there is none but there are three or four other Smiths with different first names, we are supposed to suggest them. Helen could be listed under her husband's name. If there's an 'if no answer' listing, we have to give both numbers." Seasoned operators also know the numbers for airlines, hotels, train stations, utilities. During April, when hundreds of callers a day ask for the "income tax bureau" or "the tax people," they know the number right off the bat. There are a few other clues for quick searches, but most of the short cuts are learned by experience. Right after Memorial Day, the offices get a barrage of calls for swimming pools. Around St. Patrick's Day, the demand for Irish bars reaches an inordinate level.

On a huge blackboard at the very front of the room was the speed goal for the noon to six o'clock cycle. It was 25.3 seconds. Below it was chalked: "United States Fidelity & Guarantee—new main # 393-3100."

Out of the corner of her eye, Shirley caught a figure standing at the station to her left. A supervisor was monitoring calls at random. She was marking things like voice tone, courtesy, efficiency, length of conversation. The company's policy is for "a minimum of fanfare." Operators are monitored for two calls a day by a service assistant. Each supervisor checks up on roughly forty calls a month per operator. Operators are supposed to strive for a 98 percent accuracy rate. Shirley is often at 100 percent. Some operators have a problem with transposing digits. When you look at numbers all day long, they start to run together.

Monotony bears down heavily on operators. I asked Shirley if she got bored on the job. She said, "Oh, sure, it's like any job.

Sitting great lengths of time, you can get uncomfortable and pretty fidgety. You try to devise little games. Sometimes, I'll stay on longer with a customer just to break the monotony. Then I'll race like hell to try to make up the lost time with other calls, really whiz like crazy through them. I watch to see if I'm going to get down in a well without a rope to get up."

A ballooning category of numbers that directory assistance operators find themselves preoccupied with, though they aren't ever allowed to give them out, are unlisted numbers. Unlisted numbers first came about in 1928, when the Public Utilities Commission in Harrisburg, Pennsylvania, proclaimed the legitimacy of staying out of the phone book. Since then, a passion for anonymity has seized so many subscribers that currently one out of every seven local telephonists is unlisted. The number of customers dropping out of the directories multiplies every year. In Los Angeles, 40 percent of all subscribers are unlisted; in Chicago, 30 percent; in New York, 35 percent; in Washington, D.C., 30 percent. In Omaha, about 8 percent of listings are nonpublished. The telephone company hates unpublished numbers because they cut down on calls and cost money to mind, and people looking for other people find them a tremendous irritation. The operating companies do what they can to persuade shy subscribers to put their names in the directory, but the appeal of not being listed is spreading at such a rate that the company fearfully anticipates a time when perhaps two out of three customers will consent to be listed. From the subscriber's viewpoint, of course, keeping one's number out of the book is a sure way for a person to guarantee that his telephone will be a convenience and not an intrusion, but the telephone company doesn't care. To curb this deplorable (to it) trend, AT&T charges its recluses a dollar a month just for the privilege of reclusion. The additional fee, it is hoped, will discourage the merely frivolous hermits without putting any great hardship on people for whom an unlisted number is, as serious hermits sternly put it, "a real necessity." Resourceful members of this breed, including the actor Tony Randall, have gotten around this edict by listing their numbers under gaudy and imaginative noms de plume. The phone company's distress over unpublished numbers is understandable. Apparently, it takes the information operator two or three times as long to convince a caller that an unlisted number is indeed anonymous as it does to read off an ordinary published number, and operators haven't got all day. Nevertheless, the phone company never asks people why they wish unlisted numbers, and it does seem to go all out to keep the numbers under wraps. To find out something about nonpublished numbers, I was escorted to a video display screen where, not unlike treasured corporate secrets, the region's unlisted numbers lay.

"Non-pub" receives about five hundred calls a week, the chief operator told me, from persons anxious to get through. A garage may call to say a customer filed out without leaving his key and the traffic is backed up ten blocks. Give out that number! Another caller must reach an old schoolmate to invite him to a class reunion. Dish out the number! Somebody else indignantly requests the number of her ex-husband. She has had a change of heart.

Non-pub turns them all down. If something sounds like life or death, it will call the customer itself and pass along a message, but the number remains a secret. That goes for the I.R.S., the mayor, and the police. (If they do give out unpublished listings, as some operators have done in exchange for handsome payments from credit bureaus or enterprising salesmen, they are promptly discharged.)

"We get calls because of deaths, accidents, emergencies of one sort or another," I was told by the chief operator. "What we do is agree to call the customer and have him get in touch with the caller. We have to pretty much take the calling party's word that it's an emergency, but we do instruct the operators to do some questioning. We've had people call and say they want to borrow the person's car, or they don't want to go out in the rain to tell somebody to return a book. We don't tend to regard those cases as emergencies."

"What if I'd found somebody's purse or keys and wanted to return them?" I asked.

"Then you should contact the police," the chief operator informed me.

I was given a quick rundown on the people who demand unpublished numbers and their reasons. The celebrated and those aspiring to be celebrated. Political heavyweights. Actors and actresses. The habitually private individual.

The largest category, though, is single women. They find themselves overrun with calls from would-be suitors or with obscene messages. People who have had crank calls comprise the second biggest category. Psychiatrists are also fond of remaining unlisted, so that they will not find themselves listening to disturbed people all night. People running from creditors have them. Wives hiding from a jealous husband or boyfriend. And vice versa. Then there are those people who never have been, and doubtless never will be, in demand, but want to seem like they are. "They go around saying, 'Oh, it won't be easy to reach me,'" the chief operator said. "'So here's my private number.' What a joke they are."

Herding Elephants
with Flyswatters

Unlike other mammoths of the corporate jungle, AT&T can't set its own prices. It can't dream up a new service and just go ahead and bring it out. To get what it wants and needs, it must plead its case before a squadron of regulatory bodies that have been appointed as the public's guardian angels against unduly steep phone rates and shoddy service. The friction between the two sides can become intense to the point of unseemliness. According to one popular analogy drawn between AT&T and the regulatory bodies, the phone company is portrayed as a condemned man, with the regulators cast as hangmen bent on polishing him off. Another analogy depicts the regulators as benign Santa Clauses and the phone company as a covetous child with a mile-long list of things to ask for. For most of its existence, AT&T has been the greedy child showered with Santa's gifts. Of late, though, it's begun to look more and more like the condemned man.

The regulatory world—with millions of dollars riding on votes cast by small boards of men and women—has always been marked by dissension and whispered innuendo. Critics protest that regulatory commissionships too often go to politicians who have preposterously scant qualification for the job, who are being rewarded for past patronage to the powers that are, and that once in office, commissioners often form repugnantly comfy relationships with phone company officials, the upshot being nothing more than a veneer of regulatory function. AT&T, on the other hand, often bleats like a starving sheep that commissions don't hand out nearly enough money for it to properly run its system.

Within the world of regulation, interstate rates and services, which haul in a fourth of AT&T's overall revenues, fall within the sphere of the Federal Communications Commission. The real money, though, is inside the states, seen to by a jumble of state agencies. In the last decade, the FCC has veered in the direction of deregulation. Decrees by it have sent competitors scrambling after AT&T like greyhounds legging it behind a mechanical rabbit. This, many think, widens the checks on the phone company's doings. At present, only local residential service is preserved as a full monopoly, although AT&T continues to be regulated in all of its communications services.

With the tidal rise of consumerism, commissions have become increasingly reluctant to dish out meaty rate hikes. Turnover at commissions has been raging at an all-time high (the average stay is just four and a half years), in part because of pressure applied by consumers to have governments install regulators who will once and for all put a stop to those zooming utility rates. In 1975, according to an AT&T tabulation, the phone company got 70 percent of the rate increase money it asked for. In 1979, it collected only 35 percent.

When the FCC was created in 1934, it exerted no true controlling hand over telephone rates. It neither set interstate telephone rates nor suggested an appropriate percentage return on capital for AT&T. And so the regulatory procedure bumped along in a fairly informal mode, and settled on a fairly informal limit for return on capital—8 percent. Any time AT&T's return threatened to exceed that figure, then the representatives of the FCC and appropriate officers of AT&T would sit down together, talk things over, hem and haw, and eventually work out an agreement palatable to both of them. It was close to a system whereby AT&T could determine pretty much how much money it wanted to charge its subscribers for making a phone call.

Then, in 1963, the FCC got a new chairman—E. William Henry—who was fresh and eager to put the world right. It was his belief that there ought to be a means of figuring out just what constituted a fair return for this giant utility, and so in October 1965 an ambitious (one might say overly ambitious) inquiry into interstate rates was launched by the FCC, over heated denunciations by AT&T top brass, who thought things had been going just swimmingly. An FCC spokesman, a bit annoyed at the AT&T opposition, declared that the phone company people were acting like "stuck pigs." The massive FCC rate investigation took until late 1976 to conclude, which should suggest the pace at which the regulatory process proceeds. In April 1967, the commission completed hearings in Phase IA of the inquiry, which was the part dealing with rate of return. In July of that year, it announced that an appropriate rate of return would be in the range of 7 to 7.5 percent, meaning that Bell had to reduce its interstate revenue by something like $120 million a year. No way, AT&T retorted. The FCC, in true FCC style, backed down, and in effect stated that the range it cited wasn't a binding order after all. In October, the FCC moved on to what was termed Phase IB, concerned with AT&T's rate-making methods. That was wrapped up in 1976, at which time AT&T got a thorough dressing down for wasting money, but not much else happened.

Many people presume that telephone rates are much the same throughout the country. They aren't. They differ as much as commissions do. In Detroit, for instance, the basic monthly charge for a residential phone is $9.50. In Boston, it is $10.70. In Los Angeles, it is $6.00. Probably the greatest disparity is between federal and state rates for long-distance calls. Nationwide, long-distance rates are based upon beeline mileage. The FCC sets the interstate charges, and the state commissions fix those within a state. The state toll schedules, in almost every case, exceed those of the interstate (FCC) schedule. From Los Angeles to San Francisco (351 airline miles), the rate for a three-minute daytime call is $1.30 plus tax; the charge for a 351-mile call from Los Angeles to an out-of-state point would be $1.16 plus tax. Between New York City and Buffalo, the charge is $1.41 for three minutes. You can call coast-to-coast for $1.30.

Since inflation began to loom large, rate increases have become a recurrent feature of phone service. Before 1967, more than a half-dozen rate cases a year was rare. In the last eleven years, there have been a striking 215, which produced rate relief totaling some $7 billion, enough, as one person put it, "to make a Persian prince green with envy." Lumped together, however, rates have not soared as much as the cost of living. From 1967 through the middle of 1980, interstate rates had risen just 9 percent, while intrastate long-distance rates had shot up about 51 percent and local rates had climbed almost 62 percent. Contrasted with price increases enacted in most every other industry, then, phone service has remained pretty much a bargain. Indeed, the typical American worker needs to put in only about two hours of labor to pay for his monthly phone tab. In figuring rates, though, commissions sometimes find it politic to hold calling rates steady but to push up charges for phone installation and options like long cords and custom calling features. At all events, owing to the complexity involved in figuring them out, it still is far from clear whether phone rates could be cheaper.

Just how are phone rates determined? In bare outline, rates are based on three factors: Bell's capital investment or "rate base" (the total value of the poles, wire, telephones, and so forth), the "rate of return" (or profit) on that capital investment, and Bell's expenses. Right now, the authorized rate of return for interstate service is between 12½ and 13 percent. So take Bell's capital investment figure and compute roughly 13 percent of it. Then figure out how much cash all of the telephone bills have to generate so that, after expenses are paid for, Bell will pocket a 13 percent return. Finally, work out what long-distance rates must be to supply their chunk of the bundle. On paper, this description seems fairly simple.

It's not. For one thing, commissions can't ever be entirely sure that Bell's rate base isn't inflated. Typically grossly underbudgeted, they simply haven't the staff to certify AT&T's numbers. The phone company could be blowing up the rate base like a balloon, for all the commissions can verify. "Checking Bell's figures amounts to moving mountains with hand shovels," one commissioner wryly told me.

As the rules of the game are set, it seems logical to some that AT&T would always attempt to spend every penny it could for capital expenditures, because the more it spends, the more it can earn. But for decades, sundry economists (often college professors who extract phone company fees—as much as $20,000 for protracted cases—to testify in rate hearings) have strenuously argued that if AT&T did spend too much of the kitty, it would eventually go stone broke. Anyway, most of your phone bill is affected by the third variable, "expenses." Salaries, the cost of installing a phone, advertising, public relations budgets are all expenses. In 1979 alone, they counted up to a staggering $30.2 billion. But commissions are rarely able to check expenses, either. Rate requests by the phone company can involve months of hearings, testimony from literally hundreds of witnesses, and thousands of pages of transcripts. How can a state commission, in particular, keep up with all of this when it must also look after gas, electric, water, and transportation utilities? Some state commissions have no lawyers to advise them, and a number boast no members any closer to the arcane world of economics than fleeting encounters with college mathematics.

"It's like a gullible person who strolls into a store to buy a suit," one watcher of the regulatory scene told me. "The salesman says he's got one for a hundred and fifty dollars. But he can't show it. And there's no label in it. But he swears on his head of hair that it's a good buy. So the customer, like the commission, goes and takes the suit, not having the foggiest notion of whether it's any good."

As another observer put it to me: "You know, you can't herd elephants with a few flyswatters."

Though consumerism has unquestionably beefed up the performance of the regulatory process somewhat, the truth is that complaints from consumers about phone rates remain relatively minor. Electric utilities find themselves in the role of scapegoat for consumer ire far more commonly than AT&T. Telephone rate hearings are rarely crowded, even if those who do show up are vehement in their denunciations.

Here, for instance, is a public hearing on a fairly recent New York Telephone rate increase application. It was held in a public hearing room in the World Trade Center in lower Manhattan. Roughly fifty people were in the audience, a few of them public officials lamely following up on campaign promises. On stage, sitting behind a long desk that spanned the width of the room, the commissioners had the manner of a high court, listening to testimony and arguing among themselves. The testifiers appeared to be an angry and worried group of people.

"Don't mess up the phone rates any more."

"I strongly suggest that our phone rates not go up. We are not millionaires. I don't think we can keep our phones if they get more expensive."

Everyone kept nodding agreement as accusations flew at the phone company. When a particularly barbed point was made, the audience burst into applause and the commissioner in charge rapped his gavel and sternly warned against any showing of partisan sentiment.

"The phone company is going to the Arabs when the money from these increases come in."

"The phone company will be another Saudi Arabia."

Someone else said, "No sirree. What we do not need are fatter phone bills. We deserve lower phone bills. Yes sirree."

And someone else said, "This is for the birds."

Whereupon a distinguished-looking dark-haired man, dressed in a vague imitation of a cowboy suit, straightened his spine and gave a short-bark cough for attention. He appeared to have received in his lifetime a lot of unquestioning attention.

"It's a goddamn outrage, what's happening here," the man said. "Ain't no way that the phone company is going to get this kind of money. Ain't no way, long as I'm able to stand up and speak. It's always got its hand out. It's always grumbling that its pockets are empty. Hell, those phone company types are living on Easy Street, while the rest of us are scrambling just to make a buck. I say let the government run the phones. Forget the phone company."

In a number of respects, the Federal Communications Commission sets the tone for the nature of the regulation that the phone company is exposed to, and by most standards it would seem that the FCC is a relic of another era. And since it couldn't handle its job very well when it was created, it is more hamstrung than ever now that it is confronted with conundrums like communications through a laser beam, computers taking over from telephones, new electronic methods of infringing on privacy. Ralph Nader has gone so far as to suggest that the FCC is the worst agency in Washington. A recent study conducted by the General Accounting Office concluded that the FCC suffered from poor management, low morale, and a failure to keep up with technological change in the communications industry. It recommended greater congressional supervision, a cutback in the number of commissioners, longer terms, and a public participation program for FCC proceedings. According to a previous GAO study, the FCC was also the paperwork champ of federal regulatory agencies, requiring the communications industry to spend 30 million hours each year filling out the forms that are necessary to comply with its regulations. Newton Minow, a former FCC chairman, once described the agency, after he had stepped down, as "a quixotic world of undefined terms, private pressures, and tools unsuited to its work."

There are seven commissioners, more than on any other major

regulatory agency except the Interstate Commerce Commission, and each serves seven years. The commissioners are appointed by the President, who also designates the chairman, and are confirmed by the Senate. Presidents pay fitful attention to the regulatory agencies and have frequently used them as dumping grounds for burned-out politicians or difficult characters to whom they are obliged to give a job, in the opinion of many Washington watchers. This lack of qualification, and the frequent turnover, often before terms expire, makes policy continuity and even administration of the agency difficult. Thus it is no surprise, really, that the FCC is rarely the fire-breathing dragon that consumers might hope for.

For all its burdens, the commission meets only once a week and frequently disposes of its business by lunchtime. Each Wednesday morning, the commissioners mount the semicircle dais in their meeting room and deliberate whether AT&T rates on a particular night should go down or whether a broadcaster (the agency, mind you, must also regulate the radio and television industries) may boost the wattage of his station. Occasionally it must concern itself with such matters as lewd and loud language being used by shrimp fishermen over their radios. Heady as these matters may be, however, the commissioners, from what I have been able to discern, don't find it necessary to put in overly long hours.

In his eighth floor suite, Charles Ferris wore an ordinary Washington suit, and capital pallor was in his tanned and leathery face. He had white hair and broad shoulders, and he seemed a powerful man but not forbidding. Ferris was, at the time, the chairman of the FCC.

I asked Ferris how effectively he thought regulation had worked.

He tapped some ashes off the end of his cigar and replied, "AT&T is an enormous entity. Almost one million people work there. We have less than three hundred people in our Common Carrier Bureau. To attempt to review in great detail an entity this large is an incredible task. Frankly, I'm amazed how much of a review the people here are able to give. But I think it's a very difficult task. When you compare our phone system with systems overseas, I think you conclude that we are very fortunate. How much does the American consumer actually pay for it? Could similar reliability be gotten for lower cost? Attempting to look at Bell involves second-guessing the company. And I think that's an extremely hard thing to do. The Bell System has behaved differently from a company in a competitive environment. The stringency of the bookkeeping is very, very different. One almost gets the impression that Bell puts its expenses on one side of the books and income on the other side of the books and that's it. That's the extent of its bookkeeping. In some ways, it's an exercise in mutual frustration. It's hard to get any precision."

He reflected a moment on what he had said, then added, through a haze of cigar smoke, "In the last decade, the commission has moved toward competition under what I think is a very valid premise. If the marketplace can provide the checks and balances on the company, that is more desirable than a detailed overview by a regulatory agency. That's a good solution, I think. From the standpoint of how well do we regulate now, I'm amazed at how much information gets digested, but I think the basic structure of the industry is such that regulation can never be fully adequate."

"How well do you police AT&T's investment?" I asked.

"AT&T's capital expenditures budget every year is equal to an IBM. That's IBM's revenues. I don't think anyone feels there's a real check on that."

"How can regulation of AT&T be improved?" I asked.

Ferris puffed once, twice. He scanned the room. "We are working long hours as it is," he replied somewhat mournfully. "There is so much human beings can do. We are prisoners of our frailties. I think this commission really plugs away damn hard. I'm not sure, when you take on something as big as AT&T, that gets bigger and fatter by the day, that you can do much better. Hell, we sure try."

I dropped three floors in the elevator and visited with Larry Darby, then head of the Common Carrier Bureau, through which all AT&T matters initially pass for consideration. He was a tall, bearded, soft-spoken man, who seemed better suited to an academic climate than a political one. Unlike previous chiefs of the Common Carrier Bureau, who were lawyers, Darby was an economist.

I asked him how well he thought regulation worked.

He stroked his beard, patted down his hair in back, then said, "By most standards, the quality and cost of interstate communications is good. It's very good. I think you've seen the implementation of most of the technologies in a reasonably timely way. But we've got two hundred and eighty-five people in this bureau. Roughly seventy are assigned to projects having to do with Bell. Even if I had the whole staff working on a forty-billion-dollar, one-million-people operation, you couldn't believe for a minute we had done pervasive regulation. It's too huge a task. It's a monster of a job. I think the commission's decision to have the marketplace take on regulatory chores is basically a very wise move. Regulation is essentially passive. Bell proposes things, and we either accept them or reject them. We can't prescribe what equipment they put in. Normally, unless something is way out of line, it goes into effect. We have very few tools at our disposal. We can give speeches and say they ought to do this or do that. But we can't prescribe. Until about ten years ago, I would say regulation was very passive. The time since then has been the only period there's been a real regulatory presence."

"Are rates fair?" I asked.

"You could make a case for excessive investment by Bell," Darby answered. "Do ratepayers benefit by advertising? Do ratepayers benefit by charitable contributions? Do ratepayers benefit from legal expenses involved in defending suits and initiating suits? The commission is divided on these kinds of questions. You might also ask whether Bell has engaged in sound network design. The system sure works well. No question about that. You pick up the phone and make your calls. But the thing is whether it has to be this good. It's really a Cadillac. If you're on a Volkswagen income, do you want a Cadillac system? We have a phone network designed for practically no blocked calls. You get a dial tone by the time the phone hits the ear. If you waited a few seconds to get that dial tone, you'd save some bucks. Maybe a mess of bucks. Would the wait bother people? We don't know. But if you ask, could we have spent less bucks, a system as big as Bell has a lot of fat in it. Probably if the commission were five times bigger than it is we could save the ratepayers some money. I'm inclined as an economist to think that we should have the option of the Volkswagen service. But we haven't done this."

He went on, "As inflation becomes more and more of a concern, the commission will become more sensitive to Bell's rates and be inclined to ask the questions of what do we get for that extra billion dollars, that extra five hundred million dollars. I guess the analogy is sort of zero-based budgeting with the government. This is something Bell has never been required to do. We don't have the resources to manage the company, so we shouldn't even try to accomplish that. I think the best way to regulate is to ask certain types of questions and make Bell pass certain tests. The commission should be accountable to ratepayers. I really don't want to be a regulator, because my heart is in deregulation, but Bell is a monopoly."

"Has Bell been deceitful and reckless?" I asked Darby.

"No, these are all honorable men," he replied. "I might have done things differently, but I don't believe they've been reckless."

A sizable handicap to the regulatory process has been the fact that AT&T, in its bookkeeping, does not fully allocate costs to specific services. There are clouded debates about subsidies flowing from one service to another, though just how they flow is a question no one has satisfactorily answered. Ma Bell has always maintained that it manages to keep local exchange rates low by subsidizing them with long-distance charges, predominantly borne by businesses, though many of Bell's competitors have argued the opposite, that dollars are siphoned from local service to subsidize certain long-distance business offerings. The FCC has ordered AT&T to revamp its books so that costs are clearly allocated, an enormous process expected to take years to complete. Minds have not yet been made up over whether subsidies should exist.

"There are no clear-cut answers to local rates and toll rates," Darby said. "There is no reason to think that minimizing exchange rates should be the goal of national policy. Some say lump all the costs on the businesses. Well, businesses don't really bear that. If we stuck it on the auto industry, for instance, as a consumer I'm going to have to pay more for an automobile.

"My feeling is that costs to individuals should generally reflect the costs brought on the system. If there are overriding social reasons, then exemptions should be made. AT&T says that if basic rates go up, that will defeat the idea of universal service. People will start disconnecting their phones. We don't have much evidence that this will happen. There's a lot of talk about the little old lady in tennis shoes. You've got to make sure she has her phone, and all that. Well, if you're really concerned about the little old lady in tennis shoes, rather than keep all the local exchange rates down, why not make a special dispensation instead of having her drive national telecommunications policy."

On another day, I paid a call on James Olson, a vice chairman at AT&T who has the ultimate responsibility at the company for all regulatory matters. He was in shirt sleeves (white) and had a large bandage protruding from his right thumb joint. He had cut it with a knife. I asked him his thoughts on regulation.

Straightening himself like a furled umbrella in his chair, he said, "If you look at regulation up to this point in time and ask did it work, I say it worked pretty well. Why do I say that? Under regulation, we've provided a pretty damn good telephone system. You pick up a phone and dial a number and you get through. Somebody answers and you talk and understand each other. From a cost standpoint, I think rates have a great track record. They haven't gone up at anywhere near the rise in the cost of living. From the shareholder point of view, I think we've had some disagreements on the correct rate of return, but I think commissions have generally been reasonable. I think most regulators are intelligent people who are trying to make honest decisions."

Olson went on to say that he thought it would be wiser if the FCC were split into two bureaus, one concerned entirely with communications matters and the other with broadcast, a position that has been advocated by an array of critics over the years, though the FCC has staunchly rejected the idea. Olson said he thought commissioners should be paid handsomer salaries (they earn nowhere near as much as, say, an AT&T officer), to help cut down the rapid turnover (commissioners, however, more often leave office because of a change in government than out of an apparent desire to sweeten their personal incomes). What's more, he said, the commissioners badly need more staff and more expertise to tackle the thorny issues that now confront them. He complained that want of such expertise has had a lot to do with why in some states—he ticked off Louisiana and California, known for inflicting dagger blows on the phone company—he didn't think regulation "worked worth a damn."

How well, I asked him, did he think commissions monitored AT&T's expenses and investment?

"There obviously is no way that a regulatory staff can duplicate management," Olson said. "Given the limitations of the regulatory bodies, I would agree that they have to place a lot of faith in what AT&T presents."

What about the wild and seemingly senseless gyrations in rates as you move across the country?

"I think you would eliminate a lot of confusion if the rates followed more of a pattern. This is being debated in Congress. I can see some advantages to this."

I also went to see John Segall, an AT&T vice president who holds sway over all Bell System state regulatory matters. He complained, at some length, that commissions don't always consider economic realities. He told me, "Our return on investment, almost by any measure, is too low everywhere. It should be significantly higher.

"Telephone rates have risen at a lower pace than almost anything. Yet we suffer from a tyranny of numbers. I remember when we had our first billion dollar quarter. Right on the heels of it, we got a zero award in a rate case in New Jersey. We've had a number of zero awards since then. The zero award, I have to tell you, is really the ultimate turndown. It's like the wallflower's lament: nobody asked me to dance."

It's difficult to feel sorry for AT&T. The phone company, when it wants more money, is tough to beat. In trying to get what it needs from the regulators, AT&T has engineered one of the most effective lobbying and public relations systems in industry. Critics hold it to be a remarkable tool for persuading regulators and politicians to be charitable to the good old phone company.

Like any big, practical organization, AT&T has constructed its own liaison channels to legislatures. Its chief lobbyist in Washington is John Fox, a courtly, gray-haired man who supervises thirty people and boasts a wide acquaintance among politicians. Fox and his crew make a point of being nice to everybody in the world, since everybody in the world is a potential customer for AT&T, but they especially seek warm relations with legislators and prospective legislators; their coziness with the latter comes under the heading of what the phone company calls "preventive maintenance." Washington is the most important lobbying beat for AT&T, since a running, streaming, flooding river of legislation emerges from the city on an almost daily basis. Fox's people perpetually cruise Capitol Hill and the regulatory agencies, tracking legislation and rules through a thousand drafts. A separate organization based in New York—composed of forty-five people—does nothing but grapple with matters that come before the FCC. Nobody concerned with the lobbying organizations wished to be quoted by name on their doings, though one well-versed senior member agreed to sit down for an anonymous discussion. He spoke first about Bell's relationship with the government:

"The relationship is incredibly broad and deep and involved. The range is just enormous. We constantly have right-of-way arguments, stemming from the fact that we put our lines and cables over public lands. We have a tremendous amount of business with the government over privacy. Our company is peculiar. Bugging doesn't affect an aluminum company. It's not putting them in the spy business. There has never been a year since 1962 in which we haven't had a series of hearings in Congress on privacy. The Interior Department is the biggest owner of communications systems in the country. They have all these dams which they control by communications. We're constantly trying to sell them systems. The Coast Guard, which is part of the Transportation Department, is a big user of communications. HEW is always asking us for advice and studies. We're taking a look now at medical costs in the industrial medicine field, and we're working with HEW on experimental day-care centers. In Congress, at any given time, there are five hundred or six hundred bills pending that affect the Bell System in some way. One of our jobs here is to identify the bills that would have an effect and that we may want to say something on. The government for over forty years has been expanding. It has been laying on business. It has been regulating business, saying how business should run. So most of the things that come along negatively affect us. The vast proportion of the problems in Washington are going to cost you money. We've got something like a hundred new regulations every year spewing forth from government agencies, all of which have a bearing on the phone company. You have to watch these things, or you suddenly find that to install a phone you have to get permission from sixteen agencies of government. There are so many things. What would be the rate we would have to pay for a plot of land and our access road to the top of the Rockies? We lease that land and road from the government to build unattended microwave towers on. Typically, we'll have a two-year lease. Well, a bureaucrat will come along and say they're only paying X dollars for that land and they have a million dollars of equipment up there. Well, they ought to pay according to the value of the equipment. We fight that out with the Department of Agriculture. Then someone goes and introduces a bill in Congress to make us pay more."

He spoke about lobbying: "Nobody in this office does any actual lobbying. What we do here is coordinate the lobbying efforts of the operating company people who do the real visiting. How much visiting do we do? It depends on what's cooking. Sometimes, we have people in here every week from the companies. We use a rifle shot. We visit as few Congressmen as possible, but make them count. Suppose I have a minor antitrust problem. I'd have to be out of my mind to bother Ted Kennedy about that. This is something awfully hard to measure, but I would say that the majority of our visits are successful. If you're reasonable in your request, you're going to have a good deal of success. Well, we haven't asked anything unreasonable in recent years of those birds. What other sorts of things do we do? Well, we escort Congressional people through our central offices, our earth stations, Bell Labs, our Network Operating Center. A lot of visiting goes on. We'll take people to dinner or lunch. We have theater tickets and symphony tickets and Redskins football tickets. We might take Congressional staffers to things like that. We don't do stuff like sending birthday cards to Congressmen. Hell, I don't even send Christmas cards to people in government. Sure, there are probably members of Congress who you can influence by taking them to the racetrack, but we don't encourage that kind of stuff. You do have to realize one thing. In an organization this big, everything does happen somewhere. There are exceptions to everything I'm telling you.

"You know, there are basically two types of operations in Washington. One type goes to all the events—all the embassy parties, all the fund raisers, anyplace to be seen. They are in the business of selling themselves. We don't have that kind of operation. I'm not trying to call attention to myself. I keep a low profile. I'm not trying to trade on my personality, but on my facts. A new guy on the staff will go to fund raisers and see what's popping. You buy a ticket, you go to the dang thing, you go down a receiving line, you pass on to the floor, and there's a bar set up and you have a drink and mill about. I mean, wow! It's like the guy going to the Grand Canyon. You see one and you've seen them all.

You know, I remember when people wanted to be friends with Tongsun Park. I never wanted to know Tongsun Park."

The lobbying man talked about image in Washington: "Generally speaking, I think the government thinks pretty well of AT&T. I think they have a pretty good respect for our technological ability. I think they have a pretty good respect for our service ability. Now, in some areas of government, we do have image problems. We have press problems. I have the feeling that the press is a little suspicious of us. I think the bringing of the antitrust suit has hurt us with the press. I think the whole issue of competition has hurt us. There are a lot of people here who represent competing interests who have lessened their respect for us. But we have a very stout reservoir of good will in government. I don't sense that competitors have had much success in changing our image. You know, people don't get very excited when IBM calls AT&T a bunch of big bastards. Nobody gets very excited when ITT says AT&T is trying to crush out the competition. Nobody is bleeding for IBM or ITT."

To further bolster its image, the phone company has always urged a pervasive community presence among its employees. All AT&T people are urged to hitch up with public service clubs—the Elks, Kiwanis, Jaycees, Rotary, Chamber of Commerce—and to talk up the phone company. Bell people become chiefs of local fire departments, heads of Community Chests, scoutmasters, organizers of Civil Air Patrol chapters. Prior to the 1940s, Bell policy forbade employees to seek any public office, but then AT&T lifted the prohibition and today phone company men and women serve regularly as small-town mayors, councilmen, and school board members. Bell deposits its money into more than ten thousand local banks, and it relies on local law firms to cope with a large part of its legal business. The influence adds up. What's more, an annual Western Electric tally of how much money is spent in each state is used by AT&T emissaries when they go on their lobbying jaunts. According to the last such report, Bell spent the most dollars in New York, followed by Illinois and New Jersey.

Meantime, Bell public relations people spend millions of dollars working to paint the company as a lovable Green Giant of communications. The PR departments of the assorted operating companies stay on the alert to ship out Bell System films and Bell speakers to community groups for the asking. Around forty thousand talks are delivered each year for Kiwanis, Sertoma, block clubs, churches, schools, and senior citizen groups. Films get shown on the order of seven hundred and fifty thousand times a year. Bell will literally go anywhere it is asked. It has come before inmates of the Granite Reformatory in Oklahoma City, ventured out to New England campgrounds, and spoken before a gathering of Iranian engineers.

Striving to preserve its image has made the Bell System intensely press-relations conscious. It is hard to imagine any other business in which PR and publicity activities are so closely coordinated and controlled. A fairly brief and straightforward press release from one unit may be routed for approval to several dozen executives through that and other units before it finally gets issued. The wording of a single clause may stir up a confrontation. "You learn to be awfully circumspect here about what you say," one Bell PR man told me. "You don't just go mouthing off." Any interview by the media at AT&T, if Bell has any hand in it, is almost always conducted in the presence of a PR man, who often takes as diligent notes as the reporter. I recall having lunch one afternoon with a shrewd securities analyst who was known to be a bit dour on the phone company. Several hours later, I got a call at my office from an AT&T PR man who, having heard that I had lunched with an analyst who was negative on the company, wished to offer a list of a half-dozen analysts worked up by the investment relations department who he said might balance out the picture. I never did find out how he learned of my meeting, though the odds are good that in any restaurant you eat in, in just about any city, somebody from the phone company will be there.

Millions of extra dollars go into advertising aimed at selling service extras, acquainting customers with charges, and building institutional prestige. One of the idiosyncrasies of the phone company is a policy—dating back to its earliest days—that advertising should be considered an instrument not solely of the system's attempts to sell its services, but also of its attempts to polish its image and deal politically with the public. From the early 1900s—when Bell's longtime ad agency, N. W. Ayer, worked up for such periodicals as *Collier's* and *The Literary Digest* series of full-page advertisements detailing the good intentions and the social benefits of Bell-company service—the phone company has engaged in blanket advertising, through every medium (it's a challenge to find a magazine without a phone company ad), stressing an image of quiet dignity and conservatism. The uncommonly staid ads tend toward friendly-folksy, all-is-well themes. Family groups are depicted with glowingly healthy, apple-cheeked youngsters and beaming, silver-topped grandmas and grandpas. More recent ads have been aimed at the all-important younger segment of the population and portray teenage women in curlers chatting about boyfriends. Everyone constantly calls everyone else, smilingly remembering all birthdays, graduations, and anniversaries. When it gets the opportunity, AT&T is glad to team up with some dignified event such as the now-defunct Bell Telephone Hour (which brought Van Cliburn and Gian Carlo Menotti into American living rooms) to create a benevolent impression. In 1978, for instance, it spent three-quarters of a million dollars to bring to network TV a concert by Vladimir Horowitz that attracted the ears and eyes of five and a half million people. The price tag worked out to about thirteen and a half cents per viewer, expensive by most advertising yardsticks, but worth it by AT&T's.

An AT&T advertising man discussed something about phone company ad strategy: "There's been a long controversy over what business the phone company has doing any advertising. Critics say that, look, Bell is a regulated monopoly. It's got all the phone business it needs—everybody's got to come to it—so what in tarnation does it have to advertise for? Well, first of all, we've got shareholders to think about, and we need to produce a decent profit so we can attract their investment. Besides that, though, by advertising we are able to drum up more business, which creates economies for the system that keep rates from going up, if they don't actually cause some rates to go down. So the public does benefit from our advertising. Now, we are careful about it. Being a big monopoly, we don't want to beat consumers over the head with ads. We try to take a subtle, low-key approach. Very upbeat. We try to indicate to people how phone calls are good for them, as well as good for the people being called. This is sort of a mutual reward concept. We don't want our ads to make it sound like you downright have to make calls or else. We want people to feel that going and making a call will be a happy experience."

The result of all this caution is a generally favorable climate of press and public opinion, which the phone company goes out of its way to keep track of with elaborate surveys and analyses aided by sociologists and psychologists. It once took the trouble to sponsor a study to determine whether public telephones were dangerous germ carriers; the answer was a definite no. The Bell System funds two ongoing projects to round up opinion (hopefully favorable) about itself—one a yearly report done by mail questionnaire called the Public Overview, and the other an amazing six-day-a-week operation known as TELSAM (telephone service attitude measurement). People are called on the phone and grilled about service. Chilton Research Services calls half the sample out of King of Prussia, Pennsylvania, and the Walker Research Company polishes off the other half from a spot in Denver. Everything then gets pumped into a central computer and cranked out in monthly reports for the perusal of phone company managers.

On a bright day when I visited the TELSAM office on the second floor of one of the relentlessly modern office buildings in the King of Prussia Plaza (stark, squat, plenty of parking), there was routine cacophony: a large, open citadel aswarm with bodies clutching telephones, plumbing customers' minds with their questions, and batting out answers on computer terminals.

"Was it explained to you, or anyone else, why the phone was not installed in the location you wanted?" a young woman with feral eyes was saying.

"Now, let's talk about your local calls," a thin, high voice said. "Did the last call go through the first time you dialed the number?"

"Thinking of your last call, how would you rate that operator on being courteous?" was somebody else's question.

A chipper female voice said, "Did you have trouble hearing or being heard?"

"How would you rate that repairman on being courteous and using good business manners?"

What has AT&T learned from this insistent questioning? Most people, according to TELSAM figures, always find their phone experiences excellent or good. The worst ratings are doled out to repair, which is usually an unpleasant experience for a subscriber since he is temporarily stuck with no phone. The business office category has been sinking toward its lowest depths. So has dial service. AT&T, when itself questioned about these trends, scoffs that customers are expecting so much more today than they used to. One especially unsettling concern is the lament of customers that phone people are a good deal less polite than in past times. Bell has begun to respond with some new ways of doing business. Tests were begun in several operating areas during which operators were instructed to answer the phone with their names or employee numbers to see if that personalized things more. An operator might snatch up a call and say, "Matilda Morningstar," rather than just "Operator." Early returns indicated a detectable improvement.

Despite the methodical work of the phone company to woo everybody and anybody, thereby to get the sort of favorable treatment it desires, some fairly ornery regulatory commissions still manage to flourish. One of the toughest is the Louisiana Public Service Commission. It has clamped on South Central Bell one of the lowest rates of return of any operating company. Rarely does it award rate increases anywhere near what the phone company puts in for. Louisiana was the last state to do away with the nickel phone call. Pay-phone calls were upped to a dime in a three-to-two vote by the commission in 1978, with the commission's chairman, Louis Lambert, Jr., casting one of the votes to preserve the nickel rate. "A nickel, a dime, what's the big difference?" he said to me not long ago.

One of the reasons the commission is so contentious, its critics complain, is because commissioners are elected rather than appointed (as in most states), and they use their decisions to curry public support. The commissioners, for their part, stoutly deny this.

"We're requiring Bell to prove its case," Lambert explained to me. "We aren't a charity service. We're just doing our jobs, and the chips fall where they may."

I asked Lambert why he found that Bell asked for so many unjustified rate hikes.

Without hesitation, he replied, "I always think they deliberately ask for a lot more than they think they'll get. It's the old shell game philosophy. Ask for a bundle, then settle for all you need anyway. I think they inflate their requests from two to four times what is fair, and that creates a bad credibility problem. I think they are doing themselves a great disservice carrying on like this. I frankly don't often believe them."

At the moment, Lambert was among a number of candidates vying for the governor's job in the upcoming election, which had left him especially open to criticism that he was using his decisions on the commission for political ends.

"Nah, this campaign doesn't influence my decisions one bit," he said. "I've always held the line on rate increases. Hell, my decisions are right. They've always been hard. You see, the phone company is always looking for money to rain from heaven. Well, this heaven won't give it."

9

Protecting the
Stud Horses

Theodore Vail worked it out in the early 1900s. The government could regulate the phone company (of which he was head) and put a ceiling on its profits. The plum he would get in exchange was a monopoly. Nobody else could put as much as a toe on the phone company's mountain. And so was born one of the most successful business philosophies in the world. At the time, the pact made eminent sense. Otherwise, you would have all these rival phone companies springing up, battling each other for the chance to serve the same customers. Some Americans, in fact, had already suffered through the miserable experience of having two phones and struggling to recollect, when ringing up a friend, which one to use. Phone service, clearly, was a "natural monopoly"—something where service by a single company would serve the public better than competition.

Ever since Vail's deal, AT&T's mountain has grown taller and more imperturbable, its peak as distant from the rest of the business community as the moon. But in recent years, the mountain has changed. Every time AT&T peers down through its telescope, it spots somebody else hurling up his rope, digging in his heels, and starting to shinny up. IBM, ITT, RCA, Xerox, Western Union: some of the biggest names in the corporate jungle now appear on communications products. So do the names of companies not immediately recognizable to the average homeowner—MCI, Southern Pacific, Rolm, Womac, TIE. Pick up your daily newspaper or the latest issue of *Newsweek* or *Time* and there blare full-page ads for one company or another trumpeting that it can save your business half a million dollars a year on telephone bills if you jilt Ma Bell. You can go to the local supermarket in many cities and discover telephones on sale. Drop a push-button desk set in with the canned beans, the frozen fries, and the gallon of milk, and check out. Take it home, order the phone company to remove its instrument, and plug in your very own telephone. A mob of pumped-up competitors have come thronging into the phone business. Not since olden days have the contours of the landscape of the stodgy telephone industry changed as much.

Some words about the dawn of competition: it used to be, in effect, illegal to attach non-Bell equipment to Bell phone lines. AT&T tariffs specifically prescribed that the phone company could refuse service to anybody found to have attached alien equipment to his line, the dubious reasoning being that such equipment could inflict hideous harm on the entire delicate network. In 1955, a case came before the Federal Communications Commission concerning a gadget called Hush-A-Phone, a silencer that slipped over the telephone mouthpiece and enabled a caller to speak into the mouthpiece without being eavesdropped on by others in the room. The FCC declared that Hush-A-Phone, being an acoustic device that wasn't attached electrically to the phone network, could not be outlawed by AT&T, but was a legitimate product. Oh no, AT&T said, and got its legal engines thrumming and took the matter to the Court of Appeals in Washington, D.C., which in due course overturned the decision. Still, the case filled customers' minds with the fanciful notion of hooking up non-Bell instruments to the phone lines. In fact, a fairly significant bootleg equipment business was spawned, mostly in antique and colored phones. When Bell's operating companies smoked out any of them attached to its lines, it would immediately disconnect them and sometimes cut off service for the naughty customer.

The first widespread gust of competition arrived in 1968. Thomas Carter of Dallas, Texas, had begun tinkering with electronic equipment as a young boy. In 1946, he launched a business specializing in mobile two-way radio systems. The bulk of Carter's sales were to oil companies. Their drilling crews frequently had to work in remote locations where telephone service didn't exist. Two-way radio systems were okay for these purposes, but less than ideal. If a field engineer cared to get in touch with someone who wasn't at the radio base station, the radio operator had to convey the message through a phone. Sensing a need,

Carter developed a gadget known as the Carterfone that enabled a person with a two-way radio to speak directly into a telephone by way of a base station. The person making the call phoned the base station operator of the private radio system where the Carterfone was located. The operator contacted the called party. A voice control circuit in the Carterfone switched the radio transmitter on when the party using the telephone was speaking and reverted the radio to receiving condition when he was done. The Carterfone went on sale in 1959, and several thousand units were sold over the next few years. The people over at AT&T didn't much cotton to the Carterfone, and they adamantly refused to permit its use over their phone lines. However, in a now-famous ruling that still causes the chests of non-AT&T officials to swell, the FCC decreed that AT&T couldn't prevent customers from attaching non-Bell equipment to its lines, providing that the phone company was allowed to install protective equipment between the line and the alien device. That was progress, but not much progress. The high cost of the protective equipment made most maverick equipment economically unattractive. Still, the makings of what came to be called the "interconnect industry" were established. The flood-gates were slowly opening to competition. Trickling onto the market came such items as flip-open Fold-A-Fones and French telephones and $450 nineteenth-century walnut fiddleback wall models. A market began to develop for PBXs (business switch-boards), key telephones (sets with pushbuttons to answer several lines), and answering machines. Some of them were better than anything Bell had, and, moreover, they were for sale rather than rent.

Years later, going well beyond Carterfone, the FCC set up a system of "registration" that allowed telephone subscribers to install alien terminal equipment without any protective gadgetry, provided that the foreign equipment was certified by government technical experts. The interconnect field was suddenly breathed a gigantic gust of air.

The FCC pushed on in other ways. In 1970, it authorized a spunky little company called MCI Communications to set up a communications service that would initially loop between St. Louis and Chicago. The bold action meant that independent companies (known in the trade as "specialized common carriers") could create intercity microwave relay systems for private leased-line tele-phone use by businesses, in head-to-head competition with similar

Bell facilities. Typically, the specialized carrier relies on Bell's local network to link customers to the carrier's own transmission facilities, which then take over and move messages for lower prices than those charged by AT&T. Bell flatly derided these upstarts as "cream-skimmers," since it argued that they only set up shop in lucrative, high-volume markets, ignoring the plains of Kansas and other out-of-the-way spots that the phone company was obliged to serve. In 1975, the ever-aggressive MCI unveiled a new service called Execunet, a microwave system connecting twenty-four cities across the country. Execunet went a giant step further than a private line network, which, after all, only linked a company's various offices. With Execunet, a subscriber could call his office's leased line from home and dial anybody in the MCI-served cities. This meant direct competition against AT&T's Message Toll Service. If it didn't bother you that you had to dial twenty-two digits to make a long-distance call, Execunet clearly offered lower rates, as much as 30 percent beneath Bell in some instances.

All too painfully aware that it was being undercut, AT&T howled its upset to the FCC, which responded by ordering Execunet discontinued. The FCC had been pushed as far as it would go. Refusing to accept its own death that easily, MCI trundled to the bar and succeeded in getting the commission's order overturned in appeals court. The Supreme Court's refusal to hear the FCC appeals in 1978 spelled an upset victory for the brash upstart. The monopoly crumbled further. Between the declaration of these rulings and the present day, dozens of competitors have raced to the telecommunications marketplace—all these companies piling up in rapid succession, the spirit of the first one still full of life as the latest one struggles, in a confused and distracted fashion, to get underway.

Precisely what the rules are going to be for AT&T and its competitors in the future—who can do what and what must be regulated—is still the subject of intense and often acrimonious debate in the halls of Congress and at the FCC. The problem has to do with the increasing overlap of the communications and data processing industries. Telecommunications continues to be completely regulated. Data processing has never been regulated. Therein lies a sticky problem. Right now, an unregulated company like IBM can't offer transmission services and stay unregulated, and AT&T isn't supposed to offer any data processing services. Computers and computer terminals are, in fact, specifically listed as off-limits for Bell to offer in the 1956 consent decree signed with the government. This setup made good sense in 1956. For one thing, the distinctions between the two industries were reasonably clear then. What's more, there was fear that AT&T would use its monopoly services to support data processing services, an arrangement that would mean Ma Bell could chop prices on its unregulated services and thereby undercut competitors who couldn't cross-subsidize in that way. Since then, technology has sped along at such a frenetic pace that the phone network can now store and analyze information as well as simply transmit it. At the same time, computer technology has increasingly come to involve communications. Computers now "talk" on the telephone in vaguely the same fashion that people do. Accordingly, nobody is entirely sure of where communications begins and data processing ends. The FCC has conducted two painfully slow computer inquiries that have hardly resolved the matter. "Exploring these kinds of questions," an assistant to one of the FCC commissioners told me, "is sort of like burrowing to the center of the earth." Early in 1980, the FCC issued a sweeping ruling, as a result of its second computer inquiry, that sets AT&T free to eventually enter data processing, provided that it sets up separate subsidiaries for these unregulated markets. Alas, this "final" order is far from final. There is likely to be considerable haggling to get certain aspects of the lengthy ruling revamped. What's more, the FCC's authority to unchain the phone company is altogether unclear and is expected to produce a spate of legal actions.

While the FCC grapples with this, so does Congress. For the last several years, lawmakers have been attempting to rewrite the 1934 Communications Act in a way that would be fair to competitors and AT&T alike. Two of the suggestions that have entered proposed rewrites are cutting off Western Electric from AT&T and permitting Bell to offer data processing services through separate, unregulated subsidiaries. Congress has found delving into the enormously complex issues of the communications industry as frustrating as has the FCC. There have been rewrites of the rewrites, and still no law. It seems inevitable that AT&T will probably be kept intact, but set loose to offer data processing products and services that will be unregulated. At the same time, it will continue to be regulated in basic telephone service, which is unlikely to be provided competitively in the foreseeable future. But along the way to what might seem to be a simple solution lies a complicated legal thicket. On the several days that I sat in on hearings of one or another proposed rewrite, the most striking thing to me was the apparent total incomprehension on the part of many of the lawmakers of what was being talked about. One Southern Congressman, presumably trying to sum up something or other at one afternoon's session, declared, "Well, the way I see it, Bell provides a right good telephone system, and some of these other boys are good too."

Though AT&T brass has continued to cry about competition like a wounded coyote, competitors have barely made a dent in its strength. It is still as firm as marble in its dominance of the marketplace. Annual revenues of its dozens of competitors are reckoned to amount to only about $900 million; AT&T tows in that much money every eight days. But most of the competitors have just begun to plant their crops, and their allotment of the business is expected to blossom into more than $2 billion as soon as 1985. Never have the telecommunications stakes been higher. Right now, the domestic communications industry is a $50-billion field. The data processing side is worth another $22 billion. Both areas are barreling along at almost a 15-percent-a-year rate of growth. So, if AT&T plays its cards right, the marketplace for communications will eventually become so monstrous that AT&T will continue to get bigger than ever, while still allowing plenty of room for a slew of competitors. However, if it no longer continues to scan the middle distance with slow and careful eyes for new customers, it may find itself under siege. In the words of Howard Anderson, president of the Yankee Group, a respected communications consulting firm in Cambridge, Massachusetts, "AT&T right now is like a battleship with a leak below the water line. The leak is important, but not critical. You have to solve that leak. If it continues unabated, you have to take that battleship to dry dock and turn it into something else."

The leak of competition, AT&T disclaimers to the contrary, seems plainly to have had beneficial effects for phone users. It has sparked innovation and, at least for some services and products, cheaper prices. Competitors have lined up a barrage of customers to offer advertising testimonials on how they've dumped Bell and never been happier. On the other hand, Bell has diligently rounded up an impressive wagonload of subscribers who left Mother Bell, only to be disappointed with what they got, and have since slouched back. One ace that AT&T has had in its hand is the fierce loyalty corporations have to the Bell insignia. Competitors are still looked upon, particularly by some of the bigger companies, with half-lidded eyes. It takes years of sweet-talking to get a company to go with someone else. Sure, competitors have cheaper prices, but does the stuff work? One business executive explained it to me this way: "There is something almost sacrilegious about ditching Bell. It takes some guts to even broach the subject. It's like you're having a meeting of the executive committee to talk about a new headquarters building and you clear your throat and say, 'You know, guys, instead of going the steel and concrete route this time, what about modeling clay? The stuff is better-priced.' Bell competitors have to find themselves godfathers. They have to line up these godfathers who have the courage to tell Bell to take a walk, and believe me, there aren't a hell of a lot of godfathers in the corporate world."

Competition for AT&T has several layers to it, but at bottom it falls into two broad areas—equipment and long-distance transmission. Equipment—telephones, data terminals, PBXs—has so far enticed the most players and dollars. It is about a $700-million industry. But transmission—now hovering at around $200 million —boasts some of the heaviest heavies in the corporate world, and is expected to eventually pry loose a vaster amount of AT&T business. Construed as the most dangerous of AT&T's looming competitors is no less a presence than IBM, the world's number one computer company. Simplistic views of the future picture the two as huge supertankers battering down swells of sea toward an inevitable collision. The prospect that most causes AT&T officers to toss in their sleep is that of IBM's joint venture with two other heavyweights (Aetna Life and Casualty and Comsat General)— Satellite Business Systems. In early 1981, SBS intends to shoot two satellites high into the sky to be the linchpins of a comprehensive data and voice transmission service. It will be enormously costly. Earth stations will be erected in customers' parking lots at costs expected to exceed half a million dollars apiece. They will transmit all of a client's data and voice to its various other locations. The service can't transmit anything to other companies (you'll still need Bell or somebody else for that), but SBS knows from elaborate studies it has undertaken that something like 80 percent of the communications flow of a company goes only to another company location. However, vast changes in the way a customer conducts his business will be called for with the SBS system, and not surprisingly, SBS has refined its target customer "not to the Fortune 500 but the Fortune 50." There is reason behind such apparent madness. Most remarkable is the kind of money that comes spilling out of the very biggest businesses. According to the Yankee Group, the twenty-five heftiest users of the phones spend $1.2 billion a year, or 15 percent of all intercity calling. The top thousand companies spend 65 percent of the dollars. And it is these companies—General Motors, Ford, Exxon, GE—that are the Bell System's gems, and the real brass ring that competitors are trying to snatch for themselves.

"Procter and Gamble has this product called Tide," said Howard Anderson. "It is their stud horse. They come out with Tide year after year and rake in a fortune. They take that fortune and come out with all these other products. AT&T has very few stud horses. Its big one is Long Lines. There have been small, but serious, inroads made into Long Lines by competition. We have seen only the tip of the iceberg. Long Lines can't afford to lose the big boys. SBS is going around the country now putting on dog and pony shows. They are prayer meetings. They are showing how their service can save companies money and increase their earnings per share. And these companies are sitting there, stroking their chins, and murmuring to themselves, 'Hmm.'"

In scale and intensity, the International Telephone and Telegraph Company, the so-called Geneen Machine that Harold Geneen catapulted to prominence by conceding the domestic phone business pretty much to the Bell monopoly and stalking the more fertile international grounds, may in fact prove to have the most thumping impact on AT&T. In recent years, it has rolled into the United States marketplace abiding by a cagey strategy that has scared the daylights out of AT&T managers. Rather than lead the way, ITT has sat back, twiddled its thumbs, and waited while smaller companies began to compete against Bell. After having carefully noted their mistakes, it has gotten up and tried the water. By now it has stuck its toe into every aspect of the competitive areas—business equipment, home phones, long-distance transmission—without risking too much investment in any one service. Meantime, Xerox, the copier giant, looks likely to cut a fairly substantial swath with a data transmission service that, in effect, amounts to an electronic mail system. It expects that to be working in 1981. RCA is heavy into satellite transmission of data. Industry analysts think it not improbable that such well-primed companies as Exxon, General Electric, Boeing, and McDonnell Douglas might pull on the gloves and step into the transmission ring. Also not to be counted out are the independent phone companies, which have long tied themselves to AT&T. The largest of them have grown competitive themselves. General Telephone, the biggest independent, has scooped up a Bell transmission competitor. Continental Telephone, the second biggest, bought an interconnect company and is plowing into transmission, too. Robert La Blanc, the colorful vice chairman of Continental, explained his company's role like this: "You know the guy who goes to the Moscow zoo and he sees this polar bear in a cage with a lamb. He asks the keeper how can this be. The keeper says, 'Well, you know, that's how detente works.' Then, in an aside, he adds, 'Of course, we have to replace the lamb every day.' I don't see Continental in the role of the lamb anymore."

Aside from transmission, AT&T has other headaches in the equipment field. The hot part of the market is in PBXs, computer phone systems that perform wizardry like automatically placing a call at a set time, notifying a user when a previously dialed busy line has become free, and programming the phone so that frequently called numbers can be stored and then activated by using a three-digit number. Flushed by the ebb and flow of competing products, AT&T engineered the Dimension line of PBXs for its business customers several years ago, and though it is the biggest selling system, it is widely regarded by industry observers to be less sophisticated and cost-effective than systems put out by Northern Telecom and the Rolm Corporation, its two closest pursuers. Rolm, a $100-million company situated in Santa Clara, California, the so-called Silicon Valley, has been growing at a breakneck pace. It crows that it has sold equipment to fifteen of the twenty biggest U.S. companies. Rolm claims to be shipping PBXs at a faster rate than any other independent supplier, though Northern Telecom disputes the boast. Rolm devised its equipment with a blitz of software products that can keep track of outgoing calls, restrict long-distance calling, and provide automatic call distribution (which distributes calls coming into high-volume operations such as airline information offices)—in short, meet customer needs faster than Bell or anybody else. As if Rolm and Northern Telecom aren't enough of a headache for Bell, it is only a matter of time, according to rumors swirling around the communications industry, before IBM introduces a PBX system in the

United States. AT&T officials were more than a little rattled when a new $2-million Dimension System installed in New York's august Waldorf-Astoria Hotel late in 1979 went berserk the day after it was put in. Incoming calls rang in the wrong rooms and outgoing calls became a total impossibility. Four hundred additional Waldorf workers had to be called in to cope with the havoc. They were summoned by pay phone.

Inside the corridors of Bell buildings, executives have stayed on their toes. All through the encroachments from competition, AT&T's reaction has been to slug it out, to not relinquish any of its treasured turf short of one slam-bang, winner-take-all battle. In retrospect, it was an absolutely brilliant strategy, and the genius who masterminded it was now-retired chairman John deButts. An avuncular, courtly, outspoken individual, deButts believed in the phone company the way Zionist Jews believe in Israel. To hear deButts argue AT&T's case, stepping on Bell's property was like eating pork on Passover. The whole thrust of the strategy sketched out by deButts was to do as much as possible—engage heavily in protracted court combat—to keep the competition from even getting underway. Privately, deButts had to know in his bones that the likes of IBM and RCA and ITT that were knocking on Ma Bell's door were, in a matter of time, sure to come barging in. He knew that the grounds for saving the monopoly were shaky, to say the least. And he also knew, all too well, that AT&T—with a complacent, indeed nascent, sales force entirely unaccustomed to a competitive marketplace—was extraordinarily vulnerable. So his tack was to do everything he could to keep competitors at bay, while Bell hurriedly rearranged the company, shored up its offerings, recruited a massive infusion of marketing people, and reoriented its troops to sell, sell, sell.

The most often-cited example of how vicious AT&T got during this period was its behavior toward Datran, a now-deceased company that was in the business of offering innovative computer communications systems, largely for business use. Some industry watchers, it is important to note, maintain that Datran was destined to fail no matter how AT&T behaved toward it. They say it was way overextended and way undercapitalized, and there is a certain amount of evidence that it was. Many others, however, pin the blame squarely on Bell, including the Justice Department, which cites the Datran episode in its big antitrust suit against AT&T. They complain that Datran is a classic illustration of how a monopoly can employ predatory pricing to drive a small competitor to the corporate graveyard. Datran's chairman, Sam Wyly, has insisted that Datran's bankruptcy in 1976 was brought on by a string of AT&T actions stemming from AT&T's determination to come snapping down on Datran like the bar of a giant mousetrap. He has charged that Bell improperly introduced services similar to Datran's digital service at rates slashed to 40 percent lower. After Datran's demise, AT&T's rates were indeed declared unjust. (In the spring of 1980, AT&T settled out of court for $50 million an antitrust suit brought by Wyly.)

Meantime, deButts made passionate speeches thick and fast from every soapbox he could get on, beseeching the courts to stop the onslaught of competition. He raised his voice, moaned and whined, adopted melodramatic poses, and generally called attention to Bell's potential injuries. He warned that if AT&T lost revenues to competitors, it would be forced to replace them by hiking the cost of phone service to the average consumer, boosting it, perhaps, by as much as 70 percent, a figure that hardly anyone, the FCC included, believed. He warned that the interconnection of foreign equipment might throw a monkey wrench into the whole system, causing cross talk, wrong numbers, line noise, and billing errors, among other horrors. AT&T's massive public relations machinery was set into motion to attempt to win the public to the Bell view. One of the biggest corporate lobbying drives on record was mounted to get Washington to pass a laudable-sounding Consumer Communications Reform Act, a measure that would just about ensure that the AT&T monopoly remained unchanged. The measure was so obviously favorable to AT&T that it quickly acquired the nickname, the Bell Bill. So effective was AT&T's extensive lobbying effort—almost every top Bell executive wore out some shoe leather pounding the floors of Congress—that nearly two hundred lawmakers signed on as cosponsors of the bill when it was first introduced in Congress in 1976. AT&T opponents, however, rustled up an equally impressive lobbying campaign that kept the Bell Bill from ever getting to a vote. Instead, lawmakers settled on the chore of rewriting the Communications Act.

Internally, deButts put in train a massive, system-wide restructuring. Remarkably enough, Bell had plodded on for decades organized along functional lines rather than structured according to its major markets. Responsibilities were divided according to the assignment performed, functions such as plant supervision, repair, engineering, traffic management, billing. Sales efforts were baled together with billing and customer services in what was called the "commercial" department. All phone company employees who dealt directly with the public handled both the residential and business side, even though the nature and needs of these markets had become vastly different. Of course, before the emergence of competition it didn't make much difference how responsive telephone service was to customer needs. It was good enough for Bell to decide what was best for the subscriber and just give it to him. In short, Bell's policy was that subscribers could have anything they wanted, provided Bell felt like giving it. That kind of attitude wasn't going to work with competing companies breathing down AT&T's neck, companies that were sometimes daring, sometimes careening, sometimes here-goes-hope-I-don't-flop, but always anxious to give customers exactly what they wanted. A perfect example of this was when Continental Airlines went to Southwestern Bell in 1972, wondering if it could get a new variety of call-switching and answering system to take care of phone reservations. Bell said that it would take until at least 1980 to produce the equipment. Disappointed about the wait, Continental sought out Collins Radio. By April 1974, Continental was taking reservations over an advanced new Collins system.

Responding to the spate of competition, AT&T ordered every company in the system to divide its assignments into business services, residential services, and network services (those that cut across both of the others). The turnabout began in early 1978, and optimists figure it will be years before it is all working smoothly. There was considerable initial confusion and opposition by many Bell employees and units, who thought things were fine the way they were. People began to find their jobs more confined. For instance, a repairman, who traditionally would fix sick phones in apartments and homes right along with businesses, would now specialize in either residences or businesses. Executives would likewise devote themselves to one market or the other, no longer both. It was a whale of a transformation for a company that had so long prided itself on its continuity of operation. While these changes were being implemented, AT&T vastly beefed up its marketing force, and while doing so, it did something considered taboo at Bell—it recruited almost entirely from the outside. That didn't sit too well with many people, either. In the all-important business market, AT&T has carved up its customers into more than fifty industry classifications and shipped out marketing experts to study each segment and determine how its communications affect profit and loss. Based on these studies, the market managers then proffer formal product requests, describing the general characteristics of the products and services they think their industries need. For instance, Bell came up with an option that makes it possible for different airlines located at a small airport to save money by sharing a single switchboard. Marketing managers are no longer being tracked according to Bell's traditional indices and productivity measures—which kept count of the number of orders obtained, but not the revenues. Now, they will be judged only by how many dollars they bring in, and how much has to be spent to get them.

Jan Loeber, director of cross industries in AT&T's marketing department, a man himself plucked from the banking field, told me, "The Bell System has to learn how to cope with a rapidly changing environment. This is not the way it's operated before. There's a tremendous amount of change that has to come, because of where we're coming from. Decision-making has to speed up. Design lead time has to get shorter. We have to understand software better. In the past, we tended to respond when the customer wanted some service. That cannot be. We have to anticipate. We have to be hopping all the time. The training demands on the system are tremendous. Literally everyone involved in marketing is going back to school."

I spent some time one morning with a couple of AT&T marketing people involved in orienting Bell managers to the new competitive atmosphere, and they related some of the exercises that had been cooked up for training sessions. In one exercise, half of the class of managers are blindfolded, the other half not, and then the instructor announces that he will meet everyone upstairs for dinner and leaves the room. The blinded people, naturally, seek assistance from the sighted half of the class, and grope their way upstairs. "We explain that the sighted people were trying to help the blinded people into a new environment," one of the marketing people said. "What criteria had to be used? The criteria of the blinded people. You have to go by their needs, not your own. The message, of course, is that Bell has to go by its customers' needs, and not its own."

In another exercise, the class is shown the war film *Twelve O'Clock High*. There is a scene picturing a daylight bombing raid of England by Germany. The English unit in the footage is really taking a beating. The commander is a truly understanding individual. Eventually, he's kicked out because of the losses. In comes Colonel Savage, a fiery, no-nonsense operator. He sticks all the incompetents in one plane and anoints it the "Leper Colony." He sits back while they foul each other up, allowing the proficient flyers to record significant success. Savage also promotes and heartily compliments those who excel. Then Savage suffers a bit of a nervous breakdown from all the pressure heaped on him, and the first commander returns. In the interim, he has adapted himself to Savage's tough style. The class proceeds to discuss the divergent styles at some length. Sure, the first guy is nice to work for, it is pointed out, but would you rather work for someone who increases your chances of getting killed or one who allows you a better chance to succeed? A good leader, in other words, doesn't have to be a well-liked person. The instructor then inquires whether the managers are setting high enough goals, whether they're running a tight ship. In one class, a Southern Bell manager soaked in all this discussion, then got up and said, "By Jesus, I've been getting my ass shot down and the troops are smiling. I better get in shape, or I'm out of a job."

While its marketing people are being schooled, Bell is also hurriedly trying to grind out new products and services. Its most significant new product is its Advanced Communications Service. In crude summary, it is a complex hardware and software package that will allow dissimilar computer terminals to "talk" with each other. This will mean that a user won't have to be tied down to just one brand of terminal. The network will provide text-editing and address-storage memories, so that even "dumb" terminals can be hooked up to a phone line to function as terminals for data processing or electronic mail. The network would, moreover, perform many of the control functions now done by expensive software and hardware. Some large companies currently possess more than one internal data communications network, none of which can talk to the others, creating a certain amount of chaos and underutilized systems. ACS stands as a direct threat to IBM's much-touted Systems Network Architecture, which establishes communications standards best suited to IBM gear. Though still several years away from birth, ACS has created a wave of excitement in the marketplace and frayed the nerves of more than one competitor. "On paper, ACS is terribly impressive," one communications consultant told me. "It may well be the key to the future growth of the Bell System."

I sought some outside opinion about just how well the overall response to competition was going at AT&T, and while most individuals I spoke with thought Bell was making unmistakable progress, everyone also figured it was still years away from truly mastering its new environment.

One respected consultant told me, "You read a lot about the new marketing gurus at Bell. The press releases have preceded the real action. What we're going to see in the next few years is utter chaos. A telephone installer was in here the other day, and he said that he was at a meeting where he was told that he was no longer a telephone installer. He was in the Business Telephone Delivery Group. 'What's that mean?' I asked. He said that meant putting telephones in the wall, just like he always has. Make no mistake, the Bell System is eminently viable. It will be with us a long time after I'm gone and a long time after you're gone. But it's not going to change overnight. The Bell System is an engineering company. Turning it around is like turning around an oil tanker in New York Harbor. The organization that Bell thinks it is modeling itself on is IBM. But Bell, frankly, is incompetent today. They don't have the hardware and the solutions to go head-to-head with IBM. When I have my tongue in my cheek, I call them the children's crusade. So, is the Bell System competitive today? No. Will they be competitive in 1985? Yes. It will take that long? Yes. That will be soon enough? Yes."

The consultant paused a moment, then added, "You know, the real irony is that all this high-technology competition was precipitated by the invention of the transistor at Bell Labs. That made it all possible. If Bell had known this was going to happen, all these headaches brought in, it would have taken Shockley and the others out behind the barn and put bullets in their heads."

If the communications companies themselves have a lot to say about their products, they have even more to say about each other. Friendly from the skin out, they are deep competitors, and one thing that they are (in a sense) competing for is their right to be a part of the market. A high percentage of them seems to feel that a high percentage of the others should be shut down and sent away. When they speak about AT&T, they speak not in whispers, but blow the bugles.

"The company would like to snuff everybody else out of business."

"It knows, just like everybody else knows, that competition is in everyone's best interest, but if it could have its way, it would still appoint itself to run the whole shebang."

"It's the most selfish corporation on earth. It has to eat the whole pie."

I had coffee one blustery morning with an official at IBM who has paid particularly close attention to developments at AT&T. Among other things, he said:

"We think competition has been the spur to innovation. It's not enough to invent the transistor. You've got to bring it to the marketplace. People who are trying to make a profit are damn anxious to please the end user.

"With our experience in a competitive marketplace, we have to ask a rhetorical question: Why regulate anything? We just don't see any natural monopoly characteristics in the terminal equipment market anymore, and we're not sure we see them in long-distance transmission. Now, the telephone industry thinks you're going to screw up the system. They think you put a different cover on the telephone book and you screw up the system.

"Is AT&T going to blow everybody out of the water if you unleash it from regulation? Not at all. It's just going to make everyone run a little harder. I think there's a tremendous misunderstanding about bigness in this market. There are very limited inherent economies of scale. The ease of entry has changed tremendously. IBM has a number of worthy competitors that have done very well by inventing a better mousetrap, or a better spring to go on a mousetrap. The growth rates of these companies is just amazing. Some of these small competitors claim AT&T is going to drown them. They complain about AT&T's predatory practices. I don't believe any of that. I believe small companies will do very well against AT&T. They sure as hell have picked our pockets.

"None of us in the company agrees that there are just two big companies—namely us and AT&T—that are going to carve up the market and everyone else is going to be wiped out. That's a very popular notion, but I don't believe it. We don't think it's a two-company deal at all.

"What kind of company is AT&T? As a customer of theirs, as a supplier of theirs, as an observer of them, I think they're a great company. They really believe what they say, though they've been wrong in some of their beliefs. They've had this pig on their back for so long, it's easy to criticize them. I don't think much of the criticism is justified."

The sentimental favorite of the Davids trying to slay the AT&T Goliath has always been MCI, the tiny Washington company, situated a few blocks away from the FCC, that went to court against Bell and won. Now a $150-million company, MCI thinks it can soon sprout into the billion-dollar category. It has some fourteen thousand customers, including biggies like GM, Xerox, Ford, Rockwell, Sperry, and Westinghouse. If anyone is loaded with hatred for AT&T, it should be MCI.

Orville Wright (no relation to the airplane inventor) is a round-faced, bespectacled man. Behind his desk is a map of the United States with MCI routes scribbled on it. Wright is MCI's president. "The question we get all the time is why buy from us instead of from Bell," he said. "One reason is we're cheaper. Secondly, we built our plant late in 1968. So the quality of our network is better than Bell, simply because it was built later and with the latest technology. The third reason is because we're small and customers get to know people here personally. They like that."

"How do you feel about Bell?" I asked.

"We love 'em," Wright beamed. "My people out in the field, the crafts people, get along beautifully. Many of our people came from Bell. We have our arguments with AT&T headquarters. They have been adamant that they should have all the communications business and anyone who comes in is a sinner, and they look on us as a sinner. And I think it stems from a misguided belief that they have been given a piece of property, and we're trying to take some of it away. Their feelings get hurt."

"What impact have you had on them?"

"We have no impact on them. It's like taking a little pin and sticking it in the tail of an elephant. He feels it, but it doesn't bother him very much."

"Has the company changed, because of competition?"

"They've gotten off their duff a little. They're more responsible to customers. We've prodded them into being a better company. They're a much better marketing operation than in the past. They were just a bunch of order takers. I would say to you that there are indications that they are trying to make peace, not to take the holier-than-thou position that nobody else should be playing in their ball park. Now Bill McGowan has a somewhat different view, if you talk to him."

William McGowan, the chairman of MCI, would never get a job at AT&T. He looks too mean. A cigarette was burning in an ashtray. Coffee was cooling on the desk.

"AT&T is so big that it's almost impossible for you or me to understand how big it is," he said. "I was telling my secretary the other day that when Christ was born, if you started counting at one count per second, it would take until the year 1902 to count out the annual revenues of AT&T."

That said, McGowan launched into the most scathing denunciation of the Bell System I had yet heard. It was clear that there was no interrupting him, so I sat back, pen poised, and listened to the ragging.

"I don't believe there is such a thing as the Bell System," he said. "I think the Bell System has spent hundreds of millions of dollars to convince the American public that this is one system. They have a terribly difficult time answering the question of why it's important for the company that owns all the different local operating companies to own the connecting factor—Long Lines —when there are all those independents that connect into it with no trouble. You could have a lot of kids eating sugared cereal if you spent enough money. But these are adults eating the sugared story.

"In terms of conduct, I find no evidence that they are treating their competitors in a manner that the antitrust laws require. Words are the cheapest thing to me. They say they recognize competition now. That doesn't mean a good goddamn to me. I can't take a word from Bell and take it to the bank. I care when their conduct changes, and I don't see it changing. They obviously consider themselves to be an entity above the law. That company, except for the big propaganda machine it's created, has not done anything great. It's not very hard to invent a telephone system.

"I think they should be punished. Someone should be compensated for what they've done. I know them for what they are. They break the laws of the country. They are as ruthless and as two-faced as any company can be and they flaunt it as being righteous. You know, a crook is a crook, regardless of whether he wears Oxford clothes. I think they are going to go down in history as having perpetrated as much a fraud on as many people as anyone."

McGowan's vehemence was so powerful—not to mention so novel—that I couldn't help but ask him if he thought his opinions on Bell were widely shared.

He stroked his chin, and said, "My opinions were never widely shared, except a couple of years after they were expressed."

10

"I Didn't Want Something That Would Blow Up"

Earl Syndor became one by accident. In 1965, he was puttering along First Avenue, minding his own business, heading toward the upper part of Manhattan, when a phone company truck swung out of its lane and slammed into the rear of his car, abbreviating the fender. There was hardly a grain of doubt in his mind about who was to blame. It was Syndor's sense of propriety more than his fender that was bruised. "Yet when I attempted to collect from the phone people, they unleashed this incredible barrage of lawyers," he would recall. "It seemed like the entire legal profession was on the offensive against poor me. They took depositions not for weeks, but months. Questions and questions and questions. I was so wrung out that I finally threw in the towel in disgust. It got so awfully exhausting. A man can take so much. But I figured that if this company had such tenacity to keep its shareholders from paying a little bit of money, well, that must be one heck of a company to invest in." An actor by trade, Syndor has now possessed AT&T stock for the past dozen years. "Listen, I have inveighed at least ten friends to start investing. I've been delighted with the investment. Now and then, I think of telling the phone people, 'Hey, you owe me fifty bucks,' but I more than made up for it in dividends. I haven't any plans to give up that stock till the earth ceases to spin."

For one reason or another—no one is exclusive—almost 3 million people have sunk some of their money into AT&T stock, making them the biggest shareholder family on the planet. General Motors is a distant second, with 1.2 million holders, and Exxon ranks a dismal third with 684,000 stockholders. The gargantuan size of the AT&T family can be worked into analogies that reach beyond comprehension. If the members clasped hands, they would form a line that extended more than 2,490 miles long. If by some odd coincidence, every AT&T shareholder showed up at your house one evening, it would require thirty-three days for them to get through the door. The number of shareholders exceeds the population of twenty-six states. There are so many AT&T shareholders that 200 of them die every working day.

The precise makeup of the stew of AT&T owners has always been indeterminate. AT&T records contain little more than names and addresses. Yet they do point out that twice as many women as men own the stock, and they divulge that there are more than 220,000 custodian accounts for minors. In addition, about 300,000 holders are phone company employees, and another 40,000 are institutions. Among the institutions are 9,000 corporations, 1,400 foundations, 5,000 churches, and 12,000 cemeteries. "We've never done any sampling to determine how many doctors, bakers, and Indian chiefs own the stock," a man in AT&T's Stock and Bond division explained to me one morning. "But we know instinctively about a lot of them from our contacts. By and large, they're over forty years of age. A great many of them live in Florida and California, which would suggest that they're retired. All the women owners would indicate that there are a lot of widows holding our stock. We know that people basically buy our shares for the dividend yield and its stability, not for speculation purposes. The roguish, gambler type would not be inclined to plow money in AT&T."

In the financial pages of the print media and around the water coolers at the big brokerage houses, AT&T stock has long been touted as the prototypical "widows and orphans" holding. Buy AT&T, so this line of thinking goes, and it will take good care of you. At a current market price of about $60 (the price doesn't tend to fluctuate much) and a dividend payout of $5.40 a year, you are talking about a yield on your investment of about 9 percent, which beats leaving your money in the bank, even if it falls well short of a good real estate investment. Over the long term, however, the investment has not been so wonderful. The value of the stock today is just slightly more than double what it was in 1900, while the cost of living has more than quintupled. If a daring investor—in quest of a second car or a vacation to Tahiti—had sunk $100 in AT&T stock in January 1900 (when a share went for roughly $27), and held on to it through June of 1979, the investment, adjusted for subsequent stock splits, would be worth just $217.47. Another $263, however, would have been picked up in dividends and various stock rights.

What really gave the stock the widows and orphans connotation was the risky decision by AT&T management during the depths of the Depression to keep on issuing the regular dividend payments at a time when many companies reduced theirs or vetoed them altogether. To amass the cash to meet the payouts during the dark years, AT&T had to dip into its coffers for a total of $217 million, but the tremendous quantities of goodwill built up from the gesture continue to reap benefits for the company. "I remember all that right well," one longtime stockholder told me when I broached the subject, "and my heart is still with them for paying us during those lean days. I'll always stick with them." Not once has the phone company skipped or lowered its payout, a record unmatched among corporate giants.

The attractiveness of owning AT&T stock invites a chorus of comment from the community that is supposed to know when to be bull or bear—Wall Street. The dialogue assembled here contains voices from up, down, and around Wall Street.

"It is as sweet as honey."

"I'd recommend it to my grandmother, and she believes in keeping money in her sock."

"From where I sit, AT&T is one of the safest investments in the market. It's never going to be a killer stock. But who's made a killing in the stock market lately?"

"It's an attractive defensive stock. It generally holds up in a poor market."

"I'd opt for putting your dough in a mattress over AT&T. It's done nothing lately."

"I don't know of a single time in telephone history that the risk of owning it has been as high. But, again, its yield has never been as great."

"It's wrong to think of it as just a widows and orphans stock. Some of that is still there. But it's carried away from that. It's ideal, in my opinion, even for an aggressive investor."

"The stock has always been appealing. It's like a bowl of sugar. It's always sweet. Year after year after year, it's a stock that looks good."

"Does anyone recommend against owning AT&T?"

"There have been times when I've been unenthusiastic about

the stock. There have been times when the stock has performed lousy. Sometimes, exceedingly lousy. But, over a long period of time, it's a good place to put your dough."

"In 1964, the stock was seventy-five dollars a share. I know that because I owned a bunch of it. I had to sell it because I was buying a house. My wife and I cried all night long, because we were sure that stock was going to go to the moon, and maybe beyond. Well, it didn't quite make it. In the 1964 to 1972 period, the stock performed poorly. It's only done well from 1972 on."

"What would you rather own, IBM or AT&T?"

"The common belief on the Street is that you make more money with IBM. I think that's wrong. I'd go for AT&T."

"Which would I rather own? On a fundamental basis, I would rather own IBM. On market performance, I'd rather own AT&T. If I could only buy one, which would it be? I really don't think I can answer that question. I've got children going to college and so the income is very important to me. If it wasn't, I would take the risk and buy IBM. Sure I would."

Being such a huge shareholder custodian, AT&T shoulders the weight of many tasks. Quartered at the company's Raritan River complex, a clump of buildings in Piscataway, New Jersey, is its shareholder relations department. There, a gang of fifty people does nothing but answer phone inquiries, while others reply to letters and still others transfer stock. The department is besieged by 1,700 calls and 750 letters a day. Shareholders used to be invited to call collect, until 800 numbers were installed in 1976, one for New Jerseyans and one for the balance of the country. Initially, many New Jersey residents dialed the AT&T number minus the 800 prefix, an understandable error. They got a florist in Elizabeth, New Jersey. His phone rang itself off the hook. Inquiries about yield and earnings multiples. The man was innocent of financial counsel. To soothe the bewildered florist, the company bought a handsome array of flowers and, during big offerings and dividend time, it sent someone over to answer his phone. After about six months, people wised up.

The day I paid a visit to the department, phone calls were pouring into the two rooms set up for shareholder inquiries, pressing for answers. What are my holdings anyway? So where's my dividend? My dog had my dividend check for supper (true story). I lost my certificates. Have you looked everywhere? Yes, everywhere. Everywhere? Oops, here they are in the refrigerator (true story). Raritan River is also the origin of some of the bulkiest mailings ever to congest the Post Office. Nineteen major mailings go out to shareholders each year. The largest is the annual report and proxy, which heads out to 3.5 million people. That amounts to 40,000 mailbags worth. AT&T people can't resist pointing out that if you stack those annual reports on top of each other, they will nudge past the two World Trade Center towers, positioned one above the other.

AT&T owners appear to be an uncommonly loyal bunch, clinging to their stock an average of twelve years. The average-size holding is 228 shares out of roughly 670 million shares outstanding. Much of the trading tends to be institutional (more than 1 percent of New York Stock Exchange trading is AT&T stock), and the company reckons that individuals alone hang onto their shares an average of twenty years. Many pass them on from generation to generation like family heirlooms. "I wouldn't any more part with my stock than I would with my wedding dress," I was told by one fairly ancient woman. Nevertheless, about five hundred accounts are opened and as many closed on a typical business day. AT&T owners are itchy to move, it would appear, since there are some sixteen hundred changes of address every weekday. AT&T transfer people at times encounter mighty peculiar doings. One woman wished to transfer her stock to Donald of the same last name, whom she identified as being six years old. AT&T obliged. One of the woman's sons called up to check whether or not the transfer had been made. Why yes, AT&T said. Interesting, the son replied, Donald is a dog. Back went the stock.

Undoubtedly AT&T's most novel shareholder program is its Shareholder-Management Visit program. Launched in 1956, it is thought to be unique to this day in the corporate world. It works like this: middle management employees, on their own time but under company orders, pay personal calls on owners living in their vicinity, to hear what's on their minds and to answer any questions that might be bothering them. The phone company spawned the program because it was growing fearful that the system had ballooned to such tremendous dimensions that shareholders might not relate very well to it, and if they stopped relating they might up and sell their stock. It wanted its shareholders, no matter how meager their holdings, to know that it still cared enough about them to come over and visit them at their homes. The concept has bloomed into a remarkable public relations device. Some twenty thousand visits take place each year, some more eventful than others. In Minnesota, one manager made an appointment with a woman. As he strode to the front door, he heard his name being called from behind a bush. The woman whispered that her husband didn't know she owned AT&T stock. He liked the high flyers. The visit took place behind the bush. Another manager roused the suspicions of a paranoid shareholder when he phoned to make an appointment. The shareholder, to alleviate doubt, called the police and had the manager trailed and asked for identification to prove his phone company connection. Still another AT&T visitor wound up purchasing the shareowner's home. He made the comment, "You know, this is a beautiful house, just the kind the wife and I would love to buy." "Oh, yeah? We're moving to New Hampshire." At the end of one fairly mundane visit, during which the shareholder had been uncommonly cordial, the shareholder wondered if the phone company manager, before he left, would like to hear his dog play the piano. The Bell man tiptoed out.

To get a feel for the shareowner visit program, I asked AT&T if I could accompany a few managers when they paid their calls on stockholders. The company said yes, so I arranged to go on several scheduled visits. The first one I went on was with Jim Jackson, an area construction superintendent for New Jersey Bell. We were slated to visit John Laudenberger, who lived not far from Jackson in the town of Westfield, New Jersey, a quiet residential town in the middle of the state. Jackson had short brown hair combed back, glasses, a soft-spoken manner. The night I went with him, he was wearing a blue plaid suit, a blue shirt, and a blue plaid tie.

"The only thing I know about this fellow is his address and the fact that he owns less than two thousand shares," Jackson told me as we drove toward our destination.

"How do you know he doesn't have more stock?" I asked.

"Because if he did, someone higher up in the company would be visiting him. We don't fool around with the big wheels."

The house was a lovely split level, with a well-tended front lawn. Laudenberger and his wife greeted us cordially at the door and offered coffee as we were directed to chairs in the cosy living room. Two wooden ducks reposed on the living room table between two facing couches. There was an airy orderliness to the house.

"How long have you lived in Westfield?" Jackson asked.

"Oh, twenty-six or twenty-seven years," Laudenberger replied. "We just moved into this house, though."

"Well, it's certainly beautiful."

Mrs. Laudenberger fetched the coffee and set it down on the coffee table between us. The visit continued in a small-talk vein, rambling over each other's background, a mutual interest in bridge, recent movies or books that had been enjoyed. Then Jackson handed Laudenberger his business card, after making certain to scribble his home number on it.

"You ever have any problem or anything," he said, "feel free to call me. I am at your disposal."

Laudenberger related the fact that he first bought AT&T stock in 1950. He said he had now amassed between six hundred and seven hundred shares. Until retiring fairly recently, he said he had been a mechanical engineer for Exxon.

Jackson asked him if he was aware that the dividend was going up on April 1.

"Oh, Lord, of course," Laudenberger said, letting out a small guffaw. "Things like that don't escape me. That's money in my pocket."

"Are you pleased?"

"Oh, naturally, we've been very pleased with the dividend policy."

"Good. Good."

Jackson loudly cleared his throat, slurped some coffee. "Well, let's talk a little bit about the Bell System," he said. He had brought his annual report along with him, and now he retrieved it from his briefcase. "Have you read this?" he asked.

"Oh, yeah," Laudenberger answered. "Every page."

"How did you find it?"

"I appreciate it, because it's short. It's very short for the biggest company. But it's got all I want, I guess."

"What do you think of the management of AT&T?"

"Well, the one person we see in the TV commercials and all is the chairman. I think the highest of that gentleman. I think he does a knock-up job. Sometimes, I just sit here and wonder how the heck he does do it."

Jackson laughed at that. "Even we wonder sometimes. Have you had any repairmen here recently?" he asked.

Mrs. Laudenberger chipped in, "Oh, now, nothing ever breaks in this house."

"Well, I wouldn't say that," Laudenberger inserted. "But there's nothing wrong with the Bell System."

Jackson then mentioned that the Bell System was faced with a government antitrust suit that strove to break up the phone network. The management of the company has taken a strong posture against it. Did Laudenberger approve of that stance?

"Oh, absolutely. And we're not alone. Westfield is a conservative town, and any kind of battle that takes place, the conservative wing takes control. I talked to a friend about this recently. She's retired and most of her income comes from Telephone, and she's plenty worried. She says, 'Look at the Post Office. What a disgusting mess. Why doesn't the government keep its filthy hands off the phone company? Go fiddle with something else.'"

His wife added, "I think the telephone service is superb and the cost is not out of line."

"Do you think that we've done a good job of presenting this to the public, the cost and all?" Jackson asked.

Laudenberger stroked his whiskers. His wife said, "Oh, yes, don't you think they have?"

Her husband said, "No, I don't think all the people recognize the bargain that phone service is. I'm afraid too many of us take the phone system for granted. In Latin America, where I've traveled, the phones are a joke. I think the phone company should constantly emphasize how fabulous the service is. It's so doggone good."

Finished with his questions, Jackson wondered whether Laudenberger had anything to ask of him. The man thought a moment, then said, "Oh, well, there is one thing. The wife and I have often driven past your Basking Ridge building. It's sure interesting looking. We were wondering whether we could get access to the grounds to take a little peek around."

Jackson smiled and said, "I'll make a note on that and check into it and get back to you. I don't think it's going to be any problem at all."

Back in the car, Jackson scratched down some notes on the visit for a formal report he was required to file with his supervisor. He told me, "That was fairly typical of how these babies go. I find that maybe in a quarter of the visits there is criticism on one issue or another. We talk about it some, chew it over, and sometimes they realize they didn't understand the issue that well. I don't feel my role is to convince them of anything, only to make the Bell

System's position entirely clear. If I find there is any degree of negativism, I try to explore that negativism. To be frank, most of these people have bought the stock so they can have a nice, sound investment, and they don't really follow the company very closely at all. Some of them are tickled silly just to have somebody paying a call on them."

On another piping hot evening, I got quite a different picture of how a shareholder visit can go. I accompanied Bill Mott, a traffic services supervisor for New Jersey Bell, on a visit to a married couple I shall call Peggy and Harvey Peterson, who lived in a placid central Jersey community. Their home was a somewhat dilapidated two-story, white clapboard affair. A stack of wood was piled on the porch.

When we got settled in the living room, Mott said, "Now, I don't know anything about you, whether you have two shares or two hundred thousand shares."

"Well," Peterson snapped, "you can probably see from looking around that I don't own two hundred thousand."

"Well, Harvey, let me get into a few things," Mott said. "You don't mind if I call you Harvey, do you?"

"No, I'm Harvey."

Mott asked Peterson if he had read the annual report.

"No," he said. "I don't read annual reports. I don't even read the annual report of my own company. Biggest waste of time I ever heard of."

Mott laughed nervously. Peterson's wife sat idly in her chair, saying nothing, seemingly indifferent to the entire conversation. Her eyes appeared ready to close.

Peterson said, "You know, we'd probably be burning your ears off if we weren't stockholders in this company. The phone company seems to do nothing but get rate increases. Rate increases. Rate increases. Rate increases. The customers are probably saying, 'Hey, this really stinks.' "

Mott straightened himself up in his chair, and said, "Well, we haven't really done that well on rate increases. There are so many things down the road. We need the money." He then let loose with a machine-gun volley of facts and figures. You could tell from the way he rattled off information that he had done his homework. Mott mentioned that New Jersey Bell, at the moment, was having some difficulty getting approval to charge for directory assistance.

Mrs. Peterson's eyes flashed open, her mouth began to move.

"Yes, I would think so," she said indignantly. "Tell me one lousy reason why you should do it."

"Well, for one thing," Mott said, "something like seventy percent of the people in New Jersey make only three calls a month. That's half of all directory assistance calls. We have some people who make five hundred a day, six hundred a day. They keep an entire directory assistance office open. So most of the people are carrying the freight for the minority."

"Well, I don't like the idea," she snapped. "My mother was a telephone retiree with more years than you've had, buddy boy. There's something wrong with charging for directory assistance. It's a rotten idea."

"The thing is you'd get a rebate if you didn't make any calls," Mott persisted.

"Listen," Mrs. Peterson said, her voice rising, "you're in the wrong ball park. Maybe you'd like to talk about something else."

Before Mott could turn to another subject, however, Mrs. Peterson roared back on the offensive, guns blaring: "You have lowered your standards, and I resent it. You have lowered your standards for operators. You have lowered your standards for installers. You have lowered your standards for repairmen. You have lowered your standards for every last person I deal with. You keep lowering your standards and lowering your standards, and soon the phone company will be the absolute pits."

"Well," Mott said, "do you have any good news?"

Dead and absolute silence.

Mott inquired whether they needed any additional telephone directories, or did they have any further questions. They didn't, and Mott rose slowly, like a fighter knocked down by a fluke punch, and hurriedly took his leave.

Buttoning his jacket in the car, Mott shook his head slowly from side to side, and said to me, "That's the kind of visit where there's nothing to do but bail out. Put on the chute and jump. The sad thing about it is she was right. Service is worse now. But what isn't? I felt like telling her, 'Hey, lady, shut up already. This is nineteen-fucking seventy-eight. Where have you been? Get the hell out of the attic.'"

The oldest AT&T shareholder is Dolly Warren. She is 108, and lives alone in Washington, D.C. She has owned phone company stock since the 1940s. She professes to be entirely delighted with it, and uses the dividend she earns from her 320 shares, along with Social Security money, to live on. She was married twice, but both husbands have died. "Husbands are unreliable," she told me. "Can't depend on them for nothing."

I asked her about her AT&T holdings, and she said, "It's sure been good to me, that company. I haven't got a bad word in me for them. The checks keep coming in, so something must be right. If it weren't doing right, why would that happen? You see what I'm getting at?"

Mrs. Warren whiles away her time sitting in a rocking chair, gaping out the window and watching TV. She is hard of hearing, so AT&T affixed to her phone a loud buzzer, of the sort used in factories so phones can be heard over the thunder of the machinery. "I just sit here and I have some jelly and some cottage cheese," she said to me. "I'm going deaf, dumb, and blind all at the same time. I just ain't worth a nickel anymore."

The youngest holder in phone company annals apparently was little Leonard Snyder of Philadelphia. Minutes after he came into being on December 28, 1951, his proud father relayed the news to his aunt. That called for a gift, she decided, and she at once placed an order for five shares of AT&T stock. Thirty-two minutes after Leonard was born, according to intelligence from AT&T stock and bond people, he already was an AT&T shareholder, though it was some time before he voted a proxy.

The phone company is unwilling to divulge the identity of its largest individual holder (the late Billy Rose used to brag that he was the champion owner, with some 350,000 shares), though it will confirm that the biggest owner holds about 95,000 shares of stock, an investment that carries a current market value of close to $6 million. The biggest holder of all is Bankers Trust, with some 25 million shares. It does not really own them all, though. Roughly 14 million of them are the property of AT&T employees who have bought stock under the company's savings plan. Bankers Trust is the principal trustee for the program. Even without these shares, though, Bankers Trust outdistances second-place Merrill Lynch, which has 8.3 million shares of AT&T stock.

One of the larger single owners, with 2,500 shares, is Judge Carr Bailey. He is not an actual judge. That's his given name. He is ninety-eight, a retired accountant residing in Sun City, Arizona. He can only hear you if you speak at something approaching the level of a sonic boom. Bailey calls AT&T shareholder relations people every month to find out the stock price ("I want to know it's not slipping. This is an important matter"). AT&T people know him so well that they mail him birthday cards. Once, when two months elapsed without his call, AT&T called him. He had broken his leg and wasn't much up to placing phone calls. Bailey is vigorously talkative and extremely amiable, and his enthusiasm for the company is infectious. "I tell you, you got rocks in your head if you don't buy that stock," he told me one afternoon. "Either you get it or you have your head examined. I'm not kidding. I'm deadly serious. Get the stock. Get it now. Call the AT&T folk. I tell you this, if there's life after life, I'll have my AT&T stock then, too. That answer your questions?"

Who else owns AT&T stock?

Ruth Spencer, a retired psychologist, Terrell, Texas. "Well, I would say AT&T is my first love. If I feel the need, I call them and they sure do their best to help. I wouldn't tolerate short talk out of any of them, because I'm not the hired hand, they are."

Walter Jacobs, a Bible manufacturer, Ridgefield Park, New Jersey. "I have the feeling that if AT&T goes under, then the whole country goes under."

Bert Heafner, a real estate broker, Los Angeles. "I'm so small a shareholder that I'm like a mosquito that AT&T can slap silly anytime it wants to. But it don't. It likes me."

Marjorie McDermett, a nurse, Tewksbury, Massachusetts. "I didn't want something that would blow up. AT&T won't blow up. Maybe fizzle a little, but never blow up."

George Kelty, the retired owner of the Flying A Service Station, San Jose, California. "There's no company like this that cares about its shareholders and nothing else. You write a letter to the big man there and he writes you back like you're his brother. He don't have to. The big man's got things on his mind. You yourself go out and get some of this stuff, or else you don't know nothing."

11

Hearing It
from Evelyn Davis

Here we have Spring, and so it's annual meeting time. The shareholders' meeting of the telephone company is the one formal occasion when the actual owners of AT&T can come face to face with their management and air their sometimes eccentric views on how the business ought to be run. It can be a heady opportunity. Unrestrained stockholders can grill the top men, who can't weasel or pussyfoot around. Plucky grandmothers from Peoria can afterward waltz up to and mix a bit with the directors and executives. Management holds the meeting under the pretense that the public, in the form of individual shareholders, actually has some control over the corporation. In practice, though, the shareowners really have very little say, management does what it pleases, and the democracy of the meeting is little more than a desert mirage.

Most annual meetings of corporations are traditionally held in the spring, and AT&T's is no exception, falling every year on the third Wednesday in April. The phone company used to stage all of its meetings regularly in New York, generally on AT&T premises, but in the last fifteen years, in the interest of giving as many of its shareowners as possible a chance to partake in the event, AT&T has followed a policy of rotating the site among sundry big cities. The 1979 meeting, the company's ninety-fourth, took place in Seattle. I caught a plane out there to see how it went.

On my way out to Seattle, I recapped in my mind what I knew about annual meetings. The ritual, I was aware, can follow several different courses. A great many meetings proceed in a staid fashion before skimpy turnouts, the boredom relieved only by the fact that the proceedings wind up inside of an hour. Some annual meetings flash to a conclusion in a couple of minutes. At the opposite pole are meetings, especially those of the giant controversial companies, during which shareholder unruliness annually sets a record. In these instances, pickets and demonstrations of one fashion or another are commonplace, and at times chairmen are forced to summon guards to boot out badgering shareowners. Being that AT&T doesn't do business in South Africa or make napalm, it has rarely found itself staging a meeting rocked by disruptions. During one held in Chicago, however, a protest rally was mounted by a procession of senior citizens demanding cheaper phone rates for the elderly. A noisy verbal battle ensued, until the chairman warned the demonstrators that the security people would have to eject them. They said they were leaving anyway, and turned on their heels and marched out. Another year, in Philadelphia, a clutch of phone installers picketed the meeting after they had smoked out the fact that the AT&T officers were putting up at a hotel that had purchased competitive phone equipment, an act they considered sacrilegious. At still another meeting, a shareholder completed a lengthy round of interrogation by wondering how much AT&T donated to charity. Told that the sum was $10 million, the woman said, "Mr. Chairman, I think I'm going to faint." The chairman replied, "That would be helpful."

The 1979 meeting was AT&T's first foray into the Pacific Northwest, one of the fastest-growing areas for phone service. AT&T will not call a meeting in a city until its august computers certify that there is an adequate pool of shareholders in the encircling 50-mile radius to assure an attendance of roughly two thousand people. Anything smaller, it is figured, would simply be too embarrassing. In this case, the computers reported that there were approximately thirty thousand shareholders in and about Seattle, badly in need of a chance to attend an annual meeting and since experience has demonstrated that some 7 or 8 percent of the available supply tends to show up, that meant that Seattle would do. Only a couple dozen cities in the country could meet the requirement. AT&T takes its annual meetings quite seriously. Frank Hutson, the company secretary, devotes nearly all of his time during the several months preceding the meeting date to getting matters in order. Among other things, he chats with shareowners he knows are likely to arrive armed with a tall stack of questions. A looseleaf book, thick as the Manhattan Yellow

Pages, that runs through potential shareholder questions and suitable responses is prepared for the chairman, who devotes many hours holed up with the document. Some years, mock sessions are conducted in the chairman's office, during which fellow executives pose as inquisitive shareowners. As further measure of the care AT&T takes with the annual meeting, it exhausts something in excess of $300,000 on the event.

Shortly before the meeting was to start, on a brilliantly sunny spring afternoon, I drove up to the Seattle Opera House, a huge, giddily splendid hall in the center of town, on the former site of the World's Fair, where the meeting was to take place. I felt reasonably certain that this was the first time that 3 million invitations had been sent out for any event being staged in Seattle. As soon as I arrived, it was evident that not everybody was going to show up. The hall was far from filled; a local hockey match would have done the meeting to shame. (The attendance, as AT&T later announced, was 2,744, less than one tenth of one percent of the total stockholder body; the record attendance came in 1961, in Chicago, when a throng of 20,100 flocked to the meeting.) Looking around, I spied in the crowd mostly elderly people, a preponderance of them women. I guessed that many of them were widows, and a few I fell into conversation with said that they were. I asked one woman why she had come, and she said indignantly, "Why, to see the circus." A middle-aged man told me, "I'd like to see what sleight of hand they try to pull this year." A third stockholder informed me, "I just want to make sure the top boys are alive and kicking." There were a couple of people in wheelchairs, and I spotted one man on crutches. A small coterie of deaf people had collected at a special station, where an AT&T person directed them to a reserved area in the balcony where sign-language specialists would interpret the meeting for them. A contingent of fifty security people, I learned eventually, was prowling the premises, just in case anything went awry. The meeting was slated to begin at two o'clock, and right on the dot Chairman Brown and his top echelon entered from the wings wearing dark suits and grim faces. They walked with the easy saunter of athletes. Once Brown got to the podium, he gaveled the meeting to order.

A special Bell stage was mounted on top of the regular stage, as if to afford Bell executives more security than a foreign platform. Looming behind the chairman was an enormous Bell insignia that is trucked from meeting to meeting. On each side of the big bell was a tremendous clock. The clocks seemed to have been swiped from some TV game show, though in fact they had been custom-tailored for the phone company. Owing to the unusually large size of AT&T meetings, and the need to keep the proceedings from spanning several days, all shareholders are restricted to two minutes of time when asking questions or proffering comments. As they talk, their time ticks off on the big clocks. That way nobody can accuse AT&T of letting spiels by admiring shareholders run on, while putting an abrupt end to caustic questioning. Shareowners were to speak from any of five glass-enclosed booths positioned about the opera house. The booths resembled actual phone booths, and they were indeed equipped with telephones that were plugged into the public address system. There was no charge for a call.

After introducing the other officers to a pattering of applause, Brown ushered in the governor of the state of Washington, Dixy Lee Ray, who proceeded to deliver a dry discourse on high technology, concluding that she was delighted to welcome a company "that understands that, if we do not come to our senses and utilize our knowledge, we will bring this nation to its knees; a company that is dedicated to seeing that this nation remains strong and progressive."

Brown then said that he would report on company operations. In fairly terse remarks (he commented that it was an AT&T finding that, at annual meetings, the length of the chairman's speech bears a direct relationship to the level of the company's earnings—good earnings, short speech; not so good earnings, long speech), Brown said earnings for the first quarter set a record, that "we're adding telephones at a near record pace, and we're handling about eleven and a half percent more long distance calls than we were at the same time last year." He continued, "We're confident of the long-term growth prospects of the American economy, and we're confident also that telecommunications will continue to be a prime agent of that growth." Brown went on to paint a rosy Bell System future in which "telephone service at the end of the 1980s will be superior by orders of magnitude to the best that we can imagine today. Already it is apparent that what we used to call the telephone network, and what for the most part was designed and developed to provide 'plain old telephone service,' has already been transformed into a telecommunications network. It can—at the user's command—send information in virtually any form—data, voice, graphics, TV—and from just about anyplace in the United States to just about any other place in the United States. And what makes this feasible is the growing ability to distribute intelligence throughout the network, some of it in the equipment on the customer's premises, some of it in the transmission path, and some of it in our switching centers." Then Brown got around to what he termed "The Big However." He pointed out that national debate over what future telecommunications policy should be was winding toward a climax, which caused him to view the months ahead "as an extremely crucial passage in the history of this business." While Brown said he was confident that the Bell System would remain in good shape once the debate was settled, he acknowledged that it was his responsibility to tell the stockholders that there was still the danger that AT&T's ability to manage the nationwide phone system could be hampered. Seemingly to make sure that nobody took these remarks as dark forebodings, Brown wrapped up his address with a string of more reassurances.

Next, the chairman announced that there would be an hour-long period during which shareholders could voice opinions or pose questions pertaining to the business. I knew from experience that AT&T meetings are typically dominated by proclamations from so-called professional stockholders, gadflies really. These are individuals who commit their lives to purchasing stock in companies, or securing the proxies of other stockholders, then boning up on the companies' affairs and showing up at annual meetings to interrogate the chairmen and introduce resolutions that are generally defeated by a resounding margin. Two of the most celebrated members of this curious breed were on hand in Seattle. They were Mrs. Evelyn Y. Davis of Washington, D.C., who publishes a newsletter called *Highlights and Lowlights* and is usually the most flamboyant and domineering of the gadflies, and Lewis D. Gilbert of New York, a soft-spoken and unassuming man who represents his own holdings and those of his family, quite a substantial amount of stock. What often transpires at AT&T meetings is a running debate between the chairman—occasionally other officers are drawn into the battle when the chairman sends a question their way—and the professional shareholders. Now and then, nonprofessionals get up and fan the flames, but generally their knowledge of the company is so infinitesimal that their questions are ill-formed, to the point of being laughable to seasoned AT&T watchers. So the most penetrating and embarrassing strafing usually spills from the gadflies. Unfortunately, at least to the many shareholders who so badly need representing, the gadflies often take the occasion to draw attention to themselves with overly windy, boorish, and silly speeches. Not many people take them seriously. Indeed, their behavior, at times, seems calculated as a dare for the chairman to take the rarely opted-for recourse of booting them out of the meeting altogether.

Brown had barely opened the meeting to shareholder questioning before Evelyn Davis was on her feet with a litany of questions she wished to have answered. The meeting had its first splash of derision. (Once asked why she went to meetings, she replied, "Perhaps rejection. I thrive on rejection.") She prefaced her remarks by pointing out that she was got up in her new mink coat, "fully let out," as her way of protesting a recent announcement that AT&T was contributing $10 million to six symphony orchestras. "I want to have a full explanation about this ten-million-dollar giveaway to various symphonies," she went on, "particularly since our phone bills have been going up, and why they were charged to advertising instead of charity." She added, indignantly, "I was, three weeks ago, in the Sheraton-Boston Hotel fire, wearing my mink coat, walking down twenty-seven floors, and the thing that's of interest to you about it is that the pay phones in the lobby were not working after the fire. Why was that possible?"

Brown, with a frozen gaze, replied shortly that the company felt that the orchestra contribution was valuable for the communities in which the Bell System operated and that "in raw economic terms, it's a very good advertising medium. For example, in 1972 alone, it cost about a hundred and fifty thousand dollars to move the Pittsburgh Symphony around for its tour. Now, a hundred and fifty thousand dollars is about the same amount of advertising money you spend for one minute of prime time television."

Davis was unpersuaded: "But, Charlie, we don't need advertising. If you don't like AT&T, you don't talk on the phone. We have no competition at the present time, so why there should be advertising when we don't need it, I don't see, because you have to do business with us or you don't talk."

Refusing to be ruffled, Brown replied that there was, in fact, quite a lot of competition against AT&T, and anyway, the company felt that it needed to advertise, because "we feel that we owe it to the public to explain ourselves, and in addition, to tell them about our products and our methods of service. We think that we need to keep our name in front of the public in a favorable way."

Getting around to the broken pay phones at the Sheraton-Boston, Brown suggested that the problem might have been that the box that catches coins was stuffed, which causes the phone to stop functioning. Davis quickly interrupted that the boxes weren't filled, because nobody else was using the phones. Brown stroked his jaw, then said that maybe the fire had scorched the cable.

After some more jousting that got more or less nowhere, Brown pointed out that Davis's time was up and he had to move on to another booth.

Eventually, a thin-faced man named James Rosenau from Oakland, California, got up and said, "I'm not a widow and I'm not an orphan. I feel somewhat schizophrenic here in the auditorium, because I think that I'm one of the few people here under forty years of age. And I think that some of the remarks that you and Governor Ray made earlier make it difficult for me to be in the room. It turned my stomach to hear some of the political ideology that is just assumed in what you discussed."

Brown said, politely, "Yes, sir. What is your point in connection with AT&T?"

Rosenau replied, "Well, my problem is that I'm going to be here sixty years from now, and I think that most of the people here won't be. And AT&T and the federal government both have a great deal of say in what happens, and I don't. And what I'm concerned about is how in the world do you people sleep at night knowing the state of the world and you're all in it?"

"Well, I don't have any trouble sleeping," Brown replied quickly. A peal of laughter shot through the auditorium, followed by a spattering of applause. Brown continued, "And I think it's because the organization for which I speak is not in any way doing anything that is derogatory or that is debilitating toward the society in which we live."

Gathering his thoughts, Rosenau came back on the attack: "I think that monopolism gives capitalism one of the worst names that it possibly could. And although you make the claim that there is much competition in your industry, the phone company, among the people whom I speak to in the world, is the epitome of monopoly capitalism."

Looking stern and dour, Brown said, "Well, what is bad about having a company that gives good telephone service be a monopoly?"

Becoming exasperated, Rosenau started to shake his head, then declared, "I think that I can end it here because I find it very difficult to communicate through the glass with you."

"I see," Brown said, and went on to the next booth.

In short order, Lewis Gilbert had the floor and asked Brown what the Bell System was doing for employees who were more than forty years old and had managerial aspirations.

Carefully, Brown answered, "I think we have a pretty good record with respect to that, Mr. Gilbert. As everyone knows, it's just not legal to discriminate against people because of age. And we have tried very hard to comport ourselves in a way that indicates we genuinely are interested in getting the job accomplished by the person who can do it."

Gilbert thanked Brown for the response, before launching his next question. If AT&T had the power to admit just one gadfly to its meeting, the choice of the officers would undoubtedly be either Lewis Gilbert or his brother, John. Besides their easygoing personalities, they are so polite, considering the indelicate nature of many of their questions, that I am reminded of a waiter eager to please in order to land a big tip. They invariably run through a standard list of questions—having to do with salaries of officers, the integrity of the auditors, the fees of the directors—but they rarely react in a hostile manner to the answers, no matter how self-serving they might be. In fact, watching Lewis Gilbert in action, I got the feeling that he was himself a little uneasy asking some of these questions, as if he had somehow found himself with this thankless job in which he had to ask unflattering questions of people he never would have dreamt of confronting himself, but it's that or he starves.

Clearing his throat, Gilbert now asked Brown what was happening with its experiments with battery-powered vehicles.

Brown swiveled to his right and asked William Ellinghaus, the company's president, to field the question. Tapping the mike in front of him, Ellinghaus said, "Am I live?"

"I hope," Brown interjected. "I hope the chief operating officer is alive."

A burst of laughter livened the proceedings.

Ellinghaus, getting back to business, said that some thirty-five electric vans were being tested in Culver City, California, and some electric cars had been tried out in New York, and the company was hopeful. Also, he said, some experimenting with gasohol was taking place in Portland, Oregon.

The questioning continued at a rapid pace. The gadflies would take their time, pursue their questions, keep after the chairman. Covertly, the mood of a hunt was on. They were popping baseballs at him, and he was dodging.

A tall, spare man named J. R. Lawson from Seattle then asked about pensions, saying, "Mr. Brown, I left my furs at home, but you will notice I am dressed in a full-length polyester from J. C. Penney. As a stockholder and twenty-five-year employee of the Bell System industry, I'd like to ask you to think of me. We have retired employees who have served the telephone company for over thirty years and are receiving a pension of only a hundred and eighty-five dollars a month. . . . We need an annual cost-of-living increase on our pensions in order to exist. I believe over three hundred thousand dollars is being spent today on this meeting. Retirement with dignity—is that too much to ask?"

Brown, unfazed, said, "I have to say that the Bell System has been in the leadership insofar as pension matters are concerned, ever since our pension program was set up. It was one of the earliest in this country. We have increased our pension for retired people several times in the last few years. . . . In spite of this there are some cases in which the inflation that bothers everyone has struck some people particularly hard. And I assure you that we'll take a close look and keep continued watch on how our retired people are doing."

As the sniping dragged on, and with the meeting already in progress for more than an hour and a half, Brown seemed to get a little testy. He started to shift his weight visibly from foot to foot, and his answers got crisper and crisper. Shareholders drifted in and out of the big auditorium in a fairly steady stream.

A sprightly-looking woman named Karen Kaye from Seattle addressed the chairman. "If you look around the room," she said, "you'll notice that a great percentage of the people in this room are women. I've noticed that there is only one woman on the Board of Directors, and I was wondering if you'd comment on the representative nature and why there is consistently the same group of men nominated and elected to the board."

"I have to say to you," Brown replied, "that the purpose of a board of directors is not to have equal representation from sexes nor from either geographical or political or occupational groups. The object of a board of directors is to see if we can acquire directors for this organization who are able to contribute to its management and direction by virtue of their own understanding, through their own businesses, of relatively complex large organizations and/or major scientific organizations."

As the meeting droned on, there was also a considerable number of overtly affectionate shareholders who took their turns in the glass booths and expressed, in their sweetest tones, their warmth for the company. An elderly shareholder from Ronan, Montana, got up at one point and declared, "Mr. Brown, I'd like to make a remark about the legislation upcoming. Of course, Congress has not asked me for any advice, but if they did, so far as our telephone service is concerned, I would tell them, if it ain't broke, don't fix it."

Wearing a broad grin, Brown replied, "I would appreciate your telling anybody for whom you have an address in Washington of that."

At this point, the hour-long question and comment period was up, and the management-sponsored slate of directors for the coming year was duly nominated. Ostensibly, the shareholders elect the members of the board, but they have less choice than one might expect. Every year, several weeks prior to the meeting date, management sends out in the mails a proxy statement that lists its choices for the board. A terse summary of each nominee's qualifications along with his or her photo is included. Shareholders then have the option of either voting for the slate, or marking a box labeled "Withheld." There is no opportunity to write in one's own favorites. Should you have your own slate, it's up to you to bear the considerable cost of preparing and mailing out your own proxies, which rarely ever happens. Since it's equally unlikely that very many shareholders will withhold their votes, the actual voting process is a mere formality. Management is, in fact, virtually self-perpetuating.

If you show up in person at the annual meeting, you have the option of putting a candidate into nomination by verbally declaring him, but you run the disadvantage that the vast preponderance of shareowners have already cast their votes through the mail, never having heard of your man. Not discouraged by this drawback, a man from Arlington Heights, Virginia, got up now in booth number four and nominated one Allen J. Noel, whom he identified as the labor candidate for the board. In explanation, the shareholder stated that none of the members of the current slate "appears to have background that is relevant to the unique position of the worker shareholder. But we are not a small, insignificant group. There's over three hundred thousand of us. . . . We want a money-making, secure investment. Yet, as workers, we want something more. We also want job security. . . . But we have no say in the true decision-making of the company, we have no communication link. . . . For more equitable representation and an avenue of communication, mark your ballots for Allen J. Noel."

A short while later, Chairman Brown announced that each of the management-sponsored nominees had fetched in excess of 482 million shares and were now officially the directors for the coming year. Allen Noel, he said, had attracted 11,800 votes. So much for the labor candidate.

More discussion followed. It wasn't long before Evelyn Davis was back in the glass booth. This time, she wanted to know if the company's accountants disagreed with the officers over whether certain contributions should be classified as advertising or charity. What's more, she said she would like to know whether "there have been any political contributions that have been disguised as charitable contributions or advertising expenses."

Brown, somber-faced, replied, "Well, although you and I don't agree on advertising and contributions, the auditor agrees with me, Mrs. Davis."

"Well, he has to, or he wouldn't have a job," Davis snipped.

At this point, even some of the shareholders were getting a little fed up with Evelyn Davis's unending trips to the booth. Some boos had begun to greet her appearances. Finally, a petite woman strode into one of the booths and when she was recognized, said, "The meeting is marvelous, the company is really great. My husband has worked thirty years for the phone company; it does so much for so many. And I think that its meeting should not be used by any one person to discourage people who do come to really listen to the business that they are investors in. To have someone turn it into an ego trip, to make a mockery out of it, to be so courteous and polite and have somebody abuse it, I really disapprove of Mrs. Davis's many, many trips to the booth."

A big round of applause greeted the woman, and then Brown, clearly stretching the limits of his manners, commented, "Well, I think it's fair to say that all shareowners ought to be given an opportunity to speak their piece."

"Thank you," the woman said. "You're very nice."

The words had barely left the woman's mouth, before Davis was back in her booth, firing from the hip: "I'd like to ask you a point of personal privilege. There is nothing more complimentary than to get comments from a jealous woman, who can't stand a woman with a six-thousand-dollar mink coat, somebody who's dressed in a six-dollar outfit."

"Okay," Brown interrupted.

"There's nothing better than having a jealous woman," Davis went on in a scolding tone, "and now you see why I don't want women officers and women directors. It's always the women . . ."

"Okay," Brown cut in again icily.

". . . who complain," Davis kept on. "If the men don't want to listen, they have something nice to look at."

"Okay, Mrs. Davis," Brown said.

Eventually, Davis went back to her seat and everybody calmed down.

The time had come for the meeting to consider five proposals put forth by shareholders. As in voting for directors, proposals by shareholders have the odds heavily stacked against them. Any shareholder who can prove a minimal level of support for his addition to the corporate bylaws is assured of having his proposal, along with his rationale for suggesting it, included in the management proxy. In most cases, a shareholder, whether he knows anything about these proposals or not, will automatically follow management's recommendation, also included on the proxy, which is almost always to vote against the resolution. What's more, if a shareholder signs his ballot but doesn't mark himself for or against the stockholder proposals, management allows itself to count these ballots as being voted against the proposals—which explains why shareholders who manage to get proposals on the ballot regularly walk away with something like 1.5 percent of the vote. Any management proposals that are included on a ballot typically lure better than 96 percent of the vote.

The five proposals that made it onto the 1979 proxy statement had to do with the company being required to furnish to shareholders a complete list of all law firms retained by the company and the fees that were paid, that future proxies list payments received by AT&T directors from serving on boards of other companies, that directors disclose in the proxy any union affiliations, that board members should not automatically serve perpetually, and finally, that the company adopt for its director elections the system known as cumulative voting. Under such an arrangement, a stockholder may channel all the votes he is allowed to a single candidate rather than spread them over the whole slate, and therefore a minority group of shareowners is afforded a much better shot at electing one representative to the board. Though a topic of some controversy in big-business circles, cumulative voting was probably the most worthwhile of the shareholder proposals, in light of the fact that hundreds of companies in the United States have made it mandatory in their elections. Nevertheless, Brown didn't think much of the idea. He reiterated the standard company statement on the subject, the main point of which was that cumulative voting could open the board to "special interests" and "substitute a series of narrow factions for a representation for all the shareowners." The statement was perfunctory, in that Brown had in hand more than enough proxies to defeat all the shareholder resolutions. As the tabulations later revealed, the best any proposal did was 6.4 percent of the vote, that being the one having to do with cumulative voting. To return on next year's proxy, a proposal, under SEC regulations, must attract at least 6 percent of the votes cast. So, if nothing else, cumulative voting would come back to face still another thumping defeat.

The rest of the meeting, given over chiefly to questions and comments from nonprofessional stockholders, as opposed to the professionals, was decidedly less lively than what had gone on before. A stockholder from Missoula, Montana, prior to posing a question having to do with pensions, declared, "I want to share with you my love for God, first, my family, second, my past job with the telephone company, third." An AT&T person seated near me remarked that he had mistakenly gotten the order reversed, though, if so, Chairman Brown didn't comment on it. A man from Anderson Island, Washington, spoke up about the small independent telephone company, Sound Telephone Company, that he was served by and whose service he said "has been marginal, at best."

He wondered what the possibility of Bell taking over the independent was. Brown answered that AT&T, under an agreement with the U.S. government, can't swallow up additional phone companies and so "I'm afraid we can't help you on that one." "We'll just go back to tin cans," the shareholder said. A Seattle man said, "If there's going to be a recession and all that, is it a good idea to keep my investment in AT&T stock?" Brown said that he didn't like to proffer brokerage advice, but "I feel very good about the prospects of the American Telephone and Telegraph Company." "Okay," the man said.

I profoundly wished the meeting were over. I was bored. The shareholder comments all seemed identical. The answers from the chairman all seemed identical. One by one, people drifted out and didn't return. I could hardly blame them.

Heaven help Charlie Brown! Evelyn Davis was back. She protested now that "the clocks are not kosher, one time one of the clocks showed three minutes and the other one minute." She said that the only way the clocks would improve was if the chairman replaced the company secretary with someone else.

"I will select another secretary if I think it's appropriate," Brown replied, calmly.

"I think it's most appropriate, Charlie," Davis went on, talking even faster than before. "You're making improvements, we're having a better meeting now, but until you get rid of him, of the whole old regime, and replace them with men loyal to you, it's not going to be good enough. And it is your prerogative. You're the chairman now. Remember: Power is greater than love."

The dialogue went on a bit longer, Brown obviously doing his best to control his temper, before Davis's time finally ran out. There were two more orations by stockholders on the virtues of AT&T, then Lewis Gilbert got up and, as he customarily does, motioned for adjournment. Before doing so, though, he couldn't resist stating, "Mr. Chairman, you know, anytime that Mrs. Davis doesn't like a secretary, I know he's doing a wonderful job and I would like to see everybody here applaud Mr. Hutson." At which point, the remaining stockholders did applaud the secretary. Finally, three hours and eight minutes after it had begun (two meetings incredibly enough stretched for more than six hours), the 1979 annual meeting of the world's largest company ended.

The several hundred stockholders who had stuck it out to the very end spilled out of the Seattle Opera House, and I spilled out with them. The sun had already begun its descent in the sky. In thinking back over the events of the long meeting, it occurred to me that I hadn't gained even a morsel of information about AT&T that I didn't already know. No matter how badgered he was at some points, Chairman Brown hadn't withered and burst out with some startling revelation about how the phone company was engaged in wiretapping the Polish government, or something. After all the questions, comments, answers, eloquent speeches, and considerable rudeness, all I was able to conclude was that most of the shareholders of AT&T know that they are cashing in a nice dividend each year, and as long as that dividend gets paid, that is all they need to know about their company. The estate of stockholding, for the most part, is by its nature passive. Nothing management said or did was likely to change that, but, then again, why would management want to?

12

The Troops

Peter Knego arrived in the United States with his young family in 1890, seeking a new life. Behind him lay a career as an Austrian sea captain. An ugly accident occurred on his ship, the exact details of which have been lost in history, and though he was fully exonerated, he felt unable to return to the sea. Jobs in America were in scant supply, but before long he found work on a barge that floated cargo down the Hudson River. He and his family actually lived right on the barge, but after his wife became pregnant, the perpetual swaying of the vessel left her sick many days. An acquaintance worked in Newark for the New York Telephone Company, and as a lark, Knego applied. Shortly, he found a job digging ditches for cable. He made good progress, and in time, advanced to foreman. After a while, some of his children came to work for the phone company. One of them, Michael, was even assigned to his father's crew. Knego was a no-nonsense boss. If he were to appear in a movie, it would be a prison movie and Knego would play the warden. It was said he would fire his own son. In fact, he did. He told his son he would fire him if he didn't work hard. The son didn't work hard. Peter Knego fired him. His son promised to work harder. He was rehired. The elder Knego stuck with the phone company until his death, at which point four of his six children were drawing their paychecks from it. His touting of the company did not quickly wear off. Almost a century later, twenty-eight direct descendants and relatives by marriage have joined the Bell System. About a dozen remain active. Collectively, they have put in 725 years of service.

When asked to explain the Knego clan's enchantment with the phone company, Helen Beattie, a granddaughter of Peter Knego who put in her share of years in the billing department, told me one afternoon, "I don't want to sound corny, but we're a telephone family, simple as that. The phone company has always encouraged a family feeling. They wanted your relatives and children to join the ranks. They liked that kind of continuity. The phone company has been good to us. No, it ain't made us millionaires, but we've always had bread on the table. We've all been oh-so-proud to work for it. It's fed a heck of a lot of Knego mouths. In our family, it was automatically thought that once you got out of school you skipped on down to the personnel office of the phone company and signed right up. Until your bones began to tell you something, you never left."

At present, AT&T bulges with roughly twice as many people as work for General Motors and more than the entire population of Boston. One-half of one percent of the population of every state works for one of its companies or labs. In this clutter of people, this Niagara of employees, are many stories of heartfelt devotion. They represent a significant number of arcs in the wheel of attitudes toward the company. The Bell System has long scrupulously nurtured a reputation as a "good" place to work. Without hesitation, innumerable employees I spoke with replied that what they had wanted to do most was to work for the phone company. It is difficult to calculate the stimulating effect that the place has had on tens of thousands of grammar school and high school students who have viewed a phone company person as one of the absolute best things in the world one could ever be. You want a good career, hurry and sign up with the telephone company. Wherever I went, I found considerable numbers of people who had never worked for any other employer. Some had put in forty and fifty years of service. Even as the company passes through some of the bumpiest times in its history, its jobs are still ones aspired to by many people. For it is often the matter of image that has recruited people into AT&T—and held them there. As one linesman in Nebraska told me over a foaming glass of beer, "Yessir, I never really knew what it was like to have a respectable job until I came into the Bell System. I know a heck of a lot of people who hate their jobs with a purple passion—they end up walking around doing nothing, sitting on their butts. My job is a real sweet deal."

By the yardsticks of personnel experts, AT&T has never been considered the absolute best company in the world to work for—many management consultants would stick IBM at the top of this particular totem pole—but it does smother its employees with a bounty of provender. Headhunters scouting for AT&T scalps promise good starting salaries and quick raises for those who excel (about a hundred thousand workers in the Bell System—one in ten—pull down $25,000 a year or more). Moreover, employees are assured of virtual lifetime job security. Telephone jobs have been favorably compared to civil service positions: safe, not overly draining, with a lifetime guarantee. In return, Ma Bell expects a good deal of respect. Those who step out of line face a formidable —if often subtle—wrath. On the one hand, AT&T zealously guards the privacy of its employees; on the other, it inevitably intrudes into their personal lives, encouraging, if not exactly enforcing, what some AT&T people speak of as a numbing uniformity of attitude, appearance, and action. "We are one giant family," AT&T managers like to constantly remind the troops. "And we should behave like one." Employees are bombarded with inspirational sales talks, infused with moral rectitude, and permitted no deviation from the creed. The loyal prosper—enjoying comfort and sometimes riches.

Who are these people who present themselves as being so sure of themselves, the self-styled elite of the telecommunications industry? AT&T doesn't compile and computerize official biographical statistics, but an informal composite profile is not hard to fashion on the basis of observation of, and conversation with, a considerable number of phone company employees. It seems almost absurd to suggest that a million people can be alike in very many ways, but I got the unshakable feeling that there is an AT&T mold that most employees fit. There is something of a sameness about telephone people that doesn't seem to be the case among, say, IBM people or GE people or General Motors people.

AT&T people are a fairly even split between males and females of an average age somewhere in the forties. Most are married and have children; if they are not married when they join the company, the chances are good that they will meet and marry a phone company worker. A striking amount of AT&T employees are married to fellow AT&T employees, a situation that the phone company, unlike many corporate giants, thinks is just fine. I recall talking one afternoon to a female phone worker in Springfield, New Jersey, and when she didn't have the answer to a question I posed, she said, "Hold on, let me ask my husband," and she strolled down the hallway, turned left into an office, and asked him. Quite a few employees are sons or daughters or nephews or nieces of phone people, and they see their career decision as a natural progression, a step upward that is still in the same great tradition of phone company service.

Phone workers tend to be disgorged from small colleges (few of the employees I encountered had gone to Ivy League schools), and though they are rarely wealthy, they are solidly planted in the middle class. They like to live in the suburbs, rather than smack in the middle of the big cities, and do things on weekends like play golf or cards. Indeed, the life-style of phone company people is usually in keeping with their image as solid citizens. They tend to buy their own homes, and to send their children to public or parochial schools. They generally dress conservatively, although there are no white-shirt-and-black-shoes rules. The men wear their hair relatively short. I personally counted just two beards in the Bell System, and both beards remarked to me on how they were occasionally teased as being a bit on the weird side. The world view of many phone company employees generally includes a heavy component of political conservatism. Phone people, it seemed to me, carry small-town values and principles. That means an uncommon degree of openness and friendliness, but also a sense of horror about what goes on in the big cities where a lot of workers, at some point in their careers, end up working. They seem to be straight and honest and, though sometimes targets of allegations of corruption, have rarely been caught with their fingers in the kitty. Indeed, phone people are seldom guilty of breaking any of the canons of respectability and, in a general way, are rather unobtrusive figures. From certain perspectives, they might be looked on as, well, bland.

Those who know intimately a great many phone people delight in flinging around their own characterizations of the breed, and willingly do so at the slightest provocation.

"They don't put you to sleep, but my eyelids sure get heavy in their presence. They're good people, but lord, they're dull."

"They're just basically nice people. It's unusual to hear a swear word out of them. They won't even spell a swear word."

"You can come at them with your cannons loaded, and they will still talk to you without raising their voices."

"They're straight as an arrow. Correct that. They're straight-er than an arrow."

"They're more honest than George Washington. They're more honest than the Pope. You'll never catch one of their hands even moving toward the corporate till."

"I sort of like them. They're very predictable. You never are caught off guard by a phone person."

"Phone people will tell you everything you want to know—and then some. It's the then some that empties rooms."

AT&T has a powerful conservative influence on new recruits, and it infuses them with a sense of higher purpose. Many phone company employees can cite the exact date when they started duty; it was a major event that meant important changes in their routine and perhaps even in their sense of self-worth. It made them part of an organization that is sustained by a high level of spirit and enthusiasm. Phone company people often are called on to work long hours. When a disaster strikes—a hurricane rips down some phone lines, a flood washes out cable—they may work through the night. They do so without complaint. Most of them seem to enjoy easygoing relationships with their immediate bosses, and they always call their bosses by their first names. Still, employees are appropriately subservient and obsequious toward those with higher rank or greater power.

More than a few employees I spoke with indicated that there is a lot less politicking and back-stabbing at the phone company than is found at other big corporations, perhaps because workers feel such a profound sense of security. One thing the phone company is notorious for is shuttling its employees around at regular intervals every couple of years. It's hard to set down any roots as a phone worker. AT&T will doggedly insist that, well, this is the only way to ensure that its people get a good grasp of how the entire system works, but closer to the truth, it also has the effect of keeping employees loyal to the company rather than to any community. And, indeed, phone people ooze a strong feeling of fidelity. They believe in Bell and will lash out with pat defenses at any criticism broached in their presence. The instinct is to defend the phone company as an institution against all attackers, even from within. Employees view regulators and competitors with considerable skepticism, since they feel they are not duly apprecia-tive of the hard work they have put in to make the phone system as good as it is. Many of them are inclined to believe that the federal government, increasingly less receptive to Bell's monopoly status, has gone off the deep end of radicalism. They consider phone people who have departed the system to join up with a competitor, as some do, usually for more money or swifter advancement, as downright traitors. Phone company people, I have found, don't even like to joke about anything that reflects adversely on the system. "We take real pride in the impact for good we have on the outside world," one manager told me. "We are helping people communicate. That is as basic a good as there is on this earth." A *New Yorker* cartoon flirted with the truth when it depicted a phone installer telling an associate, "To me, it isn't just installing a phone, Lou. It's giving one human being a means of reaching out to other human beings."

One afternoon, I chatted with Michael Maccoby, the author of *The Gamesman*, who has expended considerable amounts of time and energy studying Bell managers. He told me, "On the whole, I find the atmosphere at the top levels to be more colloquial than I do at other big companies. I find that there is a positive feeling that has to do with the fact that the employees are making a product that everyone agrees is very beneficial. On the other hand, they're much more cautious than other technical companies, because they have not been in a competitive environment. There's a respect for people and a respect for performance. On the negative side, there's an effort to try to mechanize the world for everyone. That can make it an unhappy place for a lot of people.

"In the past, it was the most different of the big corporations; a kind of noncorporate atmosphere prevailed there. It was oriented toward a sense of service and a national mission, and there's still a lot of that. The feeling was that we're more than a business, we're here to do more than make money. Now, they have to become more interested in making money, with more competition, and be more risk-takers. The gamesmen will begin to rise to the top. They have to be more oriented toward marketing, more flexible, less of a bureaucracy in some ways. I think the company will need to develop less rigid rules, more sense of looking for managers who are entrepreneurial, less of an insistence that you have to pass through certain rites to get to the top. More of a concern for people than in the past."

For a long time, AT&T was the corporate personification of

male chauvinism and racism. It had acquired a well-known tradition of hiring relatively few members of racial minorities, and while it was the biggest employer of women, it traditionally relegated them to low-level slots as secretaries or operators. The government took care of that. The militant Equal Employment Opportunity Commission cracked the whip and, in 1973, pressured the phone company into signing the largest corporate civil rights agreement ever struck. AT&T was going to introduce some unprecedented reforms in its hiring and promotion policies—or wish it had. The thirty-one page document, along with two subsequent decrees that the phone company signed, stipulated, among many other things, that 26,000 women and racial-minority employees were to be handed immediate wage increases that summed up to $36 million in the first year. An additional infusion of $15 million was to be dispensed to soothe prior job discrimination complaints. Hiring and promotion policies were completely overhauled to hoist thousands of women and minority workers into management slots. Moreover, men were to be installed in hitherto "female jobs" such as phone operators, and "male jobs" like linemen were to receive influxes of women.

One does not just sign an agreement and pay out some money and create job equality, and it was years of determined work by both the government and the phone company before it was agreed, in January 1979, that the vast decree could be allowed to elapse. The government cautioned, though, that it would continue to monitor with wide-open eyes the Bell System's personnel habits. Women currently hold some 36 percent of management jobs in the phone company, compared with 33.2 percent in 1972. There are four women officers, as opposed to none in 1972. A hefty increase (from 0.2 percent to 4.7 percent) came in women's employment in outside craft jobs, though AT&T is still bedeviled with problems locating females eager to climb up telephone poles or descend into manholes. Men in operator jobs surged to 7.9 percent from 1.4. Total employment of all minorities rose to 17.4 percent from 13.8, and management representation went up to 10.1 from 4.6. A scaled-down affirmative action program remains in effect at AT&T, though it is clearly less ambitious than the original and will allow minorities to move forward at a much more leisurely pace. All in all, the overall minority hiring and promotion records at the phone company seem to compare favorably with those of many other corporations, though the complaint still persists that comparatively few of the minority employees hold truly prestigious positions, and few are even threatening to move into them. It will be many years before a woman or black is chairman of AT&T.

Whatever tensions have underlain employment at the phone company, there has never been a problem filling vacancies. To keep people flowing into the Bell System subculture, AT&T has engineered one of American business's most sophisticated programs of management training and evaluation. Like seagulls around a piling, about a million eager job hunters throng to Bell employment centers every year. From this gigantic stew, only about 70,000 people are hired, around 4,000 of them into management posts. To scoop up the hottest of the hot prospects, AT&T annually dispatches 160 scouts who blanket close to 500 college campuses, sifting for glimmering candidates in the way prospectors pan for gold. They grill and pick their men and women from the top part of the graduating classes, and comb for those who have spent more time hunched in libraries than cheering their lungs out in stadiums. A phone company study found that 45 percent of those recruits in the top third of their classes were also in the top third of the corporation's salary scale for those boasting the same number of years of experience. Only 22 percent from the bottom third of their classes attained the highest salary level. Demonstrations of leadership ability also carry considerable weight with AT&T personnel hands. "If a person was on the committee for the big spring dance, we'd give him a hair of credit," a personnel man told me. "If he organized the first spring dance in the history of the college, and it was a stunning social and financial success, we'd really sit right up and take notice."

All of the Bell System management cadre is organized into ten levels (the chairman alone resides at level ten). College recruits customarily breeze in at level one. If they perform well, they should climb to the third level—the first grade of middle management—within five to ten years. With the glut of degree holders of late, AT&T has been compelled to accept college graduates for nonmanagement tasks. As it happens, a full 85 percent of all new management people at the phone company are promoted up from the ranks of crafts people, so the Wichita lineman eventually becomes the Wichita foreman.

Scientists recruited for Bell Labs aside—they are allowed certain idiosyncrasies of behavior so long as they invent —individualistic, inner-directed workers are cautiously side-stepped by phone company personnel men, who are said to instinctively bristle at the sight of the nonconformist who is not likely to become a good "System Person." "Sometimes, I can spy someone who won't work out just by the look in his eye," a personnel manager told me. "A guy who starts spouting off about how he's his own man, how he likes to make his own decisions and, if he's left be, watch out, he's dynamite, well, we watch out for him and encourage him to have a great career over at IBM." Scrupulous personnel people, on occasion, have even been known to scrutinize the background of an applicant's wife, who may be more inflexible about shuffling from city to city than her spouse.

The new recruit, if he hopes to avoid the tumbrils to the personnel guillotine, rapidly learns that the phone company insists on making just one man ultimately responsible for every project, whatever its scope. If the project flops, he shoulders the blame. As soon as he joins the Bell system, possibly as head of a small-town repair unit or an operator force, each candidate is hurled into the decision-making maelstrom, and his performance monitored more closely than an astronaut's in space. About 40 percent of managers wash out in the first ten years, when the competition and monitoring are particularly rough and tumble, though even those who do not meet AT&T's standards are readily and willingly scooped up by other companies anxious to hire men with some Bell experience.

AT&T purposely sets up a frenetic pace of internal competition at every level in its system. It pits man against man, office against office, district against district—and carefully rates each performance on report cards that are analyzed by efficiency experts. "People are breathing down everyone's neck," one personnel man said. "Everyone is constantly subject to competition." AT&T has so many operating companies, divisions, and branch offices that it has plenty of demanding and responsible jobs in which to nurture high-management-potential employees as much as thirty years in advance. "We are looking for the next generation of leaders five and ten years ahead of time," H. Weston Clarke, the bespectacled head of AT&T's Human Resources Department, told me. "We want to be sure that there are able bodies out there. Who's going to hold this spot? Who will eventually take over here? Just what is so-and-so made of? Can he go all the way? In effect, everything in personnel gets reduced to lists of names. The higher the position we are talking about, the shorter the list."

Bell's most controversial management tools are the dozens and dozens of indexes it uses to measure performance. Employees distrust the indexes and consider them dehumanizing. Supervisors complain that indexes are used too rigidly in judging their chances for promotion. Bob Gryb, a soft-spoken member of AT&T's marketing group that deals with internal measurements, explained the Bell measurement philosophy: "Let me say first that the Bell System has long been strongly oriented toward measurements. A truism of the system has evolved: If it doesn't get measured, it doesn't get done. If it doesn't get measured properly, it doesn't get done properly. The idea, as well, is to show how employees relate to the rest of the universe—better, worse, the same. Virtually every employee of the company is subjected to some sort of measurement—even the chairman. He's measured by the overall earnings picture and overall service picture of the company. Now, we have always considered ourselves a highly competitive business internally. If you look back over the last fifty years, there are probably very few managers outside the Bell System who have felt the spirit of competition as have Bell managers. Measurements are what have triggered the competition. I like to use the analogy of a guy driving a golf ball into a dense fog and not having any idea where or how far it went. If that happened all the time, the guy would just chuck golf. There's no satisfaction. What make sports so wonderfully competitive are measurements. Same with us. Lately, we've been doing some things differently with our measurement benchmarks. Basically, in the past we tended to set the objectives internally, with some customer feedback but not a whole lot. Now we are seeking out customers to set our objectives. Take telephone installation. We start out with focus groups around the country to find out what's important to customers. Then we'll do a sampling of subscribers. For instance, we've found out that the most important things with installation were showing up at the time promised and neatness of the work. So we study how close to the promised time is acceptable and what degree of neatness is important and create goals. We've also started to break customers up into different groups. The marketplace is so complicated today that not everyone has the same expectations. For instance, hospitals have different priorities than stockbrokers. A rural customer cares less about waiting for repair than an urban one. I think this is an important change, because the last thing an employee wants to do is be measured on something that doesn't count, something that the customer doesn't care about. We're also now rating performance in bands, rather than in precise numbers down to tenths of a percentage point. We were having some problems with this. A supervisor would berate an employee because his score on something went from, say, ninety-seven point four to ninety-seven point three, which was a change that wasn't even mathematically significant. Now we tell our people if their work meets the objective, is higher, is lower, or if it's unsatisfactory. This should get rid of some of the paranoia we had before."

AT&T profits from its reputation for continuity, and telephone people tend to stay in their jobs longer than most. Turnover figures are astonishingly low (7 percent a year), and the average employee sticks around for thirty-two years and one month. The routine paperwork and standardization of style that are so annoying to some phone company people assure that one employee can usually move in and pick up where another has left off. The American army traditionally bombards its lower echelons with training manuals that cover every situation a rookie might be confronted with, from assembling his rifle to making his bed. AT&T marches right along in step. "We prefer to have our men use their own initiative," a company executive said recently. "But we leave as little as possible to the imagination."

Pecking order in corporate America being such a highly sensitive subject (should a vice president notice that, say, an assistant vice president has acquired a desk that measures a clear 2 inches longer than his own, several days might well be devoted to corrective measures), AT&T takes no chances of offending its workers' sensibilities. It has drafted regulations that, in minute detail, spell out who gets what when. For instance, Level I management people sit in an open area of 75-by-100 feet, no partitions between desks, and receive 60-by-30 inch steel desks. They make do with a standard telephone with no additional lines. Lucky, though, is the group supervisor. He holes up in a two-person semi-private office. Now, a district head gets quartered in his very own private office of somewhere between 110 and 150 square feet. For the first time, he gets carpeting under his feet and the luxury of a 60-by-36-inch steel desk. He also gets a silver pitcher and two drinking cups. At the manager level, a person lands an office of between 200 and 225 square feet. Forget metal: he gets a 66-by-36-inch wooden desk. To decorate his windows, he is blessed with "see-through" curtains. He earns a speakerphone, a second phone line, a colored phone of his choice and a voice channel that presumably allows him to summon his secretary with greater dispatch than a simple shout. The director level is when offices start to really get capacious—a hearty 300 to 325 square feet. What's more, one may select from carpeting of more exquisite quality than the standard building carpeting; there is a 72-by-36-inch wood desk to command from and—yes, yes—a pair of guest chairs. The assistant vice president (now we're really getting up there) receives an office of 375 to 450 square feet, and for the first time, a private bathroom, plus a reception area of 150 square feet in which he can keep visitors drumming their fingers for insufferable periods of time. Also, draperies for the windows, a 78-by-36-inch desk (wood, of course), and three (not two) guest chairs. Also, two phones, one for his exclusive use, the other for visitors. Finally, the vice president and higher officer gets an office of 500 to 575 square feet, private toilet, a reception area of 200 square feet, and the wild freedom to let his personal whims and imagination design his own office (in consultation, naturally, with the Office Planning Interior Designer).

To assist the personnel departments in their understanding of Ma Bell's workers, assessments administered by staff psychologists plumb workers' changing moods—a tradition of exploration that reached its supreme expression in the Management Progress Study, begun in 1956 and widely described as the most exhaustive long-term dissection of the working businessman. In charge of the project since its inception has been a convivial AT&T psychologist named Douglas Bray. Bray, who got his Ph.D. in psychology from Yale, was a research associate at Columbia, where he worked with Eli Ginzberg on such projects as the achievement potential of blacks and the effect World War II had on soldiers. AT&T, however, convinced him that the businessman was where the action was. "The middle-aged businessman," Bray told me, "seems to have replaced the white rat and the college student as the psychological research world's number one subject." When he set up shop at the phone company, Bray picked 422 low-level managers at the beginning of their careers, split them up into groups and had them tested for intelligence, attitudes, and personality traits. Then he sat back and followed them—like specimens under a microscope—for the ensuing twenty years. Bray drew on exercises patterned after methods used by the Office of Strategic Services in World War II to select spies. The intelligence organization would subject its candidates to a grueling week of obstacle courses and stress interviews (including an exercise in which the candidate was told that he had flunked out). Bray's assessment routine was somewhat less of a pressure cooker, but no less thorough. Role-simulation routines were concocted. For instance, subjects were told they were partners in a toy factory where they bought, assembled, and sold parts. The participants were observed as they strove to maximize profits, some emerging as leaders, others as followers. Candidates, in other exercises, had to write stories describing what was happening in pictures they were shown. They filled in the blanks for sentences such as: "A large company is . . ." The initial assessment found the candidates to be eager to advance and optimistic about their careers. Bray wanted to know what happened to that mood as careers unfolded. Each year for the next seven, participants were interviewed, and after eight years, the managers went through a second assessment procedure. A number of surprising things turned up. Though intellectual abilities had increased, administrative skills—the ability to plan and organize work—had not. Subjects had gotten more independent. They were less concerned with the views of others. Bray continued to have the managers interviewed year by year, then conducted a twenty-year mid-career assessment. More surprising findings confronted him. "The most significant general conclusion of the study so far is that a person's total satisfaction and happiness with life appears to be almost totally unrelated to whether he or she is successful at work," Bray told me one day at the AT&T headquarters. "Career success, in short, is not a predictor of life satisfaction." What's more, Bray found a stunning negative correlation: those who scored highest in heterosexuality and mental ability turned out to be less content and well adjusted than most of the other Bell people studied. Bray hastened to point out to me that most of the subjects in the experiment possessed IQs easily above 100, and he suggested that unusual intelligence may work against a person's happiness in many instances. "The people who were better adjusted may not be quite as introspective," he said. "They don't worry about what life is all about. They are less questioning. The heterosexual finding may mean that those with an overdependence on the opposite sex may preclude themselves from pursuing other sources of satisfaction and happiness in life. Another thing that came up was that managers are not exactly dying to get ahead, not anywhere to the degree that they were twenty years ago. We found some expressions of disdain about organizational politics and criticism of decisions made by top management. With time, it seems, the place becomes a little less magnificent."

Increasingly during my explorations through the Bell System, I found that the bloom has been coming off the biggest private employer. Rapid and deep-seated change has produced a tension that underlies much of the work going on in the phone company. It is tension over the way in which AT&T may proceed, tension of technological change versus the old ways of doing things, of stasis versus economic productivity, and in part it has caused a worsening of attitudes that are altering, or threatening to alter, the service provided to customers. According to the findings of recent Bell studies, more than half of Bell System employees thought morale was deteriorating. Very few thought it was improving. Furthermore, many employees felt that, owing to unrealistic work goals, the quality of service was getting worse. Troubled by these trends, AT&T created in early 1978 a four-man task force—the Work Relationships Unit—to sniff into the changed perspective of the labor force and see what could be done about it. In announcing the formation of the body, AT&T executive vice president Charles Hugel declared, "One can't help but conclude that there is something wrong about the way we're dealing with our people that is bothering them."

Louis O'Leary, a remarkably affable man who was spearheading the work unit, told me, "The problem isn't just with the craftspeople. Oh, no. Some of the scarier trends, at least to me, are happening throughout management. The second-level attitudes have gone to hell. Fifth is very bad, too—that's policy setting, the director level. We don't have a revolution brewing. The company isn't ready to collapse. But the trends are there, and they're bad. And now we need the people with us, with today's complicated marketplace, growing competition. You might make a persuasive case that we need the people now like we've never needed them since World War II."

Craig Hinckle came drifting into the phone system nineteen years ago in search of a direction for his life. He had dropped out of college because of complications from an appendectomy and was "kicking around, just spinning my wheels, going no place fast." His father was a phone worker and told him it was a damn good outfit, give it a whirl. He applied and was hired. The pieces began to fall into place. "I used to really tubthump for this company," he recalled. "I'd wear it like a badge."

Generous by nature and swiftly articulate, Hinckle is now a switching equipment technician for New York Telephone. He said to me during an idle moment, "I've lost a lot of interest in this place lately. It used to be that a certain amount of equipment was your responsibility. It was like your property. Now you don't have that. You're spread all throughout the office. They want a guy to be universally adaptable to every unit. It's almost as if they don't want a guy to take pride in a particular unit of equipment. It used to be that the boss would come over and say, 'Hey, do this,' and if you did a good job he'd pat you on the back, and if you did a rotten job he'd kick you in the butt. Now, you get a piece of paper from a central control unit and the boss may not even know exactly what you're doing."

I asked Hinckle about the impact of technology, a factor that has perturbed many Bell System employees. Hand labor is the wave of the past. This is the age of the computer—the mainframe, the mini, the micro.

"As they put more and more equipment in, we become closer to button-pushers," he replied. "More and more, job skills we have been trained for are becoming useless. This isn't the sort of trend that comforts you much at the end of the day. The work is easier and cleaner, but it's less rewarding outside of the pay checks. A lot of guys complain about the pay. I'm not getting rich, but I'm not complaining about that side of the coin."

He reflected a moment on what he had said, then added, "It's not the old-time telephone company, that's for sure. None of us does cartwheels as we come in the door. One floor above my head they're putting in a new electronic switching system. The system I work on isn't as advanced. It takes five guys to keep that system humming upstairs, and it takes thirteen down on my floor. People aren't looked on as the resource they once were. Machines are the resource. The troops are not super-popular anymore. The phone company is getting out of the people business and into the computer business. I worry about being replaced by a computer. If they're going to bring in twenty million dollars worth of semicon-ductors, hey, I can't compete with that. Manual dexterity I have, but I can't think that fast. I'm thirty-eight, numerous pounds overweight, I'm living in a house I can't afford with two kids I can't afford. That's not the company's fault. But I imagine the day when the boss says to me, 'Hey, lookee Craig, hate to say this old buddy, but I'm afraid we don't need you anymore. So we're going to have you scrub floors. We think you'll like that.'"

One real mess of a day—a real autumn downpour—I visited a middle-level manager with New Jersey Bell. At thirty-four, he was composed and placid, a married man with a child. His wife, who was pregnant with a second child, seemed excitable. Inside, the house was serene and comfortable, with an almost Mediterra-nean bloom of light and color. There were handsome rugs, walls of books, and in every room paintings by modern artists. The manager had invited me over to tell me, with the protection of anonymity, what it was like to work for the phone company.

"I'll tell you what it's like," he said. "It's like being in ROTC. They even use some of the same words, like 'direct order.' If you get a direct order, you do it, or you're out."

"Out?" I asked.

"Yeah, out. I don't mean fired. They almost never fire anybody. You have to rape an eight-year-old girl. You really have to do something bad. In ten years, I can think of only two people fired, who were in purchasing and were apparently making deals for themselves on the side. That's part of the trouble. You like to be at a place where performance counts, where if I did something well it counted and if I did something bad it counted. Here, neither extreme applies that much."

He went on: "It's a fascinating place. They have more good people than they're ever going to use. There's tremendous competition and in-fighting among the different managers. It's all very political and bureaucratic. The difficulty is that there are just too many managers and too many levels. To do quality work, there is an unbelievable amount of bureaucracy to fight, and it takes a lot out of you. The people who are worked are worked to death. The successful person has to present the right image. Working fifty-five and sixty hours a week. Coming in on Saturdays and all that. Third level is the key. First and second levels, you can get to on ability. Third level you get to by having the right image. You have to never ruffle a feather and never be wrong. You have to be perfect. To be perfect takes a lot of energy, a lot of energy."

I asked about future plans.

"Look, I'm in it now for the long haul. I've got too many years under the belt to try to set up shop somewhere else. I'm prepared to obey the orders and go as far as I can go. It's called sticking it out. The pay is good. They generally pay people over market. If I'm going to do some dumb job for the rest of my life, I might as well do one that pays."

In a southwestern city, I lunched one day with a half-dozen phone company workers, none of whom was at all shy about airing his views on AT&T. These were some of the things they said:

"There's just all this change. The company's gotten like a monkey on your back. We're sure not the close-knit Bell Family anymore."

"Look, I've lived and breathed telephones for half a century. Sometimes I feel like a telephone. So I've got some love for this place. It's put my four kids through school, and it's kept me and the wife happy. People may knock this place, but you're not going to hear it from me."

"We're nothing but the company's oyster. They open us when they need us."

"Knowing that somebody can be clocking you at any time, checking out how you're doing, hardly makes for a sane environment. You know, you had all this junk from your parents when you were growing up. You had it in school from your teachers. Who needs it anymore when you're an adult and working? Everybody's comparing his scores with everybody else. It's sickening. I tell you, it's sickening."

Glen Davenport came into the Bell System thirty-eight years ago, with purpose ignited by the fact that the phone company had fed his father for forty-eight years. He talked one day about his job: "Well, if you have to work for somebody, this is one of the finest places to be. As long as I can remember, it's been my ambition to work for the telephone company. I had an application in to them as soon as I got out of high school, though they didn't get around to recognizing me until after two years of college. I started off as a cable splicer's assistant at seventy-two dollars a month. But I sure lived great. Now I'm at what you call third level as a division construction superintendent in Portland. There's extensive pressure today, no denying that. The employees we have now are no longer the dedicated employees we had before. The Bell Family, so to speak. They're more independent. There are two incomes in most families. Their purchasing power is greater. They don't have the fierce loyalty to the business. It's rather frustrating, you might say, compared to the days of the old-time foreman. It's a problem getting eight out of eight out of them."

On another day, I sought out Fern Asma, the assistant medical director at Illinois Bell. One of her primary functions is to counsel employees, and she spoke about the people who came to her: "We're all seeing more stress and more anxiety than we used to. A lot of our young people are coming in and saying they want to see a psychiatrist. I think we're seeing a little more alcoholism than we used to. Some people come in here because they're afraid they're going to be dismissed because of poor motivation. They complain of just plain more stress on the job. I don't think we are getting problems peculiar to the phone business. We just get people problems. You know, I think some of the difficulty has to do with the fact that we've done too good a job of communications. We weren't aware of small places in Africa where problems are brewing when I was much younger, and now we are aware of them, and so you have more opportunity to perceive stress. The younger people, I'm afraid, are not motivated to be as loyal to the company. So the older managers are coming in and grumbling about the fact that employees aren't as dedicated. The younger people complain that their bosses don't understand them. It's a two-way street."

Roughly three-quarters of AT&T's work force is unionized. Three unions represent phone workers. The biggest by a wide margin is the Communications Workers of America. One day I spoke with Glenn Watts, the president of the CWA, about what he sensed was the mood of telephone workers. Watts began as a telephone installer in Washington, D.C., then moved on to the commercial department as an account representative, before he settled in as a full-time union official.

"Compared to most places, if you look at it carefully and objectively, you'd have to come down and say it's not too bad a place to work," he started off. "But if you look at the day-to-day problems, you begin to realize that a lot can be done to improve it.

The problems I refer to are job pressures. One typical example is what happens to the modern telephone operator, whom you can characterize as nothing more than an appendage of a computer. She has to meet an index. In order to meet that index, there's pretty high pressure. Those indices are designed without what I think is sufficient concern for the human element. I think we should look at the job and see what the job should be in the modern sense. The overall morale is certainly not as good as it was ten or fifteen years ago, and it's deteriorating. I would characterize it as a serious problem. Technology is the trigger that brought it about. But the blame must be put on top management. I think supervisors are more severe than they used to be. You know, operators have got to raise their hands to go to the toilet. They've got to sit at just the right angle. This is for the birds. The workers are bearing the brunt of the pressure thundering down from the top. I don't like it."

Lou O'Leary, as entrenched as any phone worker I met, felt convinced that employee attitudes could be gotten back where they belonged. "One thing I think we're going to have to do is to train managers differently," he said. "We ought to tell managers what we want, a general approach to management. Right now, we heavily emphasize a leadership type of management. We will have to emphasize more of a consensus style. The guy who's interested in other people's opinions. You see, there is this new employee. Much less amenable to external discipline. He has the Protestant work ethic, but he wants to be talked to. If you send him across town, he wants to know why. I never had to be told why. I was told to move and so I packed my belongings and moved. The new worker wants explanations. We've got to involve the worker in the work. You don't do this by the 'How's the wife and kids' routine. The old popular human relations thing of the fifties. It's asking workers what they need. What do they need to do their jobs? You know, the basic insight we learned from the Hawthorne Studies has been lost. It showed that if you paid attention to worker productivity, then morale improved. The basic insight was that if you really gave a shit about the human beings, productivity and morale both improved. What we really have to do is create an institutionalized Hawthorne effect. We've still got a tremendous reservoir of good feeling among the workers, something that can be called 'moral capital.' But moral capital can be lost entirely in a generation, and by a generation I mean ten or twenty years. So we've got to get cracking. We're talking about reversing morale. It involves an awful lot of psychotherapy. You know, a lot of our managers won't even admit they're troubled. The key moment in psychotherapy is when someone says, 'Yeah, I've got a fucking neurotic problem.' Up to then, it's all fun and games."

13

Another Hundred and Fifty Big Ones

If the telephone company has to replace a telephone pole, the cost can run up toward $400. If it orders a new microwave tower, the cost is $500,000. If it orders an electronic switching system, the bill may be $30 million, but the price is in line with the microwave tower and the telephone pole, and seems on the whole accepted by phone people. Money gets spent by them by the wheelbarrows, which is why it's probably impossible to make sense out of AT&T without knowing something about how it raises money.

Every corporation intermittently goes scrabbling in the money markets for dollars to borrow, but this is the telephone company and the procedure is truly complex. AT&T's ravenous appetite for the long green is not due to size alone, but also because the phone business finds itself so impelled to spend. It is a capital intensive business—meaning, in short, that compared to the amount of money ingested, a large capital investment must be expended. The applicable rule of thumb, according to phone company financial hands, is that it takes an outlay of $2.60 to return $1.00 of revenue, whereas the typical manufacturing company lays out a spendthrift $.55 to get $1.00 back. Money experts at AT&T take fund raising pretty much in their stride (they are handed checks for $100 million and simply shrug), but nonetheless it is an article of faith that the phone company must drum up approximately a billion borrowed dollars every four months. The mere contemplation of what seems an act of bravado would give rise to a cold sweat on the forehead of the chief financial officer almost anyplace else. Bravado, on the other hand, is commonplace at the telephone company.

Midway in my wanderings through the phone company, I came to wonder about the way in which AT&T managed to raise such colossal sums of money, and decided to call on the company's chief financial man, under whom the green waters run extremely deep. His less than palatial office is a short stroll down the corridor from the chairman's, on the carpeted twenty-sixth floor of 195 Broadway. Big wooden desk. Mounds of paper. Comfy chairs. No signs of a monstrous vault with bags of cash stashed inside. William Cashel, Jr., the tender of all the money, is a tall, angular man with close-cropped dark hair, slightly formal in manner but without starch. He has about him a certain quality of Eastern tweed. When I asked him if he could explain the financial bill of particulars, he crossed his legs and started off by saying, "We always need money. That's a given. We always need these big chunks of money. Other companies can postpone an expansion or the construction of a new building if it happens to be a lousy year in the financial markets. We can't. We have to respond to customer needs and raise money in the financial markets every year. A good portion of our expenditures, I should point out, go simply to stand still. Our subscribers are constantly on the move, and we are therefore continually ripping phones out and then putting them back in somewhere else."

The system's budget for new construction expenditures, Cashel went on, ran in the neighborhood of $15 billion a year. That should install a lot of phones. To add some perspective, he mentioned that this was something like three times more than what any other American corporation would be spending, and roughly 5 percent of the capital expenditures scheduled for any given year by all U.S. companies lumped together. I was curious how this massive figure was arrived at, and Cashel responded that basically it was put together on a piecemeal basis. The operating companies, he explained, submit budgets for their territories based on what their planning people figure their projected needs to be. "They essentially look at the growth in business, how much modernization they're doing, what old plant has to be replaced, and how much customer movement is going on," Cashel said. "It all adds up. For instance, we're putting in slightly more than one ESS system per day at a typical cost of twenty-five million to thirty million dollars. As these budgets trickle in, AT&T's construction plans department responds by submitting each of them to a fusillade of tests. Is all this in line with expected telephone growth over the next five years? Is the revenue growth keeping pace with the growth in phones? Then the company economist moves in full throttle and applies various economic tests to the budgets and then gazes into the future at likely money-market conditions to see that the funds are out there to support these budgets. I look everything over to make sure it's in order, and then the total budget is brought before the Board of Directors for final approval. I should point out that the budget includes everything that's bought by the companies—central offices, buildings, desks, couches, pliers, paper, motor vehicles, clock radios, you name it. And there are budget people out in the operating companies who are revising the budget daily. They are literally changing the numbers every day. The engineers are continuously reevaluating their needs, and as their plans are finished the needs are added to the budget. We talk about the budget here as a living, breathing thing. It really is." Once the budget gets the blessing of AT&T's board, then it is up to Cashel to go and drum up the money.

"If I had to raise it all, I would probably by now be operating out of a room with padded walls," Cashel said. "Fortunately for my sanity, a large portion of the money comes, you might say, naturally. In some recent years, we had to satisfy as much as half of our capital needs from the outside, but now we pluck about three-quarters of the money right from our treasury. We pick up another billion dollars from our dividend reinvestment plan, which is a way for shareholders to put their dividends right back into more AT&T stock, our employee savings plan, and our employee stock ownership plan." That is all a big help, but it still leaves about $2.5 billion for Cashel to come up with.

Where does one find that kind of money? It's not possible to just hold a forked stick and wait for it to swing down. The options to sort through are several, Cashel said. You can sell stock. You can sell new bonds. You can sell a combination of the two, such as preferred stock or convertible debentures, or resort to any of a host of additional mystifying divertissements such as serial bonds, straight preferred, convertible preferred, straight preferred with a sinking fund. Back in the robust stock market days of the 1960s, Cashel explained, AT&T met a considerable amount of its money needs by selling common stock. Late in the decade, though, the stock market began to falter, regulatory pressure picked up, and

AT&T's stock price tumbled to a point where new shares couldn't be issued on terms likely to entice very many existing shareholders. In the most recent decade, therefore, AT&T has for the most part sold bonds—also known as debt securities—to institutional and private investors.

Cashel said that a big part of his job was juggling the amount of debt and equity the company had. Too much debt is an unhappy situation, because it leaves the company on shaky footing, and if the debt gets too great, the credit ratings will suffer and force the company to pay higher interest rates than it would care to. Equity money has great appeal, inasmuch as there are no interest costs, plus the money never has to be paid back, but, at the same time, too much equity erodes profits and leaves a corporation financially listless. Keeping the debt-to-equity ratio at just the right level was described by an AT&T financial man as a matter of striking a balance between "eating well" (too much debt) and "sleeping well" (too much equity).

"Since 1965, we have had a debt-to-equity ratio objective of between forty percent and forty-five percent," Cashel said. "In 1975, for a brief spell, we got up over fifty percent, which worried us a lot, mainly because the credit people started giving us some awfully sour looks. We haven't reached forty-five percent yet —we're just a shade over forty-six—but we're moving nicely in that direction. It takes a lot to move a mass this size. It takes years to move a single percentage point. When we had a massive equity infusion in 1977 by selling twelve million shares of AT&T stock, the total impact on the ratio was less than a percentage point. It surprised the hell out of me. I looked at the result and said, 'What?' I couldn't believe it. So you are talking about quite a heap of money. It's like moving an iceberg."

Shuffling around enormous sums of money didn't seem particularly to faze Cashel, though he related to me a tale of just how frenzied and frustrating things can get for the chief financial officer. Back in 1970, AT&T found it necessary to raise something like $1.6 billion, and so for the first time ever, it shrugged off its traditional conservative posture, cast its fate to the wind, and opted to issue common-stock warrants, a risky financial beanstalk that it had rarely even considered as an option. The way things were set up, each stockholder got one warrant for every ten shares that he held; each warrant gave the owner the right to buy a share of AT&T stock at any time up through May 15, 1975, at a price of

$52 a share. Since telephone stock was selling for $52 at the time the warrants were issued, it seemed like a bonanza for the warrant holder. Over the subsequent few years, AT&T stock spiraled up and down in price, which didn't particularly trouble telephone company executives, as long as the stock was selling at more than $52 when expiration day rolled around. Then the warrants would of course be exercised and in would pour a cool $1.6 billion to the AT&T tills. The alternate possibility was almost too dreadful for AT&T's financial officers even to mention: the stock wouldn't be selling for that much, the warrants would expire without being exercised, and not a dime would flow into the treasury.

As May 15, 1975, neared, the whole experiment was unwinding like a thriller. Telephone had taken a downward toboggan ride to a market price below $52. Gloom had descended over 195 Broadway. If it were possible for AT&T officers to sell their mothers to get the stock price up above $52, they might have sold them. Within days of expiration date, the stock began to jiggle slowly upward. Would it make it or wouldn't it? was the question on every broker's mind. Tongues clucked. Investors shifted uneasily over their stock tables. Some of the warrants were exercised as deadline day approached; but most investors were still holding back. Telephone closed on the final day at a cliff-hanging $51.88. Nine-tenths of the warrants were allowed to perish unused. Into AT&T's cash registers came $160 million, a measly one-tenth of the sum that had been hoped for.

"It was a case of poor luck beyond our wildest dreams," Cashel said, cringing at the mere thought of the debacle. "One result of it all is that I don't get very many people coming up to me and recommending we issue a bunch of warrants anymore. No sir. Investors don't have a short memory."

To get an adequate perspective for how the money is raised at AT&T, Cashel recommended that I follow, from start to finish and close at hand, one particular operating company bond offering. After studying the upcoming schedule, I elected to visit New York Telephone, which was slated to shortly go to market.

Through the entranceway at New York Telephone's headquarters, at the corner of Forty-second Street and the Avenue of the Americas, and up the elevator to the office of Grace Fippinger, vice president, secretary, and treasurer. Short curly hair. A wide grin. A head for money. One of the highest-placed women in the phone company. "The key to these issues is planning, which is done five to six years ahead," she said. "It's fairly tentative planning that far out, then we really get down to the nuts and bolts two years out. When we first looked at our construction needs a couple of years ago, we determined that we would probably need to raise somewhere between a hundred million and two hundred million dollars this year, and we'd probably need it sometime in the second quarter of the year. What happens when one of the operating companies wants to issue bonds is that it has to notify AT&T of the date it prefers, and then AT&T checks the request with those from the other companies. The last thing we want to do is to compete in the money markets against one of our own companies. That's like Dad stealing from Mom. We've got operating companies going after money every single month, and what AT&T tries to do is to space them two or three weeks apart at a minimum. We finally decided that we wanted to raise a hundred and fifty million dollars, and we thought June twentieth seemed like a reasonable day to try to get it. That turned out to be about two weeks after New Jersey Bell was scheduled to go to market, so AT&T gave us the green light."

As a general rule, the bond issues are bid for competitively by the two immense Wall Street underwriting syndicates—the so-called Morgan Group, which is headed by Morgan Stanley & Company, and its rival combination, which rotates leadership, and would in this instance be spearheaded by the First Boston Corporation. On some occasions, a few other syndicates join in the competition, with the winner assuming the responsibility and privilege of distributing AT&T bonds to investors, hopefully at a handsome profit to the underwriters that comprise the syndicate. "When we have these bidding competitions, we're not interested in looking just for bargain basement prices," Grace Fippinger said. "We want it to be a good business deal for the underwriters, too, because we're going to have to deal with them again next year. The bidding generally is very competitive. Sometimes the prices are so close that the bid has to be taken out to three or four or even five decimal points to decide who has won. Last year, the winning bid was a hair lower than I expected, which was a pleasant surprise. I'm never really surprised. If, for some reason, the bids both turn out to be too high to make any sense, we would simply refuse them. We've never done that, though other companies have on very rare occasions. I would expect in this instance that we would get a cost to us of about eight point nine percent or so, about what New Jersey Bell came in at. That's how things look now, at least, and there's still a couple of weeks till bidding day. A lot can still happen."

Fippinger said that she was entirely cool and collected about the offering at this point. "Why shouldn't I be?" she said. "There's plenty of time left. Wait until bid day. I'll be a disgusting bundle of nerves."

Bob Perkins has about him the look of the successful high-level American company man. He is a balding, chipper man who heads the syndicate department at First Boston. Sitting in his somber office, he said this about the New York Telephone issue: "It's pretty automatic that we bid on phone company issues. It's historic. Right now, Bell bonds are among the least risky long-term debt we bid on. They offer probably the highest liquidity of any securities that are competitively bid for. The phone company usually calls us about five weeks in advance of the bidding, sometimes eight to ten weeks. On rare occasions, we are notified just two weeks in advance and we have to really hustle. This happens when AT&T spots a really good market and decides to run and seize it. In this case, we knew about the issue for over two months. The first step for us is to notify the syndicate department and make sure our group is large enough to handle the amount of money being asked for. We had seventy-five firms join up for this one, and more than enough resources. Then we put the event on our bidding calendar, send out letters of agreement to underwriters, and start moving toward the date of sale. Once the syndicate is formed, there's not that much for us to do up until the bid. With these things, all the action takes place on the last day."

Tom Saunders, the main syndicate man at Morgan Stanley, told me a little about Morgan's preparations: "We always set out to win the Bell issues, they're just among the best things out there. There's a very broad list of potential buyers for them. As soon as we are notified of an upcoming issue, we invite our underwriters who traditionally bid on the company to join up. We had eighty-one sign for New York Tel. Right now, we have no idea what our bid will be. This is a last-minute type of thing. You have to look at how the entire bond market is doing. Then you look at how New York Tel trades relative to other telephone bonds. What the perception of New York Tel is compared to other telephone issues. It should trade within five basis points of Illinois and New Jersey Bell, some say. Some say it's a solid Triple-A, but slightly below others, which would put it in the middle of the pack. Some say it's a below-average service climate in New York and an unfavorable regulatory climate. So you see that all your factors come to the circus here. You try to assess all news developments that affect the market. You take the pulse of every living factor that could play a part. You're looking at everything you can get your hands on. The closer you are to the bid, the more information you have. In theory, this makes it less risky. But, let me tell you, it's still a very risky business."

On June 15, five days before the bid, an event known as a due diligence meeting was held at AT&T's headquarters. The purpose of the meeting was to allow the company to air any pertinent facts about the upcoming offering. Representatives from New York Telephone and some of the underwriters assembled in a not overly large conference room. The telephone people chatted about the operating company's financial health and future prospects. They said the company was doing just splendidly. They said prospects were extremely good. They mentioned a key telephone company barometer called the overall volume of business, which is revenues deflated by rate increases. It offers an idea of the strength of local phone usage, and is vital to planning. New York Tel said that its overall volume of business had been rising at more than 6 percent a year. Questions were asked. Questions were answered. Fairly routine.

Meantime, the underwriters had begun to canvass their major accounts to scout out what sort of pre-sale interest there was in the bonds. This interest is known in financial parlance as the "book," and it is critical in deciding on a bid. Bob Perkins on the book: "Legally, the underwriters can't take any actual orders yet, but what happens is the sales organizations of the different firms call their big accounts and feel them out about the issue. They mention some rough prices that the issue might go for, and see what sort of interest there is at each price. The book is built from the moment the syndicate is formed up to the bid, in theory. In practice, the book is built several days before. That way, it's more reliable. If everything goes well, you would have a sparkling book and sell the issue within an hour and a half. Recently, Bell issues have in fact sold very well, though this particular issue was a problem last year. The market turned down and the issue hung around in the syndicate for eight to ten days before the price was finally lowered. No money was made on it. You can't hold these issues forever. You have to turn them. You're borrowing money to hold on to them. In practice, we rarely hold them much beyond a week. Usually, they're gone within a day or so."

Tuesday, June 20, dawned dark and ominous. On Friday, the prime rate (the minimum interest rate charged a bank's most credit-worthy customers) had shot up to 8¾. (And in subsequent months would advance well into double digits.) The basic money supply, expected to drop a bit, remained the same. That was interpreted by financial specialists as a negative. A few more people had added their voices to the chorus of predictions for double digit interest rates. What's more, the Federal Reserve Board's Open Market Committee was meeting in Washington to determine federal policy, leading to plenty of uncertainty.

Grace Fippinger was pacing in her office. She was not calm. "All of these things are working against us," she said with a wan smile. "Sometimes I think the whole thing has to do with psychology. At any rate, I'm now expecting the cost to the company to be in the high eight point nine to low nine point two range."

A financial man pointed out: "Every hundredth of a percent will cost New York Telephone six hundred thousand dollars over the life of the issue."

"Did you have to bring that up?" Fippinger said. "My stomach is in enough knots."

A telephone call came in for Fippinger from one of the brokerage houses. She picked it up, listened without revealing any expression. "Now, Jamie, that's not very good news. Is that the best you have to offer me on a day like this? Some bearer of good tidings you are. . . . Well, I think there will be aggressive bidding. There's not much else business out there. I think the two bidders will show up." The bid was scheduled for noon.

At 11:00, representatives of the seven principal firms in the First Boston syndicate sat down in a plush conference room in First Boston's offices near Wall Street. They considered prospects for the market. The book showed that, at a yield to buyers of 9 percent, there was plenty of interest to "handily sell a hundred and fifty million dollars in bonds." But it was agreed by the underwriters that that sort of yield would not make for a winning bid. So they decided to gamble. They would cut the rate of return, hoping to get rid of enough bonds by the technique of swapping other securities for them, which might then trigger a wave of interest that would lure cash buyers in at the lower yield. It was a roll of the dice.

At 11:15, the managers convened in a more capacious room with the sixty-odd smaller underwriters that composed the balance of the syndicate. The bid that the principal firms had agreed on was announced to them, and each underwriter was individually polled to see whether it would stick or drop out of the syndicate. Most thought it was too much of a gamble and jumped ship. Twenty-four stuck. The seven lead firms, which had originally been slated to take $84 million worth of bonds, agreed to absorb the "slack," giving them a full $130 million worth, just about the maximum that they were prepared to buy. "That's a ton of bonds," a First Boston man said. "I hope to hell they sell."

Similar proceedings went on uptown at Morgan Stanley. The eight major firms also concurred that there was plenty of pre-sale interest at a 9 percent yield. Because of the murky climate surrounding the Federal Reserve Board meeting, Tom Saunders felt, "We were in a time period that was the worst one you could devise. We were in no man's land. We were in that foggy area where you have to speculate. So we speculated." It was speculated that the bonds would probably sell at slightly under 9 percent, with swapping.

Morgan Stanley, like First Boston, felt that the "window," or time frame in which the bonds would have to be sold to do well, was at best twenty-four hours. In a declining market, which this was, important bonds like those of the telephone company either are snapped up right away or are ignored.

Just sixteen underwriters dropped out of the Morgan Stanley syndicate, leaving a total of sixty-four. There was more than enough money, though, so no slack had to be picked up by the principal partners.

The small, carpeted, unstylish bidding room on the thirty-second floor of the New York Telephone headquarters was empty at 11:30. Yellow chairs had been rounded up and arrayed in rows, and a wooden table was set up in the front. A small white clock reposed on the right side of the table, the official time. There was a pitcher of ice water and a stack of paper cups. Looking at the setting, one might suppose Tiffany lamps or antique silverware was about to be auctioned off, rather than $150 million worth of telephone bonds. Outside in the hallway, Bob Perkins and Gary Hovis, a First Boston assistant vice president who would enter the bid, were chatting. A platter laden with an assortment of muffins and pineapple-and-cheese canapés had been placed on a folding table, with a coffee urn and cups nearby. The two First Boston men were munching danish and sipping coffee thoughtfully. They had just arrived from their office by cab. The subway would have been quite a bit faster, but an unwritten rule at the firm is that you never take the subway. You could get stuck in a tunnel. If you're in a cab and it wrecks—as happened to a friend of Gary Hovis who was assigned to an important bid—you can always hop into another cab. First Boston's bid, as was the custom, had not yet been determined. Hovis would get it, just minutes before it was due. He would get it, appropriately enough, by phone.

"Well, I've got some good news," Bob Perkins told an AT&T financial man. "My daughter just got a ninety-eight on her math Regents test."

"Gee, that's wonderful," the AT&T man said. "You must feel awfully proud."

"Yeah, I do."

"What brings you here so early, Gary?" a New York Telephone executive asked.

"The danish."

"And you, Bob?"

"The coffee. The New York Tel coffee is first-rate. They ought to sell coffee rather than bonds."

Three Morgan Stanley men, led by David Goodman, a tall, debonair-looking man, bounded in at 11:40. Hellos to everybody. "Bob." "David." "Gary." "David." Others followed by the elevatorful. Most of the action was still around the danish. A knot of New York Telephone and AT&T financial types were talking about numbers—interest rates, yields, closing prices. Figures were being hurled into the air. 8.889. 8.988. 9.029. Something like athletes debating their most current batting averages.

"What's your guess, Sam?"

"My guess is there will be two bids."

At ten minutes before noon, Gary Hovis repaired to a small private room set aside for his syndicate and phoned his office. The bid wasn't ready. It was still being fine-tuned. He said he would wait on the phone. He was a bit fidgety. He drummed his fingers on the table. The practice is to release the bid at the last possible moment—to release it on the very brink of auction time—so you are able to take into account the latest information available from the financial markets, which can, and do, turn on a dime. ("Who knows," Hovis had explained to me earlier. "Who knows, the government could fall in Washington. That would sure change a bid fast. That would change a bid to no bid.") The other advantage of deciding on the bid late is to avert leaks that might get over to the other syndicate.

At two minutes till noon, Hovis was finally read the bid. He read it back. Mistakes have been made. "If I ever made a mistake on a Bell issue, I wouldn't return to the office," Hovis said. "I am deadly serious. I would find a new way to support myself."

David Goodman, planted in another private room, got the bid from Morgan Stanley at almost the same time. He wrote it down, then handed the phone to a colleague to read it back. Morgan Stanley worries that sometimes a person writes something down wrong, then says it back right.

His lips pursed, Gary Hovis walked smartly into the bidding room with a minute and a half to go, almost bumped into a chair, and dropped an envelope with the bid on the head table. He sat down next to his First Boston colleagues in the front row, crossed his legs, and leaned back. About fifty people had filled up the room and were talking noisily. David Goodman bustled in with a big grin with half a minute to go. He looked more debonair than ever. He dropped his envelope on the table and sat down in the front row next to his associates. He crossed his legs and leaned back, as if the more relaxed you looked the better chance you had of winning. Each envelope also contained a good faith check of $4.5 million. The rest of the money was due the following week. Once, when a $200-million bond issue was up for bid, the winning firm mistakenly included a good faith check for $600,000 rather than $6 million, but the eagle-eyed telephone people caught it.

Grace Fippinger, presiding over the affair, was now at the head table. She peered at the white clock, which said exactly 12:00, looked out at the assemblage, and picked up the envelopes. A former Southern Bell treasurer used to shuffle the envelopes, even though there were just two. Fippinger simply said, "I have two envelopes here and I don't expect a third," then ripped open the First Boston bid. Calmly, she read out the figures. It would produce a yield to investors of 8.94 percent. The key figure, though, was the cost to New York Telephone, which worked out to 8.989. Murmurs through the crowd. Without any discernible change of expression, Fippinger tore open the Morgan Stanley bid. The yield would be 8.98. Cost to company: 9.026. More murmurs.

Trailed by her financial cohorts, Fippinger retired to a private room to check the figures over, notify the Public Service Commission, and consult with New York Telephone's president, who had to give the final okay to the bid. Ten minutes later, she returned and announced to the people in the bidding room that First Boston's bid had been accepted. Morgan Stanley got its check back.

"I'm genuinely surprised that First Boston went that low," a Morgan Stanley man said as he gathered his things together. "I figured we had the winning bid."

"Well, that's the first step," Gary Hovis said. "Now all we've got to do is to sell them."

Grace Fippinger said, "You're never happy. I'm glad that it's under nine, after all that pessimistic news. But you're never really happy." The difference between the two bids, in terms of cost to New York Telephone, was $1.3 million over the forty-year life of the bonds.

By the end of the day, the First Boston syndicate had sold about 50 percent of the bonds, mostly by swapping—not a bad showing, though nothing spectacular. The next morning, however, the market weakened considerably and, after an hour of trading, it was clear that the response to the bonds was pretty dismal. At 10:45, the managing partners conferred and agreed to break up the syndicate, a step that allows bonds to find their own price level—in this case, a lower one than had been set. By the day's end, it was evident that First Boston would lose a modest amount of money on the issue, as would the syndicate as a whole. The gamble hadn't come off.

A First Boston man on the sale of the bonds: "Well, as it turned out, we guessed wrong. Not totally wrong. If the market had held up for another day, we might have got out of this all right. Most of the firms that expressed pre-sale interest on a cash basis simply did not buy. They simply did not buy."

Tom Saunders had this to say about the bonds: "We felt when we heard First Boston's bid that it had no chance of working. I will not accept the notion, I will not buy it, that the market changed and so the deal didn't work. Look, every fact was available in the marketplace. We discussed them, and bid accordingly. Anybody who tells you that the market changed on the facts is dead wrong. I'm not saying the decision was easy. But their bid was not prudent. Saying the market is to blame is grasping for straws in the wind."

An AT&T financial man said this: "The winning syndicate and the losing syndicate always say opposite things. The loser always says the other firm wasn't wise. I'll tell you, nobody in this business has a corner on being right."

There was still a week to closing. It wasn't automatic. If some material effect came about, the whole deal could be dumped. In November 1974, smack in the middle of the closing period on a $600 million AT&T issue, the Justice Department decided to file its massive antitrust suit against the phone company. That was a material effect. The investors wanted out. The issue was canceled, money refunded. In January, AT&T went back to market and raised the cash anew—at a slightly lower interest rate.

At 10:00 on a hot, muggy Wednesday, Gary Hovis met with New York Telephone legal people at the Bank of New York, 90 Washington Street, to sign the raft of closing documents. No additional antitrust suit had been filed, the government had not fallen, nothing else menacing had happened. The atmosphere was one of barely controlled confusion. Documents were brandished back and forth across an oblong table. "You sign this, Gary?" "I think so. Uh, maybe not." After all the signatures were in place, clearance was given to release 2,403 debentures totaling $150 million. Two First Boston messengers carted them away in bulky black suitcases. A certified check made out for $144,134,229.17, the balance due after commissions were deducted and interest added, was turned over to New York Telephone.

A short while later, Hovis trundled uptown to officially turn the check over to Grace Fippinger, who had been unable to make the 10:00 session. It was basically a ceremonial gesture, good for some publicity shots. Hovis strolled into her wood-paneled office, extended his hand, and gave her the big check. "Why thank you," she said. "It's certainly been a pleasure doing business with you."

"Hey, how come this check says it's made out to Pacific Telephone?" a New York Telephone man said, feigning puzzlement.

"Oh, get lost," Hovis said.

"Wait," said another New York Tel man. "This reads a

hundred and forty-four thousand dollars. That's not quite right."

"Hey, lay off," Hovis said.

A barrage of publicity pictures was snapped by photographers.

A treasury man pocketed the check, shrugged into his jacket, and headed down Forty-first Street with it. Nobody mugged him. He trooped into the Citibank branch at Fortieth and Broadway, marched up to one of the bank's officers, and said he had a little money to deposit. "I was tempted to use the quick deposit slot," the treasury man said, "but then thought better of it." Within fifteen minutes, the check was credited to a New York Tel account, where it would be used to pay off some short-term debt. "Well, that's that," the New York Telephone man said. "Another hundred and fifty big ones in the kitty."

14

Listening In

There are those who would say that every crackling sound erupting from a phone connection means that someone is relentlessly listening in on their doings. While suspicions of electronic eavesdropping play on in their minds, wiretapping stands real. As the central carrier of private communications in the country and, therefore, the chief guardian of phone privacy, the telephone company has for many years played an ongoing poker game against intruders who monkey with its lines. To hear the company tell it, it has consistently held the winning hand.

"From the time our business began, the American public has understood that their telephone service was being personally furnished by switchboard operators, telephone installers, and central office repair workers who, in the performance of their duties of completing calls, installing phones, and maintaining equipment, must of necessity have access to customers' lines to carry out their normal job functions," I was told by H. W. Caming, an AT&T lawyer whose bailiwick is privacy and fraud. "We have always recognized this and have worked hard and effectively to ensure that unwarranted intrusions on customers' telephone conversations do not occur. Our mission is to have the phone conversation be every bit as private as the face-to-face conversation, whether two wives are talking or two senators. And I can say, without any equivocation, that customers should feel secure about their telephone conversations."

But nobody really knows with any certainty how many secrets get stolen over the phone lines. The feeling of many security experts is that there can be no real assurance that your phone is safe. If someone wants to hear badly enough, he'll hear. The safeguarding of the average phone user is not widely thought of as the most significant or pressing problem that besets the phone industry. Who cares what most people say? But a suspected criminal or anyone embattled in a marital dispute has pretty good reason to think that somebody is out there listening. An installer I spoke with in a Southwestern town told me unblinkingly, "You're kidding yourself if you don't think tapping goes on all the time. Sure, it goes on. And I know phone people who help out with it and don't ever get caught."

Robert Smith, the former assistant director of the Office of Civil Rights in the Department of Health, Education, and Welfare, and now the publisher of a newsletter called *Privacy Journal*, has for many years been what might be called a privacy scholar, and he says, "I don't think the company is a major violator of privacy. But neither do I think it is a very strong advocate. I think the phone company's record on privacy is very mixed. My impression is that it waits until it's pressured into becoming concerned about privacy, rather than being at the forefront as I think it should."

Every year, roughly ten thousand fretful subscribers call up AT&T convinced that their phone is hot as a poker. Free of charge, AT&T will hustle some security people over to scour the lines. By and large, the company finds plant trouble to be the source of unease. Anyone who detects background noise or clicking on his line and concludes, aha, someone is tapping my phone, is usually wrong. Most modern-day taps are powered by their own batteries, or else they drain so little current that the larger normal power fluctuations make them undetectable, even with sensitive current meters. Clicking on the line can be brought on by faulty connections in the phone, central office equipment or cable, defective switches in the central office, damp cable, and power surges when batteries in the central office are charged up. A good tap records conversations on a machine that switches itself silently on and off as you talk. The tap is designed to work without extraneous noise, unlike your phone. Fiction and thriller films have nourished many a needless worry in people's minds, no doubt, by perpetrating the myth that noisy lines are evidence of a wiretap.

Nonetheless, the searches by Bell security people, plus routine repair service, turn up some 200 listening devices a year. In the last decade, the annual roundup has fluctuated from 163 to 249. Just about all of these have been taps, gadgets that cut into the actual phone conversation and pick up only what's said over the telephone. A smattering have been microphones, or "bugs," that have been planted in the phone. A bug, in effect a miniature radio station, soaks up room conversation even while the receiver sits in the cradle.

Electronic eavesdropping, of course, is a crime. The Omnibus Crime Control Act of 1968 outlawed it, except under court order by federal law enforcement officials and local prosecutors in states with wiretap laws (currently twenty-two plus the District of Columbia). Violation of the law is punishable by up to five years in jail and a $10,000 fine. Legal tapping can also be mandated by the government in the name of national security, a procedure that many civil libertarians, for good reason, consider widely abused. Between 1968 and 1976, the latest date for which numbers are available, the federal government and the states placed 5,495 legal listening devices (and overheard 3.6 million conversations). About 200 devices are installed annually for national security reasons. AT&T rarely unearths a legal tap, since those tend to be of the most sophisticated sort and are generally installed with phone company knowledge.

Anytime the subject gets around to wiretapping, Bell people are quick to point out that the company takes great pains not to involve itself any more than is necessary in legal taps. It maintains that it fears too much participation might unduly corrupt its employees. Listening in on what people say on the phone, after all, can be fun. Under the law, the phone company must divulge line information and furnish a private phone line for taps. But the company never actually places the devices. Nor does it supply tapping equipment. "No," Caming told me, "we don't keep recorders and transmitters in stock in our central offices. We don't give out phone company uniforms to the FBI so they can slip into homes unobstructed and put their taps on."

When AT&T roots out a wiretap, it always notifies the customer about it, even if the device happens to be legal. It doesn't, however, characterize what it finds. It simply declares that it has found a listening device. There are two exceptions. In Minnesota (by law) and New Jersey (by policy), if a legal tap turns up, the company merely states that no unauthorized device was discovered. When evidence of any tap is found, the first step the company takes is to check with the FBI and the local prosecutor's office to see if the tap is indeed legal. If not, the company asks the customer if it's all right to leave the device intact for forty-eight hours to give police the opportunity to smoke out the perpetrator.

Legal taps, of course, are left on, though authorities tend to remove them once the phone company has informed them that the customer is conscious of the tap, since their usefulness has become compromised.

What motivates people to tap? Corporate intrigue and criminals tapping criminals account for a fair proportion of taps. But about three quarters have to do with sex, AT&T has discovered. A husband suspects his wife of infidelity (or vice versa). A tap may well confirm what's going on. Sometimes, parents have reason to believe their sons or daughters are heavily into drugs and have taps placed on their phones to get to the bottom of things. Some private investigators have been found willing to do the dirty work of installing taps, if you meet their prices. A crackerjack job, it is said by those who would know, runs around $5,000 a month.

Perhaps a more interesting question than how much tapping is discovered by AT&T is how much snooping isn't found.

"You're talking about the dark side of the moon," Herman Schwartz, an attorney and longtime student of electronic eavesdropping, told me. "All we have are impressions. My impression is a lot."

Anthony Pellicano is a courtly licensed private investigator now in the countermeasures business. Countermeasures became very big right after Watergate, when everybody who was anybody (and also apparently a lot of people who weren't anybody) thought they were being bugged or tapped. Pellicano is based in Westchester, Illinois, but he's willing to roam. If you're able to pay $400 an hour, he'll "sweep" your premises for taps and bugs. Business, he told me when I caught up with him in between sweeps, is fairly brisk. However, he said that he turns up something in just one in a hundred cases. He pointed out that "ninety-nine percent of the people who call me call over the suspected phone or in the room they think is bugged. Real smart. Really smart." He said that in any sort of domestic squabbling "you should expect almost a fifty-fifty chance of some form of eavesdropping going on. After all, you can breeze into many electronics stores and pick up an adapter that lets you hook up a recorder to your line. I find a good amount of amateurish taps like that." Like some other experts I spoke with, Pellicano said he didn't think very much corporate tapping took place. "It's so much easier and less risky to pay off someone for this information," he explained. "The top espionage people in the country find the weakest person in a corporation, and then they induce him. Much easier than tapping. There's no law against paying people for information." When he is not wending his way through rooms hunting for listening devices, Pellicano whiles away endless hours trying to decipher what was on the infamous eighteen-and-a-half-minute gap on the Nixon Watergate tape. He acknowledges that the odds are probably a million to one against ever getting to the bottom of the gap, but he said, "I'm that kind of guy."

Plenty of companies, I managed to gather, are itchy about electronic ears. Every year, several hundred call on Burns International Security, the vast worldwide detective agency, for sweeps. Typical charge: $1,000. Charles Bates, the overladen director of investigations at Burns, told me that he figures a device is found in roughly 5 percent of the probes. (It should be said that guesses furnished by countermeasures people on how often listening equipment is found could be skewed by the knowledge that if they lead people to believe that nothing is ever found, there wouldn't be very much call for their business.) Bates came to Burns a couple of years ago, after thirty-six years as an FBI operative (he headed up the Patricia Hearst hunt). Did he think telephone talk was safe? "The telephone is absolutely not secure," he said to me. "When I was in the FBI, we automatically assumed that the telephone wasn't secure. We never discussed anything of any classified nature over the phone. Same way here at Burns." Another security man told me, "If you've got something you don't want overheard, I'd never ever say it over the phone."

Michael Hershman, who was the chief investigator on the National Wiretap Commission, a panel appointed by Congress and President Nixon to review the effectiveness of federal wiretapping law, said to me, "Certainly a great deal of tapping could be going on without anyone knowing the first thing about it. But I don't really think this is something that, for the ordinary citizen, should cause a chilling effect. There's no motivation for anyone to tap him."

Bugging by phone (naturally, one can also bug by vase, by picture, by fountain pen, and by cigarette lighter) apparently isn't as popular a scheme to purloin information, a very good reason being that one needs to have access to the premises to plant a bug. Still, AT&T has happened on some crafty ways to bug by phone. There is the hookswitch bypass method (with several variations), which circumvents the cutoff switch on a phone so that it remains "live" even after it's hung up; in one version, a tiny wire is added to the maze of wires curled inside a telephone. A more nefarious instrument is the so-called harmonica bug, which is harder to discover. It is, of course, tough to find a bug that isn't operating, which is at the heart of the harmonica bug principle. The bug is planted in the victim's phone, and when the eavesdropper wants to activate it he calls the number and, before the first ring, blows a medley of notes into a harmonica, which, when sent over the line, activate the bug. The bug, in effect, answers the phone and keeps it from ringing. When the eavesdropper has had his fill, another blast on the harmonica switches the bug off. The bug can be flicked on and off from any phone anywhere in the world.

Bugs have been found in the most curious places. In October 1970, Governor Marvin Mandel of Maryland discovered a hook-switch bypass bug in one of the phones in his office while a routine countermeasures check was being conducted. The bug, as it turned out, was on a special Civil Defense hot-line phone, part of the National Warning System. A special telephone hookup to allow communication between federal and state government during a national crisis, the system makes use of the Pentagon's classified telephone network. As a result of the bug found on the Mandel phone, other governors had their lines scoured and at least five more bugs were uncovered. Governor Lester Maddock of Georgia, rather than test his phone, simply yanked it from the wall. AT&T, which put in the phones, maintained that they had probably been hot-wired by mistake.

What about the phone company itself? Does it pry into our conversations? Few security people accept without qualification the sanctity of telephone personnel. AT&T does routinely cut into a smattering of calls to phone company offices and plant repair stations in order to assure itself that its employees are fielding them properly. What's more, supervisors randomly listen to a minute fraction of operator-handled calls. Customer-to-customer calls are never overheard, AT&T says stoutly, except portions of those that AT&T is pretty much convinced are fraudulently placed. Title II of the Omnibus Crime Control Act gives the telephone company carte blanche to overhear its customers, so long as the listening fits under either of the broad headings "rendition of telephone service" or "protection of the rights or property" of the phone company. The definition of these terms is left pretty much to the telephone security force, making it possibly the most powerful private police force in the country, since there is no legal requirement even to notify courts or the police that such a tap has been attached.

When Bill Caming appeared in 1977 before the National Wiretap Commission, he resisted the suggestion of some Justice Department officials that the law be changed to require telephone security people to secure court orders before tapping somebody's phone, as the police must do. That just wouldn't work, he testified, because in most cases of suspected fraud, the security force wouldn't have persuasive enough evidence to get a warrant. The commission, as it turned out, went along with the telephone company and made no recommendation that the law be revised.

Calls placed between two subscribers can be gotten into. When a person moans to an operator that he can't get through to somebody he's dialed for days, please check the line, there are verification operators, as well as certain regular operators, who can deploy special trunk lines to silently break into a call. When they do so, company rules stipulate that they are to stay on only long enough to ascertain whether people are talking. What's to stop some bored operator with verification privileges from plugging into calls and listening away? Several security people I talked with said they knew a great many phone workers, and the word they have gotten is that bored operators do sometimes dip into calls. A former Pacific Telephone Company operator revealed some years ago that company technicians working in telephone switching centers often search the lines until they come across an interesting conversation (they especially like those having to do with sex, she said), and then switch it onto the loudspeaker for the pleasure of their fellow employees. One woman allegedly heard the voice of her husband on the loudspeaker making a date with another woman. The company axed her when she began to listen in on her spouse on a regular basis. AT&T, when asked about this, insisted that these operators are rigidly supervised, and if they're caught listening—as a small number have been—they are immediately mustered out of the force.

Now and then there have been whispers, occasionally turning into shouts, that phone company people have been cajoled or paid off to cooperate with the police or friends in illegal taps. That act is very forbidden fruit in the Bell System and will result in dismissal and possibly prosecution. "But it's always hard to get the goods on somebody," a private investigator told me. "I've got a lot of friends at the phone company, as any investigator has, and if I need cable and pair information on somebody, I can get it. It's as easy as picking up the phone." According to Bill Caming, about forty Bell System employees—mainly linemen and installers —have been nabbed taking part in illegal taps in the last decade. He said that all employees who have access to line information are sternly warned on an annual basis of the dire consequences of leaking information. "The rules are very strict for them," Caming went on. "They must obey orders far more severe than Caesar's wife." AT&T scoffs at any insinuation that there's a surfeit of taps by pointing out that its force of ninety thousand repairmen and linemen is instructed to hunt for listening devices while doing things like bringing to life dead phones. Half the devices the company finds, it says, show up during routine work.

That may be so, but wiretapping, as anyone at all familiar with the technique knows only too well, is preposterously hard to detect, especially topflight jobs, and often taps are installed on phones for very brief periods of time. Any notion that it's relatively easy to get at a tap is completely misguided. Bugs at least must be physically present in the room, but a wiretap can be installed anywhere along a customer's phone line—in other words, along miles of cable. Even a concerted effort to find the tap doesn't stand that great a chance of success, and routine repair work, which tends to concentrate on the portion of the line that is faulty, has even less chance. Considering that phones and lines may go years between visits from servicemen, no customer should count on the phone company to uncover any taps into his conversations.

When I asked a security expert named Allan Bell whether AT&T's searching is very effective, he replied abruptly, "Hell no. We've watched telephone repairmen go through their paces, and there's no way in the world they're going to hit on many taps." Bell is the president of Dektor Counterintelligence and Security Incorporated, an undercover snoop shop run by former government intelligence agents. "They're just blowing their own horns if they tell you they do a knock-up job," he added. "It's rough, rough work finding wiretaps." Mike Hershman agreed with him. "I think the phone company does a decent job, but frankly it's perfunctory. They don't do a very thorough search."

The whole eavesdropping problem extends beyond American borders and carries much darker implications. The government believes that the Soviet Union and perhaps some other countries have been snooping in on U.S. calls, mostly government ones, by picking off microwave transmissions from the sky and sorting them by mammoth high-speed computers. As a result of this concern, in late 1977 the government approved a broad and costly program to guard calls. AT&T is now shuttling many government calls by more secure underground cable, and a greater quantity of equipment that scrambles conversations is being installed.

Another disquieting matter is the fact that transmission of data to and from computers over telephone lines doesn't appear to be protected by federal wiretapping statute. The tapping of a single computer-telephone link could, inside a few minutes, invade the privacy of thousands of people, since huge stacks of personal data are stored in computer files and whisked over phone lines. Legislation is being worked on to address this sticky matter, though there's no telling when it will come to pass.

Then there are devices generically known as "pen registers" that are used from time to time by the police. Attached to your phone line, the instruments make a paper-tape record of the number you call, the date and the time you called it, and the length of the call. It does this for both local calls and long-distance ones. The pen registers aren't covered by the Crime Control Act, but only by the far looser restrictions required for a routine search warrant. So what? Well, by merely plugging earphones or a tape recorder into the registers, they suddenly become wiretaps. Police, in a number of instances, seem to have yielded to the temptation. AT&T, to its credit, has battled aggressively against pen registers. But it has lost. In December 1977, the U.S. Supreme Court ruled five-to-four in a New York Telephone case that the registers were perfectly okay, a stiff blow to the containment of wiretapping and to guarantees of phone privacy. There are no figures on how many pen registers are in use, but guesses range into the thousands.

There are gizmos aplenty to palliate the incurably paranoid. Hardware is being aggressively peddled by counterintelligence firms. Buy it and it sniffs out bugs and taps. F. G. Mason Engineering Incorporated, Fairfield, Connecticut, is one of the biggest hardware suppliers. Its annual sales approach $1 million. You can pick up a $1,000 telephone analyzer or you can fork over $30,000 for a receiver system designed to smoke out almost any sort of transmitting device hidden in a room. About 80 percent of

F. G. Mason's customers are foreign governments, the remainder American companies. Dektor Counterintelligence carries in its line an ingenious item sporting the romantic name, "Cloak." It's particularly appropriate as a gift for the man who worries that everyone is constantly interested in what he says. The Cloak is, in effect, a $3,500 telephone that replaces the one installed by the phone company. It features a special panel that lights up or goes beep-beep if you're being bugged. It will catch most wiretaps commonly used, Dektor promises, though it won't, unfortunately, pick up a sophisticated tap. No hardware will. At the end of the day, you can unplug your Cloak and take it to bed.

There are nonelectronic ways in which others, unbeknownst to you, can find out whom you're talking to. One is to get hold of your toll billing records. These records generally contain the date, time of day, duration of call, number and telephone exchange called, and the tariff charge for each toll call. They also list credit card, collect, and other charges outside the local calling area, as well as charges for directory advertising and telegrams. They can form a fairly revealing portrait of whom you know and what you're up to. The records are generally stored at the phone company for about six months, after which they're destroyed. With the possible exception of a few state statutes, there are no laws barring AT&T from turning over toll records to anyone it wants to. Up until 1974, the phone company was fairly free with these records. Not only would they be released upon receipt of a subpoena and as a result of an administrative summons (as from the Internal Revenue Service), but also, in many cases, upon a request from a prosecutor or police chief. A flurry of disclosures in early 1974 indicated where AT&T's sympathies lay in preserving the privacy of its customers. Phone company officials revealed that their operating company in Washington, D.C., the Chesapeake & Potomac Telephone Company, secretly gave copies of its toll call records for four Washington newspaper bureaus to government agents. These were those of the St. Louis Post-Dispatch, Knight Newspapers, the New York Times, and Jack Anderson. In the case of the Times, the records the IRS obtained were of the entire bureau for the preceding seven months. One reporter in the bureau hazarded a guess that the records were requested because he had been looking into reports that the IRS was investigating a large contributor to President Nixon's reelection campaign for a possible criminal violation. The IRS later explained that it was checking out a possible leak about the tax case of a *Times* reporter. The other records were requested by the FBI, evidently in connection with the investigation of the leaking and publication of the Pentagon Papers. Toll call records are a useful investigative tool, since although they reveal nothing of the substance of a phone conversation, they can aid in identifying contacts and associates and confidential sources of information.

In March 1974, apparently as a result of pressure put on it by the general public, AT&T revamped its policies in regard to toll records so that no records would be released except under subpoena, administrative summons, or court order. What's more, the company made it mandatory to tell affected customers within twenty-four hours of release of their records, except when law enforcement officials request that they be given more time so as not to impede a criminal investigation. In such instances, word comes within five business days after the investigation concludes. When records are handed over under a national security request, however, customers are not informed at all. According to the telephone company, records of something like twenty thousand customers out of the sixty-three million it serves are released every year. The bulk of them end up figuring in criminal or government investigations. A small proportion are involved in civil suits. It's not all that difficult for a jilted wife, say, to obtain such records for a divorce proceeding.

The tape recording of conversations made over the phone is still another sensitive matter in privacy-land. Telephone tariffs prescribe that an electronic warning beeper must be used when recording a conversation over the phone. There are a few exceptions: shows recorded for radio broadcast, or calls placed to police emergency numbers. (About twelve states require consent by both parties for a recording to take place.) Violation can lead to termination of service. But the rule is all but unenforceable. Anyone can attach a suction cup to a phone and record away. Hardware won't detect the presence of any recorder on the line, so who's to say if someone's got a tape going unless you spot him doing it. AT&T readily admits that the regulation about warning beepers is widely abused, and the FCC has proposed to scrap it in favor of a two-party consent rule. That, the phone company just as readily admits, won't be much easier to police, since the person on the other end of the line can't tell whether a recorder is being used. I know a number of journalists who regularly attach suction cups to their phone headsets and tape record interviews without bothering with a beeper or caring to ask the persons being interviewed whether they mind. When I've pointed out to these reporters that this violates telephone tariffs, that their phone service could be terminated, they have politely told me I was crazy.

Some court decisions handed down in recent years have not done much to bolster the ordinary citizen's right to telephone privacy. In a case involving the San Francisco branch of Macy's, where the security director put in an extension wire through which he listened to and recorded employee conversations, the court decided that an employer may listen in on his employees' conversations when the calls pass through his own switchboard. Another decision with dark implications for privacy was the ruling in *Simpson* vs. *Simpson*, a divorce case in which a husband wiretapped his wife. The U.S. Fifth Circuit Court decided that an individual may wiretap his own phone, even though his spouse may not have been advised of the tap.

"You shouldn't really worry that much about phone privacy," one security person said to me, "because there's not that much hope that it'll improve. But the thing to remember is that privacy in general isn't so hot. For instance, what's to stop somebody from secretly carrying a tape recorder in his clothing and taping away? I carry one myself."

15

Blue Boxes and Phone Phreaks

Someone makes a long-distance collect call to a pay phone that a friend is stationed at. The friend accepts the charges, but of course there's no one to bill. A man calls home person-to-person and asks to speak to himself. Naturally, he's not there. He leaves word for himself to call back at 6:05. That information, exchanged free of charge, lets his wife know he's heading home on the 6:05 train. Someone calls up a refund control operator on a pay phone. He lies that he just lost a dollar in the phone. A credit is applied to his home bill. A person makes a brief long-distance call, then notifies the operator that he misdialed the number. Policy is to take his word. The call vanishes from his bill. Someone is particularly adept at electronics, so he builds himself a "blue box," an ingenious contrivance that enables the user to dial anywhere, anytime, free.

These are just a small sampling of the numberless schemes devised to outfox the phone company. People have tried them all. They have gotten away with them all. Enough have tried and succeeded, in fact, that AT&T, the butt of most toll theft, figures that it is hobbled by provable losses from fraud of around $40 million a year. But that's just what it knows it's been robbed of. With so much chicanery that it fails to catch, it thinks the actual numbers are much higher—perhaps double. That isn't all that much money stacked next to revenues from phone usage—a staggering $27 billion in 1979—but the phone company is convinced that if it didn't work hard at ferreting out crooks, the losses would explode into the hundreds of millions of dollars and possibly strangle the entire phone system. "Fraud remains at a high level, and you might say it's straining to burst its shackles," Bill Caming told me. The cost of theft is actually dug out of the pockets of everyone who has a phone. As Caming worded it: "Toll fraud involves the commission of theft of the company that must be borne ultimately by our subscribers. It attacks every last customer's pocketbook."

The blue box is the most nefarious fraud device in telephony. Borrowing its name from the color of the original boxes, it is the weapon of the so-called phone phreaks, the loose federation of whizkids who dash phantomlike through the phone company's long-distance lines and have achieved almost a cult status. The gadget, however, has proven to be a popular intoxicant to a motley crew of users: businessmen, film stars, doctors, lawyers, college students, even high school students. Out of 653 blue box users the phone company has managed to interrogate in the last few years, nearly half were businessmen. The next biggest category was criminals, who find it alluring because it leaves no record of their calls. An inventive twenty-seven-year-old MIT student was convicted for making blue boxes and selling them at $300 a box. Two hundred boxes, ready for delivery, were found piled in his apartment. Bernard Cornfeld, the millionaire financier and playboy, was convicted of blue box calling. So was nightclub singer Lainie Kazan. Actor Bob Cummings was placed under arrest and charged with blue box use, though he avoided trial under a double jeopardy ruling. "People aren't doing it just for financial reasons, that seems awfully obvious," Caming told me. "There seems to be a tremendous appeal in getting something for nothing."

I spoke with Caming in his spare, modern office in Basking Ridge, New Jersey. He is in his fifties, with short-cropped white hair, deep-set eyes, and an expression that is a combination of whimsy and intentness. I asked him how a little blue box was able to place the entire telephone system of the world at the mercy of its user. Caming reached into one of his desk drawers and yanked out a shiny blue box that had been engineered to slip easily into a pants pocket. "This is typical of many of them," he said, holding it aloft. It was a small rectangular gadget with thirteen tiny pushbuttons protruding from it. "It's a little bigger than some. But it fits nicely into a Marlboro cigarette box or a box for business cards." With a certain practiced air, Caming began describing what you do with a blue box. Naturally, he wouldn't in his wildest dreams actually initiate a blue box call, even for demonstration purposes, so he contained any temptation to scoop up the receiver of the phone on his desk and explained the process verbally. "Generally, you begin the call by dialing a no-charge number, like to Information in a distant city or to an eight hundred number like Sears Roebuck or Montgomery Ward or one of the airlines. You hear the ringing of the call. So far, everything is legit. Now, I press a button—this one at the top." A high-pitched cheep sounded from the box. "That is a twenty-six hundred cycle tone, the telltale blue box tone." Caming explained that the entire long-distance switching system is operated on twelve electronically generated combinations of six master tones. You hear those tones sometimes in the background after you've dialed a number. (These are not the tones you hear in Touch-Tone phones.) "What that twenty-six hundred tone does is more or less dislodge the call. When that's detected by our equipment, it indicates that the circuit is ready for the next call. The tone is similar to a tone we have in our equipment to signal that the equipment is ready for a call. Then the blue box has the capability to do what only an operator can do. You push a button called the Key Pulse button." Caming pushed it, and a different tone sounded. "The KP signals to the equipment that a call is coming through—a toll call. Then you dial the number you wish on the blue box. You can dial anywhere in the world at this point. You can call London. Call Hawaii. Call Hong Kong. After you dial the number, you press the start button, which sends the call through. That call never registers in our billing system. When you ultimately hang up, say ten minutes later, the equipment will show only that you hung up on a free call. What's more, you can make more than one call if you do it within a certain number of seconds. There's a several-second lag before there's a disconnect. It's like if you hang up, it's a few seconds before you get a dial tone."

Caming twirled the blue box in his hand, seemingly entranced by the knowledge that something so small and harmless-looking could have caused his company and him so much anguish. "So this is the blue box," he went on. "What does it cost? Probably twenty-five to fifty dollars if you have the know-how to make it. What does it cost to buy? Up to three thousand dollars. By the way, if you happen to have been blessed with perfect pitch, you don't need a blue box. You can simply whistle the tones into the phone and fool the equipment. A number of people have done it."

Caming then remarked that there is also a less popular device that's been christened the black box. It is installed at the jack of a phone and avoids any charge for calls to that phone. "When you have ringing," Caming explained, "you will normally have current on the line to cause the ringing. When you pick up, that signals that the call has been completed and the billing should begin, if there's billing involved. The black box intercepts the call so that it cuts off the ringing. Thus no billing. Calls, however, would have to be made at appointed times, so the recipient would know when to pick up. The more sophisticated black box in use today, though, has a switch that kills the ringing before the phone is answered. That means that if you call me from a phone booth, you'll get your coin back because it looks as if you didn't complete the call. The device is of no particular benefit to the person getting the calls, except if he happens to be a bookie. Bookies, I would suppose, are the biggest black box culprits." A man who adopted the pseudonym Alexander Graham Bell, I had been told, claimed to have invented the black box, and he supposedly sold both black and blue boxes to gamblers.

"What's the going price of a black box?" I asked.

"About three dollars to make," Caming said. "And from a hundred bucks up to several thousand to buy."

Caming mentioned that there is also a red box that simulates the sounds of coins dropping into a pay phone box. "Of course, this has limited use," he pointed out, "since it's only good in a pay phone and is kind of cumbersome to use for very expensive calls." People have also tried, with some success, tape recordings of coins dropping into the coin box of a public phone. Some years ago, an undergraduate at the University of Texas was casually making a phone call from a pay booth when some friends, as a joke, turned the booth on its side. Not overly bothered, he continued to feed coins into the slots and discovered that the odd position caused nickels to sound like quarters to the operators. Fellow students wallowed in discount rates for months before Bell caught on and bolted the booth in place. Other people, known to the phone company as "stuffers," have found it profitable to shove tissue paper into the coin return slots of pay phones. Later on, they return, remove the paper, and retrieve any coins that were blocked. One stuffer that the phone company nabbed some years ago crowed that he pocketed between $50 and $100 a day using the tissue dodge.

AT&T is certain that it's losing $1 million a year from the colored boxes. However, it figures that there are so many undetected improper calls being placed that the actual deficit probably ranges between $10 million and $20 million a year. It has been rounding up several hundred boxes annually since the early 1970s. The federal penalties are stiff: a maximum of five years in jail and a $1,000 fine. But the phone phreaks, for the most part, remain undaunted.

Electronic theft was in full swing when AT&T caught wind of it in 1961. It first learned of the nefarious electronic boxes through police raids and informants, as well as from some irregular signals on its network. The first actual blue box user that AT&T ran across was a college student in the state of Washington. When it found out about the theft, AT&T was faced with a perplexing problem. Did it have to undertake the Herculean task of redesigning the entire signaling function of the telephone system, a chore that could cost as much as $1 billion? Or could the problem be throttled in some cheaper fashion? The first thing the company decided to do was get a fix on what it was up against. Accordingly, Bell Labs was asked to mint some fraud-detection equipment, and by 1964 it came up with electronic scanning units. The monitoring equipment was dispatched to central offices in St. Louis, Detroit, New York, Miami, Los Angeles, and Newark, suspected centers of toll-fraud doings. The scanners would randomly tap into a trunk line and fish out a call, automatically recording the opening minute of conversation. If the scanners detected that the tape was clean of telltale signals, the recording was promptly erased. But if the tape sounded suspicious to the scanners, it would run on, sometimes for the full length of the conversation. Tapes of suspect calls were then shipped to New York by registered mail, where AT&T security people analyzed them further. The project plowed on until May of 1970, at which juncture about 30 million calls—out of roughly 1 trillion placed—were sampled. Something on the order of 1.8 million calls were actually recorded, many of them proving to be legitimate after security listened to them. But about twenty-five thousand seemed fishy, and the phone company netted more than two hundred convictions from the project. AT&T didn't publicly divulge the scanning operation until early 1975, immediately sparking heated protests from consumer groups and furrowed brows from civil libertarians and Congress. However, several subsequent court cases did uphold the phone company's right to snoop on conversations of subscribers it had reason to believe were dodging toll charges.

From the project, AT&T concluded that it had a grave problem on its lines, but not one serious enough to warrant a redesign of the whole network. It figured that vigorous detection and prosecution could outwit the crooks. And thus AT&T's security force resolved to pursue cheaters almost with the intensity with which detectives stalk gang rapists. Bell Labs, in the interim, had cooked up more advanced scanning equipment that was rushed into central offices throughout the country in 1970. Bell also happily discovered another fruitful source of help. "We built up a good supply of informants," Caming told me, "who contact us or law enforcement people to tip us off to toll fraud or the manufacture of these boxes. Some awfully big cases have been cracked by tips from informants."

Still better monitoring equipment was devised in the last couple of years, so that much of the phone system is now ceaselessly scanned, at bewildering speed, by computerized machinery that picks out blue and black box calls and almost instantaneously taps out on a teletypewriter the calling number of the user. "We're like a searchlight at an airport that constantly revolves through the sky," Caming said with satisfaction. "With our present system, any blue box or black box call will surface eventually, almost without exception."

In New York City, he pointed out, phone security people recently broke up a ring of three blue boxers who were "selling" calls to indigent people. They duped their victims into thinking they were benefiting from discount rates, when, in fact, the fees they collected were steeper than the actual tariffs. More than three hundred people were bilked by the ruse, until the phone company detected the flood of calls and started charging victims for them. The perpetrators, though, were never nabbed. In late 1979, however, an entrepreneur operating a similar business was caught by the phone company. The suspect, a thirty-six-year-old night switchboard operator at New York University, allegedly used a blue box to complete overseas calls through the switchboard for hundreds of customers, who paid about a tenth of standard overseas tariffs. The phone company estimated that he had robbed it of $1 million over a four-year period, netting for himself roughly $100,000.

Chinks still remain in the phone company's armor. All of the phone network still isn't monitored by fraud-detection gadgets, and furthermore it's almost impossible to catch blue boxers who work through pay phones and keep their calls short. Things may improve in the 1980s, when a good deal of the country will have its long-distance calls flash across a common channel interoffice signaling system. Since, under this technology, billing information shoots over a different path from the conversation, blue box calls will be all but impossible.

Who are these phone phreaks? The most infamous of the fraternity is Captain Crunch. His real name is John Draper. He acquired the nickname by starting off using a toy whistle from a Cap'n Crunch breakfast cereal box, which the Captain learned just happened to produce a perfect 2600-cycle tone. He was born in 1943 in San Francisco and started out as an engineer working for himself. Around 1969, he got into blue boxes. According to the Captain, he was accidentally contacted by a blue box user who switched him onto a conference call with a bunch of other phone phreaks. The incident printed itself on his memory. "I was interested not in making free calls, but in learning about the network." Among other things, the Captain discovered that every exchange in the country had open test numbers that will allow other exchanges to test connections with it. When two people from anywhere in the country dial consecutive test numbers they can talk together just as if one had called the other's number, with no charge to either of them. Among his talents, the Captain has perfect pitch and ears that he describes as "a twenty-thousand-dollar piece of equipment."

The Captain, however, ran afoul of the law. He was arrested in California in 1972 on a charge of fraud by wire. He paid a fine of $1,000 and was put on five years probation. In 1976, he was caught again (he lamented that he was set up by informers) and traded some secrets about his techniques for a token five-month jail sentence and five years probation.

When I spoke with him, the Captain was living in New York's Soho district and billed himself as a telecommunications consultant to small businesses. Hire him, he said, and he'd slice your phone bill (legally). "I cut one company's bill in half by reconfiguring their WATS line," he told me. "I can't tell you the name of any of my clients. After all, Captain Crunch is an evil figure when it comes to the establishment." The Captain, who had long dark hair, wire-rimmed glasses, and a mustache, said he had no phone of his own.

He claimed he was scared of phones. He said he worried that a friend would make an illegal call and get him in trouble. He said he was a big patron of the pay phones, and insisted that he plunked real coins in them like anyone else. "I don't ever anticipate having a personal phone again," he told me.

The Captain said he no longer consorted with other phone phreaks, though he crowed that there were tens of thousands of them still cutting into the phone lines. "I think that blue box use is increasing, not decreasing," he said. "Every time someone gets busted, more people become aware of blue boxes and they're tempted to use them. At least a hundred people are using blue boxes every day in every city of a hundred thousand or more. I know this just from the amount of people I've been in contact with. I saw two people in the Port Authority a couple of weeks ago using blue boxes. When I pass through O'Hare Airport, I continually hear—cheep, cheep, cheep. Now, if I'm seeing people use them, you better believe those boxes are being used. The important thing is to make your calls at a pay phone. The phone company is really catching people at home. It's almost impossible these days to get away with it at home. A friend of mine said that right after he made a blue box call, the security department at the phone company called up and said they'd be over in twenty minutes to pick up his box. Well, he wasn't there when they came, so they disconnected the phone." The Captain went on to say that many of the die-hard phone phreaks have junked their blue boxes, now that the phone company has gotten so sophisticated, and have shifted to nonelectronic means of theft, which he said were pretty easy to get away with.

I asked the Captain how he felt about the phone company.

"Well, the system is okay, but I think the people who run it should take a better attitude toward the customer." He said that he knew of an experimental phone company installation out in Iowa that could be programmed to do just about anything, including tapping into anybody's phone line. He called it a "super-snooper" that he said was part of an all-out assault by the phone company to ferret out crooks. He speculated further that he thought the phone company would use it to let the CIA and the FBI illegally tap the phones of people they were investigating. After the Captain's charges about the Iowa "super-snooper" got into print, AT&T said it thoroughly scoured its Iowa's facilities and didn't find anything of the sort.

I asked the Captain what he would do to improve the phone company.

"You could take the Robin Hood view and steal from the rich and give to the poor," he said. "Make the businessman pay more and the resident pay less. You could have the phone customer pay a flat rate—say thirty bucks a month—and for that you could call anywhere. At first, the system would be overloaded. Everybody would be calling all over the map. But after a while, you'd get sick of calling everyone. You wouldn't want to call Aunt Jemima anymore. Calling patterns would drop to normal. So you'd get rid of all the time charges in the system, and you could dispose of all this equipment needed to supervise these calls. I'm not saying my way is infallible. But it might work. It just might."

In March of 1979, some months after I had spoken with him, the Captain was sentenced to a year in San Jose Prison for violating probation by placing fraudulent long-distance calls. He was allowed to serve his sentence under the federal work furlough program. "You have to pay for your long-distance phone calls," the judge who sentenced him admonished. "Is that a very difficult concept to grasp?"

Oddly enough, one of the redoubtable phone phreaks of yesterday now works for AT&T. Joe "The Whistler" Engressia has been blind since birth. He has perfect pitch. He can whistle phone tones better than phone company equipment. Since he was four years old, The Whistler has had one direction in his life, and that was to learn all he could about the phone company and some day work for it. "When I was four, I learned how to dial the time," The Whistler told me when I got in touch with him. "Phones always entranced me. I used to play Telephone Man. I told my mother I was going to grow up to become a telephone man. The phone was just all sorts of adventures for me. I learned to type over the phone. This retired secretary who didn't have much else to do used to call me and explain where the keys were." At seven, he learned his first phone stunt. One of his baby-sitters put a lock on the phone dial to keep him from always playing with the phone. He got mad and started banging the receiver up and down. He discovered that by banging it once it dialed. Another bang, another dial. Soon, he learned to control the dialing by varying the intensity with which he pressed the hookswitch. When he was eight, he learned about whistling. He used to dial nonworking number recordings to listen to them. As he listened, he would whistle. Once, while he was whistling, the recording clicked off. Shortly, he figured out what was going on.

Engressia went to the University of South Florida, and while he was there he would whistle long-distance connections for fellow students. In 1968, however, the phone company smoked him out. He was disciplined by the college, and the whole case got into the newspapers all over the country. He cut out calling for a while. In the months after his curious talents were exposed, though, Engressia began receiving streams of calls, some from other blind youths with whistling talents and some from blue boxers. Blue boxes must be within 2 percent accuracy to work, and owners used to call Engressia and have him tune their boxes by ear. "Didn't pay as well as piano tuning, but it was steady work." Engressia, in effect, became a link for the phone phreaks; he brought them together. A nationwide underground gradually grew up. They called each other and exchanged tricks.

At age twenty-two, The Whistler first got out on his own, when he moved to Memphis. "I resumed making whistled calls. It was a bit expensive being on my own. I was getting ninety-seven dollars a month total income from welfare. No one would hire me. One guy told me, 'Gee, that's great, you got your clothes on straight. How did you do it?' Now, of course, there weren't too many ways of putting your pants on crooked, even if you were blind." To augment his income, Engressia sold courses for a correspondence school and cemetery lots by phone. He relentlessly pursued knowledge of the phone system. He would regularly show up at a central office switch room, explain in a polite voice that he was a blind college student interested in telephones, could he please have a guided tour of the station. Naturally, he was escorted around, touching switching circuits, crossbar arrangements, panel units, figuring out the phone system. He would travel hundreds of miles in every direction on the bus just to examine some new equipment he had heard about. Repeatedly, The Whistler tried to persuade the phone company to hire him, but he had no luck. So he decided to get arrested. "I figured you can say a lot of nice things and not get a mule to move. Then you can hit it over the head with a two-by-four and it will start running like hell. I decided to have my whistle be the two-by-four." The Whistler had a blue box made for him, and in May 1971 he called the United States Embassy in Moscow. He had a bunch of phone phreaks on the line with him. A marine guard picked up. The Whistler said that he was a disc jockey from a San Francisco radio station, and the listening public was just wondering how it felt to be out there, all alone, in Russia. The marine guard explained, at length. Prior to placing the call, The Whistler had told the phone company that he was experiencing some trouble on his line, and so it readily detected what was going on. A few days later, The Whistler was arrested. He pleaded not guilty to possession of a blue box and theft of service. The judge reduced the charges to malicious mischief and found him guilty. He was sentenced to sixty days in jail, but the sentence was suspended after The Whistler promised not to monkey with the phones anymore.

Out of the experience, he found a job cleaning phones for the Millington (Tennessee) Telephone Company. "It wasn't quite the sort of job I expected to get. I really wanted to work for Bell, but they wouldn't touch me." The Whistler told me that he gave up cleaning phones in 1972, then became a phone solicitor for a small outfit. The company went bankrupt, and so in 1975 he moved to Denver into a high-rise apartment. He long nourished a dream (second only to working for Bell) to live in a high-rise. "To me, the high-rise represented independence and orderliness. You had all the facilities inside and instant service. You could lean out on the balcony and hardly hear the ground. I used to have an envelope labeled 'high-rise.' It began with twenty-six cents in it and I would periodically stash some money in it until I had two thousand dollars." While living in his high-rise (twelfth floor; it had to be above ten for him to feel comfortable), The Whistler would appear at public utility hearings on phone rates. He attended the annual meeting of Mountain Bell, the regional AT&T operating company, and he would regularly call up maintenance people and tip them off to phone problems he detected. "Finally, I got in touch with a Mountain Bell personnel man, and after months and months of interviews—they were really very suspicious of me—I was hired as a troubleshooter in the network services center. I still don't believe I have this job. Sometimes I sit here at my desk and I feel my Bell insignia on my chest and I can't believe it. It blows my mind. I must be the luckiest person on earth."

Engressia began to demonstrate some of his talents to me. He said he was a bit out of breath from talking so much (we were speaking on the phone), so he played me some tunes on his push-button phone. "Swanee River" pulsated across the long-distance lines, followed by "Dixie." Then a high-pitched voice said, "This is Mountain Bell Telephone. Have tone, will phone." Finally, Engressia came back in his own voice.

I asked The Whistler, who's thirty now, if he was currently in contact with phone phreaks, and he said he rarely heard from any of them. "I was never a diehard," he said. "I wasn't interested in ripping off the company. I was interested in the pure joy of the system. It's an incredible jigsaw puzzle that never ceases to amaze me. And it's really not worth it to fool with Bell. Over the long run, it's pretty hard to get away with it. It's like robbing a bank. You may rob ten banks and then feel pretty swell, but at the eleventh bank you get killed."

The Whistler used to talk a lot to Captain Crunch back in his phone phreak days, but he rarely hears from him anymore. "Once in a while, the Captain gives me a call," Engressia said. "I ask him how it feels being this one man against the big Bell System, and he says, 'Well, it can get pretty lonely out there, but somebody's got to do it.' "

A brooding presence of nonelectronic tricks are played on the phone company. They're not easy to squelch, either. In 1979, for instance, AT&T estimates that these shenanigans drained it of roughly $39 million in toll revenues. The heftiest chunk of the fraud is accomplished by the credit card dodge. Either stolen or bogus cards are used to place calls. All it takes is for someone to overhear a businessman reciting his card number into the phone and he's got a billable card. Underground magazines are fond of printing articles describing how to fabricate credit card numbers (certain combinations of numbers are consistent in them), or they simply publish exhaustive lists of numbers certified to work. Some diligent individuals have trained scanner receivers on conversations between mobile phones, as a means of getting hold of credit card digits. Considering that there are nearly 8 million cards in people's wallets, the potential for abuse is great.

Unauthorized third number billing—charging a call to a fake number or a real number you have no business charging calls to—cost AT&T about $19 million in 1979. Phone phreaks have urged people to feel free to bill calls to places like the FBI or the White House (though AT&T, when I asked it, said this hasn't been a problem). In Kearney, Nebraska, some years ago, a traveler from

New Jersey figured he'd call home free by plucking a name at random out of the local phone book and charging the call to that name and number. Unluckily for him, he picked out of 12,000 names the manager of the local phone company. The operator readily recognized the name and called the police.

Credit card and third party fraud is tough to stop. Operators do check credit card and third party numbers to some extent, AT&T says, but the certification process is by no means definitive. When an undue amount of fraud crops up, fishy card numbers and third party numbers are circulated among operators. Call patterns are analyzed. But the phone company admitted to me that an abuse here and there probably will slip through.

Some advanced new hardware, years in the making, will be hustled into use within the next couple of years, I was told. The phone company boasted to me that the equipment should substantially stamp out most credit card and third number fraud. But it's keeping the details of the hardware under wraps. "We wouldn't be very smart giving away the key to the vault, would we?" a telephone man explained.

Sundry other tricks, like calling collect to coin phones and code calling, sock AT&T for millions of dollars in losses, as well. The company has prosecuted entire businesses for imbibing in code calling. Department stores and sales firms, using the cover of person-to-person calling, have fashioned codes to order merchandise from suppliers. Someone calls a supplier and asks for Mr. Trapper. He's told he's out (since he doesn't exist). The person says he'll call back in thirty minutes. That could translate to an order of thirty cases of ball bearings. Truckers have been known to deploy similar codes to inform collection points of when they are likely to arrive with goods.

It happens to be illegal to notify someone that you got someplace safely by arranging to call at a specified time and let the phone ring three times before hanging up. That is passing information across a phone line without paying for it. AT&T, when I asked them about enforcement, admitted that it's just about impossible to ever convict anyone of this ruse. Likewise, if you call up refund control and request a refund for money you claim you lost in the phone, the practice is to believe the customer and automatically grant the money. However, if you begin to pocket $10 or so every month, you can bet that the phone company will check you out.

To help root out nonelectronic fraud, the Bell System maintains seventy-four Centralized Ticket Investigation units spotted around the country. Experienced operators in these units try to puzzle out who should pay for unbillable calls. A visit to one of the biggest CTIs was arranged for me, provided I didn't disclose the location or quote anybody by name. It was a big, rectangular, fluorescent-lit space. Ticket investigators were huddled over tickets representing calls. A few were on the phone. Along the wall sat microfiche machines where master lists of all operator-handled calls made in the area could be peeked at.

The CTI director, a cordial, gravelly faced man, explained the operation. "We do about seven thousand investigations a day," he said. "The first thing is to see if there's a simple error—a number transposed from a credit card, an incorrect area code. Almost half of the tickets are easily corrected in this way." Investigators latch on to possible fraud—which shows up in about 10 percent of the cases—by riffling through call patterns and frequently used fraudulent credit card and third party numbers, and by resorting to what the director called "a sixth sense that these people develop." He said that the general practice was to pass on a fraud case to security for final investigation and possible prosecution when it gets to $50 and there's a suspect, or when it hits $200, suspect or not. One case that was masterminded by a band of college students had ballooned to $8,000 worth of fraudulent calls a month before it was cracked.

In late 1976, more than a hundred prisoners at the Metropolitan Correctional Center at Foley Square were caught having made $100,000 worth of fraudulent long-distance calls. Using bogus credit cards and third number billing, the convicts made something like two hundred calls a day on the jail's twenty-three pay phones, some of them as far away as South America. The mischief came to light when people started complaining to the phone company that they were being billed for calls they hadn't made. After the CTI tracked the problem down, the phone company threatened to yank all the phones from the jail, until a prison lawsuit was filed charging that removal would violate the prisoners' constitutional right to communicate with lawyers and relatives. Finally, the phone company arranged a plan under which the pay phones were rigged so that only prepaid calls could go through. The volume of calls reportedly dropped drastically once the inmates had to pay for them.

The general feeling around AT&T is that it will probably always have to live with the specter of fraud. "As in any struggle between the forces of evil and those who try to stem them, there will always be some crime," an AT&T security man told me. "Thank goodness, the average customer is honest. If he made a call, he'll tell you he made a call. Thank goodness. If he wasn't honest, we'd be in a hell of a mess."

16

The Ralph Nader of the Phone Company

Along Route 281 north of San Antonio, the urban plastic has not yet arrived and cattle and goats continue to graze. The region, with its gently rolling hills, meandering rivers, and palmy pleasantness, is a dreamy weekend retreat for the well-fixed Texas city dweller. It is a wonderful place for a real estate broker—most particularly in the commercial concentration on the very fringe of Blanco, population thirteen hundred. This is the site of Jim Ashley Real Estate. One hot summer afternoon, the telephone rang there. Jim Ashley answered it.

"You mean that many feet, or twenty-five thousand dollars?"

"Yeah, I can do that."

"I can do it."

"Yeah, I think we're in some trouble there. Damn it all. Well, blame it on old Ashley."

"Heck," he said after hanging up. "It's always seemed convenient to blame it on old Ashley."

Selling tracts of land in tiny Blanco, where the hours go slowly and the sidewalks, by Jim Ashley's estimation, "roll up around eight o'clock," is how the days pass for the man who calls himself the "highest-level defector in the history of the Bell System." "This is a company that don't ordinarily fire its generals," he told me. "Well, you're looking at a general who's been fired." The land business, as it happened, was booming. The phones were jangling off the hook. New salesmen had to be brought in. It was a long way from six years ago, when Jim Ashley started to make accusations of dirty dealings at the Southwestern Bell Telephone Company, his employer for twenty-three years, that culminated in the most lurid trial the Bell System has ever been mixed up in. It was a remarkable scandal, one that invited widespread attention not only because of the specific charges involved but because of the novelty of the case. For, though individuals from time to time had accused the phone company of doing something or other in a shady fashion—ripping off the public, tapping into phones, plotting a takeover of the government—precious little ever seemed to come of the charges. Indeed, the phone company had methodically built and clung to a reputation almost beyond quarrel as a staid and proper corporate citizen. This time, things were different.

Jim Ashley was born in May 1929 in Sondheimer, Louisiana, a tiny lumber town perched in the northern portion of the state. At the time, his father was a distributor for an oil company but was a man who found it difficult staying with any job for very long. He was sure there was gold in his future, he just needed to find the right job that would lead him to it. As a result, young Ashley was raised in a seemingly unending string of small towns in Louisiana and Mississippi. He never settled in any one place for more than a year. His father meandered from selling to managing a service station to supervising an auto agency to building homes. The gold never came. "We were always the new kids on the block," Jim Ashley remembered. "And we were always the poor kids on the block. We were okay, but I grew up, because of my dad's nature, with a great deal of insecurity. I was driven to get into some field that would provide me with security. I didn't want my kids to go through what I had to go through. One thing that was also instilled in me was a desire for honesty. The day FDR died, you know, a guy left his wallet in my dad's service station. There was eight thousand dollars in it. I found the guy and gave him his wallet back, and I got a two-dollar reward. Ultimately, you'll see where this brought me into conflict with my employers."

Ashley eventually enrolled in North Texas State University, where he met his wife, Bonnie. He worked in a flour mill to help meet his expenses, and he was exceedingly active in school government. He served on the college senate and spearheaded a committee designed to police businesses that gouged students. Ashley got his degree in business administration and interviewed with a number of college recruiters. "I was close to going to work for a large department store chain, but I also spoke with the Bell people, and I was told that Bell was really looking for the cream of the crop and that my future could be unlimited at Bell. I was rather excited about that. Damn, if you've got to be so good to qualify, it must be some place to work. I didn't know much about Bell. I knew about linemen and installers, but that's it. I liked the fact that I was told only the fittest would survive. I liked the challenge. So I went to work for Bell in June 1951. I went through two years of very intensive training. About fifty percent of it was training and fifty percent of it was indoctrination—coming around to the Bell way of thinking—why Bell is good, what dangers there are to society if Bell is weakened. I guess it was the closest thing to sophisticated brainwashing that you could have. I became a dyed-in-the-wool, dedicated Bell person."

Ashley was picked to specialize in what is known as the commercial office of the telephone company. The commercial office consists of the people who meet customers, who scribble down orders for service, and who then process those orders. Also, it is charged with the forecasting of requirements for additional facilities, with rate procedures, and with customer outcry. Traditionally the department is made up largely of women. Ashley started off in marketing in Fort Worth, and quickly passed through a parade of jobs—in Lubbock, in Wichita Falls—then fetched up in Arlington, Texas, as manager of the business office. One of his chores was rate negotiation. "This was probably the basic thing that was the catalyst of all my disagreement with Bell. A scheme was devised within Bell to use Texas to subsidize some of the states that had tough regulation. Texas was the only state without a regulatory commission. Rates were decided on by city councilmen on a city-by-city basis, and they were pretty easy to bamboozle. Consequently, Texas was consistently one of the biggest earners of all the states. This was the principal villain in the whole picture, that Bell would use Texas to subsidize the tougher states.

"One of the goals in rate negotiation was to create a favorable political climate that would give us more than a fair hearing when we came up for a rate increase. We were taught to always be a public relations leader in a community. We were to join the Rotary. We were to become involved in the Chamber of Commerce, and always the United Fund. If there was a United Fund drive for five thousand dollars, you'd try to raise ten thousand dollars. You'd do it by putting ten or fifteen Bell people on the drive for a month or so. Once you achieved the goal, you'd be looked on as a dynamic leader. In Denison, Texas, I exceeded the United Fund goal by twenty-five percent over the previous record, by doing this sort of thing. I was always a member of the local country club (which Bell paid for) and played golf and entertained with the top citizens of the town. The upshot was that whenever we went in for a rate increase, there was never any meaningful opposition. Everyone was our friend. Our buddy. I also decided what banks our money was in, what service stations we got gas from, what auto dealerships we bought from. I decided according to how influential those businesses were. City councilmen, you see, always have businesses, and we'd swing some money their way. Our objective in the rate cases was a hundred percent. Always a hundred percent. In other words, either we got what we wanted or it was our careers. It was a win-or-else situation. And we won every damn time.

"I must say, I was convinced that this was right. We were so indoctrinated that the bleeding heart liberals were out to get us and that we should fight fire with fire and the end justified the means. We were convinced that this was a good cause, as good as they came. So we were geared up to bamboozle the hell out of the regulators. They were the gas station owner, the auto dealer. They didn't know a blessed thing about regulation.

"In Texas, the rate base was based on fair value of our equipment—what we could sell it for—rather than net book, like in other states. This made it very simple to vastly inflate the rate base. We inflated the hell out of it. A telephone pole might be worth ten dollars and we'd say it was worth thirty dollars or a hundred dollars. Who's going to question it? The grocer? Who's the expert? So it would look like we were earning very little money on our rate base. The regulators would realize that we had to get an increase or we wouldn't be able to provide service. One thing we would do is go in to the mayor or whomever and say we need this much, you want us to ask for more so you can cut it back and everybody looks good. I would say this fat was added in at least fifty percent of the rate cases."

In 1965, Ashley was chosen to become division manager in Kansas. A man named T. O. Gravitt was his boss. Gravitt was a poor boy from Oklahoma who never managed to get to college. He joined the telephone company as a rural equipment salesman in Oklahoma in 1947 and rose through a spectacular twenty-seven-year career to the vice-presidential level. He was a swaggering, widely liked individual who, in traveling to business appointments, flew his own plane. Kansas, of course, had a state regulatory body, and Ashley says he was astonished to find out how differently rate cases were handled in Kansas, how much more stringent things were. "I became convinced then that we were vastly inflating the rate base in Texas. I talked to Gravitt about it, and he shared my apprehensions." In Kansas, influence peddling still went on, Ashley maintains. Regulators and politicians were wined and dined and exorbitant tabs run up. Money was put in the "right" banks. Free credit cards were distributed to regulators on the premise that this would better enable them to test the long-distance network. (The practice was abruptly scrapped after the scandal broke.) Dossiers, he says, were kept on regulators, gleaned, among other ways, by illegal wiretaps. "In Kansas, I learned about organized political slush funds. The system was that you had a chief lobbyist who collected money every month from all fifth-level supervisors. They would in turn falsify expenses to make up the difference. When the IRS began to require receipts, Bell came up with another scheme. Everyone was given a thousand-dollar-a-year raise. After taxes, that was about six hundred dollars, and you were expected to donate fifty dollars a month to this slush fund that was then used to support politicians favorable to our cause."

In time, Ashley was assigned to the San Antonio office as its general commercial manager. He was making $55,000 a year, supervising about fifteen hundred people (twelve hundred of them women), and was in charge of collecting roughly $30 million a month in revenues. Gravitt, meantime, had become the top man in Texas, an $80,000-a-year job. "We used to meet and discuss the Texas situation. Let me not mislead you. It's not that we were great crusaders and were trying to right terrible wrongs. We just didn't think we had to do this. Why should we subsidize the other states? We started working with other people who felt as we did to try to correct some of these things.

"I think the motivation for what subsequently occurred is the guys up above said, 'Hey, these fellows are rocking the boat and so

we better slap them on the wrists a little bit and get them in line.'
So word was passed out that, look, what we got on Gravitt, what
we got on Ashley. What we got on those boys. As Gravitt came up
the ladder, he made some enemies. Among them were the security
people. He found out that during an investigation of one of his
people there was wiretapping used. Gravitt blew his stack and
really burned the security force. So when the call came down, what
can you get on Gravitt and Ashley, it fell on willing ears."

On October 7, Ashley's boss, C. L. Todd, blustered into his
office and asked Ashley if he'd take a ride in his car with him.
Ashley obliged. They drove to the La Mansion hotel. Before they
got there, Todd told Ashley that he was being suspended for
numerous improprieties, mostly of a sexual nature. He was
accused, among other things, of arranging illicit parties and
promoting those who indulged in the parties. He was escorted to a
room in the hotel where he was interrogated at length by two
security people. They told him what they had on him, and he
denied it and told them they could get themselves sued for making
accusations of that sort. On the same day, according to subsequent
testimony by Zane Barnes, the president of Southwestern Bell,
Gravitt flew unannounced to St. Louis and showed up in Barnes's
office. According to Barnes, he said he knew that security people
were swarming all over Texas investigating him. He claimed he
hadn't done anything, and Barnes says he told Gravitt that they
weren't investigating him but that Ashley had been suspended and
his name had come up in some of the interviews. According to
Barnes, Gravitt again professed innocence and went on to say that
some awfully bad things were going on in Texas. Barnes says he
assured Gravitt that if there were, they would be taken care of.

Meantime, Ashley and Gravitt conversed with each other by
phone. According to Ashley, both feared they were being tapped,
so Gravitt would generally contact Ashley at one of his neighbors'
phones. When he was forced to call him at work, he would furnish
Ashley with a number to call him back on. By prearrangement, he
says, they reversed the fourth and seventh digits. Hence, if the
number Gravitt gave was 245–1824, Ashley went to another phone
and dialed 245–4821, which would most often turn out to be a pay
phone. A few days after his suspension, Ashley said a friend of
Gravitt's called him about a plane incident involving Gravitt that
worried him. Gravitt had been flying his plane from Dallas to San

Angelo, when, he had later claimed to his friend, he had fallen asleep with the plane on automatic pilot. He had awakened over the Gulf of Mexico. The friend thought it might well have been a suicide attempt. Ashley quickly flew to Dallas and met Gravitt at a shopping center. Ashley says Gravitt assured him that it wasn't any suicide attempt, that he was simply wrung out from the pressures and hadn't been sleeping nights. "He said that it was pure baloney, that he would never commit suicide. That statement weighed heavily on my mind later on."

On October 14, four days after that meeting, Gravitt strode into the garage of his sumptuous $120,000 north Dallas home, shut the door, flicked on the ignition of his Oldsmobile, and settled back to die of carbon monoxide poisoning. His wife had been out shopping. Later on, Gravitt's family and Bell colleagues discovered a ruminant nine-page memo in his briefcase accusing his company of political payoffs, illegal wiretapping, and using questionable bookkeeping to secure telephone rate increases. There was also an arresting hand-scrawled message that said:

Ever since last Thursday, I have not been able to keep my head from spinning. It hurts and I feel bad. I am afraid of brain damage. My right arm has started to go to sleep.

This coupled with the fact that the Bell System has permitted some of our people to question over 150 people and in so doing, had caused irreparable damage to my reputation. Questions like:

1. Have you bought him gifts at his request?

2. Have you fixed him up with women?

3. Have you gone to bed with him?

4. Has he made a pass at you?

This is unfair for a company to do without letting me be present. They have accused me of being partners with contractors. This is totally untrue.

I did try to get reimbursed for my airplane. It was used on company business and to haul politicians.

They have accused me of having financial arrangements with [the name of a company is illegible in the note but is apparently a printing company]. This is totally untrue. I have known Bill [last name illegible] for 10 years. We have been in each other's homes.

> *I work through Western Electric and [the name of a man*
> *here is illegible] in trying to get another traffic record in*
> *Texas. Bill [name illegible] turned out to be the best qualified*
> *and cheapest. He never gave my company one cent, only*
> *quality work.*
>
> *I think records should be subpoenaed according to*
> *attached memo.*
>
> *Also a memo showing a few things others have done.*
>
> *There is bound to be much more. Watergate is a gnat*
> *compared to the Bell System.*

Ashley said Gravitt's funeral was "like a New York Mafia funeral. All the guys who, if he did commit suicide, drove him into it, were there. Todd was there and asked me what I wanted. I said I was going to fight you bastards. He said he heard I wanted to be the Ralph Nader of the telephone industry. He said that, if I pursued this, wherever I went on earth, there would be Bell people hounding me." Todd later denied all of this under oath, as he did Ashley's claim that he was offered a settlement by Todd that would have amounted to half a million dollars if he dropped his charges and quietly resigned from the phone company. Ashley visited the Gravitt family, found out that they were determined to sue, and decided that if he "took the half million dollars and ran, I'd always be branded. So I made the judgment that I was going to sue. I was going to ride this one out to the messy end." On October 31, Southwestern fired Ashley.

In mid-November of 1974, Ashley and the Gravitt family filed a $29-million libel and slander suit against Southwestern, AT&T, and C. L. Todd. The suit also alleged defamation of character, invasion of privacy, and wrongful death.

In all likelihood, the suit would drag on for years and run up legal fees bolting into six figures. Neither Ashley nor the Gravitts had access to that kind of money. Ashley paid a call on an upper-crust San Antonio lawyer named Pat Maloney to see if he would take the case on a contingency basis. At the time, Maloney had never thought much about the phone company. "I had absolutely no feelings one way or the other, except to think they had a pretty good phone system. I was blissfully unaware of their existence other than paying them a monthly bill." Maloney had never heard of Ashley before, either. "But I'll never forget the day

Jim walked in," he recalled years after the trial. "I never saw a man so whipped in my life." Maloney said that there was no doubt in his mind that Ashley was telling the truth. "Every day I have to judge if a guy's lying to me. Most of my cases are on a contingency basis, so credibility is most of what I do." To be sure, Maloney confessed that he had grave doubts about tackling the case. He reckoned it would cost at least $200,000 (it wound up costing double that) and be all-encompassing of his time. He asked his colleagues for advice, and to a man they said don't take it. "We've had many an unpopular cause, but old Ashley led them all. We didn't have a band in front of us or behind us." But he elected to take the case. Ask him why, and he says, "I just thought it was the most challenging thing I ever saw. I've always been a sucker for a steep hill."

Once he filed the suit, Ashley says that he experienced some strange doings that flooded him with severe doubts. "The day after Gravitt's funeral, my neighbor's car was up on blocks and got loose and plowed through my bedroom wall. It was during the day, so luckily none of us was home. Then there was a team of SEC investigators in town. One day, they were returning to their hotel room when a gang of hoods suddenly opened fire on them. One investigator was hit in the necktie and the bullet was miraculously deflected. It was funny that the hoods never asked for any money. Another time, I was driving home from Houston in my car when I heard music playing, though the radio wasn't on. I figured there was a bug in the car that picked up the music. I had a watchdog, and somebody shot it dead. I got another watchdog, and it was poisoned. It seemed that strange things happened to anyone who opposed Bell.

"One day I got a call from a high Bell official who was my friend, and he advised me not to sue. He suggested we meet and talk. We set up a meeting at a restaurant. I walked in and sat down. After a while, I began to think he wasn't going to show. Then his wife sauntered in, purchased some gum, never even looked at me, then walked past my table and dropped a piece of paper on the floor and went out. I picked it up and it said, 'I'll leave the parking lot, drive two blocks, and park on the right. Drive past me and I'll drive behind you to make sure you're not followed.' There was a map leading to a cove, where this official was to pick me up in a boat. So I pulled into this isolated cove, and it was pitch-dark. I heard the putter of a boat, and there was this guy. He told me not to say a word, but to put this hood on. I put it on, thinking this was awfully silly. We went out to the middle of the lake and pretended to be fishing. This friend asked me if I was guilty, and I said I was innocent. He told me to forget the suit, but I said I couldn't. After I left him, I felt that if this guy, at his level, was so fearful of this thing, what in the world was I facing?"

While the suit stumbled toward trial, the Texas State Legislature passed a bill calling for state regulation of telephone rates, and the governor signed it. Legislators had tried without success for thirty years to regulate Southwestern Bell's charges; the scandal apparently won the necessary votes.

More bad news for Bell people started to seep in from another operating company, the Southern Bell Telephone Company. Until his forced resignation in September 1973, John Ryan was a $64,000-a-year vice president of Southern Bell in charge of all service for the state of North Carolina. In January of 1975, in interviews with the *Charlotte Observer*, he acknowledged that he ran a political fund that was composed of salary kickbacks from an average of six to eight of his immediate subordinates in the North Carolina operation. He said the kickbacks amounted to roughly $12,000 a year, which was funneled to candidates expected to be favorable to the interests of Southern Bell. He said that one of the most important races in North Carolina from a Bell standpoint was the gubernatorial contest, since the governor was the person who appointed the members of the Public Utilities Commission, charged with setting telephone rates. Ryan went on to say that he issued contributions to all candidates in the 1972 contest. Though he said that he never received any direct order from Southern Bell to make these contributions, or to be the keeper of the fund, as early as April of 1962 he had been awarded a raise and told explicitly to use it for political donations. He said payments simply arrived at his desk without being asked for. Southern Bell subsequently stoutly denied that it had ever authorized Ryan to make illegal contributions, and it maintained that Ryan was forced to resign because company officials felt he was much too deeply enmeshed in political and civic affairs to pay suitable attention to his managerial duties. For his part, Ryan insisted that he was booted out because he strove to elevate women into managerial slots appreciably faster than the company cared to.

The Southern Bell case eventually took on some bizarre twists of its own. The company, after an internal audit, grimly confessed that some $143,000 of company funds had been mishandled or misappropriated. The North Carolina Utilities Commission responded by fining the company triple that amount as a penalty. After two batches of indictments of Southern Bell officials were issued, culminating in Southern Bell pleading guilty to falsifying expense statements for the purpose of misapplying funds for political purposes and getting saddled with an additional fine of $310,000, John Ryan was brought to court and acquitted of the charges filed against him. A suit that he, in turn, brought against Southern Bell for allegedly firing him illegally and libeling him was settled out of court in October of 1978 for an undisclosed sum of money. Ryan moved down to Miami, where he, at last report, was not working.

Meantime, a flurry of investigations was loosed on Southwestern Bell, Southern Bell, and a few of the other operating companies by the Justice Department, the SEC, the FCC, state legislatures, and public utility commissions. Few charges were ever to bloom from these probes. A majority report by the Texas Senate Subcommittee on Consumer Affairs, however, did scold Southwestern Bell's top executives for living an "opulent" lifestyle at posh country clubs at ratepayers' expense. The report also drubbed the utility for throwing business to some public officials in order to influence their votes in Texas rate cases. In 1975, William Clark, a member and former chairman of the Missouri Public Service Commission, resigned in the face of almost certain ouster after he divulged that he had been a guest of Southwestern Bell on a three-day hunting expedition to Texas in 1969. Ashley had fingered Clark in his deposition for the slander suit. Later in 1975, AT&T announced that an internal audit that it conducted of all its operating companies had unearthed "scattered instances" of "improper use of corporate funds, mostly for political contributions." It found $2,200 of improperly spent money at Southwestern, $142,000 at Southern, and $9,520 at the balance of the operating companies between the years 1971 and 1974.

As these disclosures seeped out, telephone employees in Texas began to feel the public's wrath. As C. L. Todd recalled at the time in an interview that appeared in a phone company publication: "Just the other day, one of our service representatives was humiliated in a local store when she tried to pay her bill with an eight dollar and eleven cent check. She was told in loud tones—before a group of people—that no check for telephone people would be cashed in that store. One employee took her family to church—which she attends regularly—and found that other people avoided sitting on that bench—until a woman announced in loud tones that she would sit there if no one else would."

In January 1976, while the big slander suit was still snagged in legal skirmishing, Ashley and his wife dropped another bombshell. They filed an invasion of privacy suit against Southwestern Bell, accusing the company of wiretapping their phone. It went to trial that November, at which point Ashley testified that "wiretapping is a sick obsession with the telephone company. They've got to listen." He contended that long-distance records of city councilmen were regularly scoured by the phone company to glean information for dossiers. C. L. Todd disclosed, among other things, that nineteen Southwestern employees over the past twenty-five years had been dismissed for violating company privacy rules, but he denied that wiretapping was sanctioned by the company. As he pointed out during a talk he delivered: "If you sold oranges and nothing else—if that was your sole reason for existence—would you put ground glass in them? I think not. But that's what we would be doing if we wiretapped." The main thrust of evidence of tapping that Ashley and other witnesses presented had to do with a mysterious "battery" that Ashley insisted he found on the ground outside his house. He said it was used to bug his phone. Also, he testified that he came home one day to discover two phone company installers checking out his kitchen phone, though he had not reported any trouble. A neighbor had let them in. Ashley was never able to produce the battery—he said that he had slipped it into a desk drawer at his real estate office, and it had subsequently vanished. Fairly flimsy evidence of tapping, it would seem, yet after a stormy three weeks of testimony the jury returned to its room to deliberate and reappeared with a verdict finding Southwestern guilty and ordering the company to pay the Ashleys a cool $1 million. Grinning broadly, Ashley declared, "There is still a Santa Claus." Southwestern quickly filed an appeal.

In early August of 1977, almost three years after the first hints of scandal hove into public view, the big slander and libel suit finally rolled into a courtroom. Before a tidy but buzzing crowd unfolded some of the most lurid testimony to be heard in a corporate lawsuit. Reporters scurried about, taking down the juicy material.

Since Pat Maloney hoped to, among other things, prove that Southwestern Bell drove T. O. Gravitt to his death, one of the first witnesses to be called was Gary Byrd, a psychiatrist employed by Maloney to study Gravitt's suicide. Byrd testified that he performed a so-called psychiatric autopsy. He sent a 566-item questionnaire to seven people closest to Gravitt, including his widow and Ashley. Each was instructed to respond in the way he or she thought Gravitt would have answered. Then a computer was called on to do an analysis. Byrd said his conclusion (and the computer's) was that Gravitt was insane immediately prior to his death, and that he was driven by an "irresistible impulse" triggered by the Southwestern investigation. Later in the trial, Southwestern Bell countered with its own expert, a Harvard psychiatrist who told the court that the "bad part" of Gravitt's life was about to be exposed and "he didn't want to face the music."

A number of Southwestern Bell managers were then produced who testified that they had made contributions to a political fund, then recouped the money by filing false vouchers claiming use of personal cars for business purposes.

Louis Sommer, a rate engineer under Ashley in San Antonio, testified that voucher falsification was not uncommon. Furthermore, he said that both Ashley and Gravitt had been critical for years of some of the Southwestern rate-making policies. Asked to characterize Ashley, Sommer replied, "I thought he was the meanest man I ever worked for, but he was also the greatest motivator that I have ever known."

Bill Holman, a colorful manager in Austin, mounted the witness stand and said that he didn't agree with the method of coming up with the rate base, and neither did Ashley or Gravitt. He said he recovered political contributions through false vouchers. What's more, he confessed that he had arranged for a city councilman to purchase some property from Southwestern in order to curry favorable influence in a rate case. On another occasion, he transferred and promoted the daughter of a city councilman to sway the official to approve a rate increase.

A Dallas attorney, Ed Brown, testified that Gravitt told him, a few days before his death, that company employees had been used as "pimps" to secure women for high officials at AT&T.

Some revelations about Southwestern never got aired in the courtroom, because the judge presiding over the case ruled that they weren't pertinent, though they provide extremely interesting and disturbing glimpses of the inner workings at the phone company. For instance, depositions from Ashley and others disclosed that a former Southwestern Bell chairman, R. A. Goodson, once received a jeep valued at $2,500, a jeep the phone company had purchased for a Texas hunting ranch. In his deposition, Goodson called the vehicle a "misunderstanding." He said he never used it and reimbursed the company for it, though he confessed that the reimbursement was made following the filing of the Ashley-Gravitt suit.

The ranch itself seemed to operate under a shroud of secrecy. An 11,000-acre hunting preserve situated in Uvalde, in south central Texas, it was leased by Southwestern during the 1968–69 and 1969–70 hunting seasons. Public officials, journalists, and phone company executives, including then-chairman of AT&T, John deButts, were invited to the ranch to shoot at deer and quail from padded swivel chairs and carpeted shooting blinds. In his deposition, the Southwestern vice president of personnel said that he was told by his boss to lease the preserve in his own name and pay for it by personal check for which he would be reimbursed, because "I could get it cheaper" if the owner of the preserve didn't know the user would be Southwestern Bell. The ranch lease cost $30,000 for the two seasons, the phone company said. Not surprisingly, the preserve is no longer used.

The Texas Senate subcommittee also unearthed a five-day company conference of 136 Bell executives that was conducted in 1973 at the Six Flags Inn in Arlington, Texas. Bell seemingly spared no expense. According to the subcommittee findings, the conference cost telephone customers $1,650 for golf balls and tees, $500 for bag cleaning and shoe shining, $450 for golf caps, $3,600 for golf carts and lease of the golf course, $13,000 for liquor and beer, $18,800 for meals, and, among other expenses, $300 for daily room delivery of the *Dallas Morning News* and the *Wall Street Journal*.

Ashley, when it was his turn to take the witness stand, told his story of being framed by Southwestern because of his crusading acts. He confessed that he falsified expense forms himself, but claimed that he did it to disguise political payoffs. "I didn't take one penny of Bell money for my use ever. I spent a lot of money on whiskey and a lot of money on politicians."

Southwestern Bell presented a number of officials, including C. L. Todd, who testified that neither Ashley nor Gravitt had ever raised any ruckus about rate-making policies. Under questioning, Todd said that a number of other phone company employees had been found to have filed false vouchers or done other improper things, and they had been disciplined.

In scrambling to the defense, the company presented evidence that Gravitt had renovated his office at a cost of $220,000, adorning it with onyx decorations, gold-plated fixtures, teak wall paneling, and a system of lights, draperies, and locks that could be conveniently adjusted from a control panel on his desk. The company said that such expenditures showed that Gravitt wasn't fighting all that hard against corporate rapacity. Maloney retorted that such expenses were modest contrasted to what other company executives spent, but no evidence of this was ever offered.

Then, in the most scurrilous portion of the trial, Southwestern Bell called thirteen female witnesses and, one by one, they indexed for the jury a book of sexual escapades—a short course in office sex.

One woman said on the stand that Ashley had a widespread reputation of "being a woman chaser, likely to have women around him all of the time." Another female employee said, "He was known to be a dirty old man, and if you went to bed with him, you might get promoted." Still another witness said that she went on a plane ride in Gravitt's plane, and at one point he put it on automatic pilot and brusquely attempted to make love to her. Someone else charged that Ashley on occasion exhibited pornographic videotapes in his conference room to company employees. The videotapes were introduced into evidence, but weren't shown in the court.

A key escapade, testified to by a number of the women, was a three-day event in September of 1974 that took place at the San Antonio TraveLodge. Ashley, in his testimony, brushed it aside as a cocktail party he threw for a visiting councilman and a phone company manager from Denison, Texas. He said that, to the best of his knowledge, no sex went on there, though he said that he spent the night at the motel—alone. Ashley did tell me that "had there been sex there, it wouldn't have been unusual. Hanky-panky within the phone company is as old as the phone company. Promiscuity is all over there, but they were trying to say we were using our positions. That's not the way it works." According to the testimony of the women, however, there were three women employees invited from Southwestern, and at one point in the evening, they said, they paired off with the three men. There were two bedrooms in the suite, and the two women testified that they stole off to the bedrooms, one with Ashley and one with one of the other men, and had sex there. The third woman said that the man she was left with repeatedly attempted to make love to her on the couch, but she refused. "He didn't turn me on," she testified. Asked why she refused sex, she replied, "Well, everybody enjoys a good screw nowadays, but he just didn't turn me on. I have to get turned on first."

Some of the most important testimony came from Effie Montoya Rumsey, a management trainee at the time who had worked under Ashley in San Antonio. She testified that she slept with the councilman at the TraveLodge party. Asked why, she said, "I did it because, as I stated earlier, Mr. Ashley had told me that when he tells me to take care of somebody I should know what he means." She said she slept with Ashley on several occasions, because he made her feel "overly obliged." Addressing the question of Ashley's reputation, she remarked, "Mr. Ashley's reputation has always been one of vindictiveness, ruthlessness; he has always been known for his obscene remarks, his reference to sex in any respect, his promiscuity." She further testified that she was having an affair with a district manager of Southwestern in Midland, Texas, at one point, and one evening, after sleeping with him, he asked her to have sex with Ashley, and she obliged.

A woman named Juanita Bryant testified, "Mr. Ashley, when he would enter an office, would look at the girls' bosoms and at their legs, and he would only be interested in knowing whether or not he could proposition them if the opportunity came, and even if the opportunity did not come."

Another woman, when she was asked to supply an example of Ashley's crudeness, responded: "At one time, he urinated in a tree in my office."

"What happened to the tree?" she was asked.

"The tree died," she said.

A woman named Bernadette (Bunny) Heroux said that she slept with both Ashley and Gravitt, as well as some others. She testified that, among other things, she would come into Ashley's and Gravitt's offices and play with their penises until they climaxed.

On September 12, after five weeks of testimony from some fifty witnesses, the ten men and two women of the jury retreated to deliberate. Their verdict, when they returned, was that Ashley and Gravitt had indeed been slandered with an improper investigation by Southwestern Bell and that the company had indirectly provoked the mental illness and suicide of Gravitt. AT&T and C. L. Todd were cleared of all charges. The jury ordered Southwestern to pay Ashley and Gravitt's estate a total of $3 million. After the verdict was read, an exultant Ashley, one arm embracing his tearful wife, said that he was proud of his self-described role of nemesis of Southwestern Bell. "I think a Ralph Nader of the telephone industry has long been needed," he told reporters. "I'm very proud to be one." C. L. Todd derided the verdict as a "miscarriage of justice," and said it would be promptly appealed.

In February of 1978, an appeals court reversed the verdict in the wiretapping case, wiping out Ashley's award of $1 million. An appeal by Ashley to the Texas Supreme Court was subsequently denied. In November 1978, an appeals court overturned the slander verdict as well. The court ruled that Bell had a right to investigate allegations of sexual misconduct and other misdeeds when it got such reports. Pat Maloney declared, "Bell can count this as their most influential day. The people can count this as their blackest day. The rich get richer. It has always been my experience as an attorney that the further you get from a jury, the less the people prevail." No further vindication was actually to come. An appeal was issued to the Texas Supreme Court, which upheld the lower court ruling.

The Southwestern scandal remains a paradigm of uncertainty. The full truth will probably never be known. It provides the basis for whatever one wants to make of it. It seems somewhat unlikely that the Bell System could be as thoroughly corrupt as Ashley and Gravitt implied, or could be, in fact, much more corrupt than big business at large. It also seems improbable that thirteen women would get on the witness stand and testify to such sexual promiscuity if some of it wasn't going on. At the same time, things that weren't exactly cricket clearly did go on at Southwestern Bell and elsewhere in the Bell System, and the sensational nature of the case probably did some good in cleansing the company to some degree. To a certain extent though, the Southwestern ruckus seems to me a gigantic example of corporate infighting. It was all very suggestive and beguiling, but one wonders how much meat was there.

Though the scandal remains an overhanging cloud, with each passing year the cloud seems to drift higher in the sky. The durable remnants of the episode are a Texas Public Utility Commission with a tough stance on rate increases, some lingering suspicion in customers' minds about what goes on behind Bell's doors, and some evil memories for certain principal players. As a company, Southwestern Bell remains exuberantly solvent. In 1974, the big operating company earned $314.5 million, and ranked second in earnings among the Bell subsidiaries, behind only New York Telephone. In 1979, Southwestern earned $567 million and ranked first.

"The whole thing is kind of a dead issue," one Southwestern manager told me. "It just never seems to enter the conversation. People don't have it much on their minds anymore. They've got other worries. Mostly, they're concerned about getting gasoline and heating oil."

Still, the top officials of Southwestern remain extraordinarily touchy on the topic of the scandal. Zane Barnes, the president of the company, steadfastly refused repeated requests to be interviewed by me, and he said that other Southwestern executives were not to discuss the case with me either. He even declined to give a reason, though I had heard that he was mightily displeased by what he considered to be highly unfair and distorted coverage of the scandal by the press. The Southwestern people were the only Bell employees, of the several hundred I had asked, who ever turned down a request for an interview.

Bill Holman, the former division manager in Austin under Jim Ashley, had no problems talking to me when I phoned him. He said that a year and a half ago, at his request, he had been transferred to a lower-rung position in Dallas. He was in charge of all customer complaints from the state of Texas. Despite the lower position, he said he was earning more money. He said he wanted the job because "I just didn't like Austin." I asked him if he knew of any firings since the case (knowing that he himself could have been considered prime firing material). He replied, "I don't know of a soul who was fired. I think I would have known had there been any. Nope, we're still all on board." He said he had never been admonished in any way by the company and didn't think many people had been.

When I asked him about Jim Ashley, he said, "When I worked for him, I didn't see this side of him. It was a difference between him and the company. I bear him no animosity."

Did he think false vouchering still went on?

"Let me put it this way," he answered, "I don't get involved in making out vouchers anymore unless when I go on an out-of-town trip, which is very occasionally, and I just cover expenses. I don't even like to hear the word 'voucher' anymore."

When I got in touch with Oleta Gravitt, T. O. Gravitt's widow, she politely declined my request to visit her. She said it got to be too painful for her to review the case. But she spoke with me on the phone a bit about how her life was going. In 1976, she married Robert Dixon, a manager in the chemicals group of Phillips Petroleum. She had been introduced to him by T. O. Gravitt's brother. They were living in Bartlesville, Oklahoma, and were financially secure.

"You never get over the hurt," she said. "The hurt is always there. I don't want to feel bitter against anybody. You can't live with hate, because it's so destructive. So I don't want to feel any hate. You feel frustration. You feel deep, deep hurt. But I don't want to feel any hate." She hesitated, then went on, "I pray some day that the phone company's conscience will bother them and they will tell the truth. They have to live with their conscience, and I'm not so sure they can."

Mrs. Dixon said that she did some fishing for bass and catfish "though I'm not sure which is which," she liked to garden, and she was basically a homebody. "I'm trying to go on with my life without this concerning me," she said. "It's always in the back of your mind. But you have to carry on. In time, the extraordinary becomes the ordinary and you go on."

Michael, her elder son, was selling real estate in Dallas, as he had been when the scandal broke. Patrick, the younger son, had recently left the Navy and was hunting for work as a commercial airline pilot. Both of them told me that they rarely talked about the case anymore.

Pat Maloney has done all right by the Southwestern case. "It was a gigantic process," he told me in his posh San Antonio office, housed in what formerly was a bank and which had the look of a small castle from the outside. We were drinking beer in his "Lone Star Room," on the top floor, where there was an impressive bar, comfortable furniture, and sliding glass doors that debouched onto a lush roof garden. "It was four full years of tremendous endeavor, both financially and physically," Maloney said wistfully. "But we pulled through nicely." Toward the end of the trial, after shelling out some $400,000 of his own money, Maloney said he began to feel a financial pinch. But he rebounded.

"We can only look back fondly," he said. "It's sort of like the Marine Corps. You don't want to repeat it. The case provided us with a national reputation and platform. We had a reputation, but not on that scale. Since the case, we have had far, far more business than we ever had before. It quadrupled. We have to turn away cases. As you might guess, these are cases by people with grievances against big corporations. Employees who feel that they've been wronged."

Maloney refilled his beer mug, took a swig, then continued, "Since that case, I am so totally accepted and regarded among advocates. That was the high point, the apex, the pinnacle. I am far better off financially now then ever before. Now I even look warmly on Bell, though I know them to be so damnably corrupt, because they have allowed me to attain the professional reputation that I have."

In a sense, it seemed to me as if Maloney perhaps secretly missed the case.

"I doubt I'll ever see a hill that steep again," he said. "That mother was slippery."

When I found Jim Ashley at his Blanco real estate office, nearly five years since his dismissal from Southwestern Bell, he was chipper and full of fun. He was just finishing up surveying some maps with a client, a man in ragamuffin jeans and a gingham shirt. After he bid the man good-bye, Ashley plopped heavily into his desk chair, and I asked him if he was bitter toward Bell.

Sitting in the dulling light of the late afternoon, the phones in the office finally quiet, he reflected, "I have no hatred for Bell per se. My quarrel has been with their corporate people. I think Bell provides a fine service. I think it needs to be better regulated. I'm shocked at my experiences with the legal system. I am convinced that the system is swayed in favor of the powerful and the rich. I don't regret having worked for Bell. I think, historically, Bell has had some fine qualities. I don't think it's that much different from other corporations. It's just so much more dangerous because of the power it has. How much power is it for Gravitt to be able to place a hundred million dollars a month in bank deposits? How powerful are you with customers if you're letting contracts for three hundred million dollars a year? Legal fees? How much influence do you have in the legal industry if you keep large numbers of law firms on retainer for fifty thousand dollars or a hundred thousand dollars a year? That's one state. Multiply it out. I'm saying you just can't realize how damn big this company is."

Ashley raised himself in his seat, folded his arms across his chest.

"No, I'm not bitter toward Bell," he continued. "It gave me a lot of good training. I think Bell people are basically fine. I'm not eating myself away with bitterness. I just feel strongly that Bell has to keep its act clean."

"Is it keeping it clean?" I asked.

"I think the Texas Commission would never be around today if not for my suit. That's done some good. I think there has been a lot of surface good done. Mother Bell has been forced to do some sweeping up. But I don't think it will hold true for the long pull. It's the same management, remember. They still feel that what's good for Bell is good for the country."

Any bitterness Ashley might have felt has doubtless been somewhat assuaged by the considerable financial prosperity he suddenly found himself in. He had been doing well at the phone company, but he was doing far better now, in large part, it appeared, because of the ruckus he stirred up. His business, he told me, embraced six offices. He had forty-five employees. The company was raking in between $15 and $18 million a year, Ashley said, and his personal income was "well into six figures." Ashley lived on a 28-acre ranch, with a stone house, parts of which dated back a hundred years. He owned two horses. The Blanco River gurgled not far from the front door. Ashley described living there as "like joining the cast of the Waltons."

I asked Ashley how he spent his days now that the corporate life was behind him.

"I work," he said. "Real estate keeps me pretty busy. I like to garden. We have a couple of horses that we like to ride. I like being a homebody, frankly. Not a whole hell of a lot to do in Blanco."

I asked Bonnie Ashley, who had stood by her husband all through the mess, if she felt any bitterness.

"Let me express it this way," she said. "I wouldn't trade my life today for my life then for anything. This is a genuine, wholesome life. That was a fake, artificial life. So far as bitterness, I don't think there's any bitterness. I don't think much of those Bell people. They were not honest. They were malicious. I think the phone company would like to forget Jim, but I don't think they ever will."

The suit had done wonders for business, even now after the initial victories had been converted into defeats. I asked Ashley about the impact on his business, and he said, "I've literally had hundreds of people call me and visit me. We've had people come in and say they wanted to do business with me because I'm the one who had the courage to fight Bell. If you took a poll, Ashley or Bell, I think I'd poll ninety-five percent. The reversal has helped me even more. People were incensed. They couldn't believe that money could overturn jury decisions. In the eye of the public, I've won my cases. Many of my allegations have been proved."

"Do you miss the corporate life?" I asked.

"Not a bit," Ashley smiled. "I've had my chances to go back. I've had some lucrative offers from Bell competitors. But under no circumstances would I go back. I like the more civil life I'm leading now. More important, if I do well in the real estate business, I profit. If I do poorly, I'm penalized. In the corporate world, how well you do is largely tied to politics. And that's for the birds."

And then he had to make a call. He excused himself and picked up the phone. The label on it identified the manufacturer—GTE.

17

Where Fingers Walk

The most widely read book in the country is not the Bible. It is not the dictionary. It is the Yellow Pages.

Anyplace in the United States, if you were to throw a pebble into a crowd, chances are you would hit somebody who had used the Yellow Pages in the past week. Day by day, city to city, the Yellow Pages are the most evident link between consumers and businesses. The precise extent of their use is not generally realized. The truth is, according to market research by AT&T, that the fingers of more than one hundred and nineteen million people walk through the Yellow Pages something like 17 billion times each year. What do they dig for? They mainly sift for information on auto repair, on auto parts and supplies, restaurants, building materials, hotels and motels, and banks. A phone company analysis suggests that the bulk of Yellow Pages users proceed to follow up their consultations with a phone call, a visit, or, in moments of great patience, a letter.

In all, the Bell System puts out for subscribers' fingers a profusion of twenty-nine hundred separate directories. In addition, the sixteen hundred independent telephone companies grind out another twenty-four hundred of them in corners of the country where no Bell phones ring. And there are a miscellany of perhaps a thousand neighborhood directories churned out by non-telephone companies, ranging from PTA or Chamber of Commerce handouts to fairly good-sized books. By far, though, the Bell System is the Olympus of Yellow Pages. It would take an Everest climb by any of its competitors to catch up. And, to Ma Bell's considerable delight, except in California the Yellow Pages are not subject to any regulation, unlike the myriad telecommunications services AT&T engages in. This is one big reason why the pages are possibly the most prosperous thing AT&T does. In 1979, for example, revenues from the Yellow Pages stood at about $1.81 billion. The net profit on that was roughly $404 million. Although the revenues count up to only one-sixth of those of the vast Western Electric, the profits amount to almost two-thirds of Western's. The Yellow Pages have done a lot to put AT&T on Easy Street. Every year, the golden harvest escalates breathtakingly.

Classified directories have a lengthy history. They are even older than telephone service. Before the phone was invented, R. R. Donnelley, the giant Chicago printer, used to publish lists of city businesses. When the phone was invented, Donnelley shrewdly threw in phone numbers. The first Bell System directory came out in New Haven, Connecticut, in 1878. It was all of a single page—in white. It included six business listings: Physicians; Dentists; Stores, Factories, etc.; Meat and Fish Markets; Miscellaneous; and Hack and Boarding Stables. Cheyenne, Wyoming, had the distinction of being the first city to publish on yellow pages. The reason is unclear, though subsequent studies by Bell Laboratories have proven that, after black on white, black on dark yellow affords the best visibility. Black on blue limps in third. These studies hurried the replacement of the early canary yellow color with the current deeper shade. The five thickest Yellow Pages today appear, in order, in Chicago (a yellow mound of 2,896 pages), Houston, Los Angeles, Orange County, and Manhattan.

The Yellow Pages' raison d'etre, of course, is to serve as a directory for commercial enterprises, but with so many of the bulky beauties in circulation, auxiliary uses have inevitably cropped up. For instance, a number of pianists have been known to put them on their benches when they play. Directories have been chopped up as confetti for numerous ticker tape parades. Secret agents have been known to employ them as coding devices, often rooting their alphabetical key in the first and last listings on a given page. South American companies reportedly have found them handy for lining the walls of railway cars and payroll trucks to make them bulletproof. People have used classified directories as the informal equivalent of safe deposit boxes, stuffing them with love letters, deeds, wedding certificates, savings bonds, lottery tickets, stamp collections, insurance policies, and money. A New England shopkeeper, phone historians report, once stashed $1,500 in his phone book, only to discover the directory missing one morning. The local telephone company collected old directories when it issued new ones. The man was invited down to hunt through the collected pile of more than a hundred thousand directories. Three days later, the shopkeeper found his money, in the seventy-five thousandth book.

Edward Hancharik, AT&T's dapper, personable director of directory operations, speaks about his books with a palpable fondness. Hancharik is a born salesman, able to spice the honeyed smoothness of the modern public relations man with a touch of the old carnival pitchman's uninhibited spirit. Most of his working hours and apparently his night thoughts as well are concerned with publicity relating to the Yellow Pages in one way or another. He looks on any suggestion of regulation with comparatively temperate enthusiasm. Why regulate, he asks, when anyone can put out some Yellow Pages, and he staunchly maintains that the meaty profits garnered by the books do substantial good in keeping phone bills affordable. "We're glad we make so much money, because we can help keep those phone bills low," he crowed to me one day recently. "Nothing wrong with that. We have never had any sort of monopoly on the directory business. No monopoly at all. Anyone is free to enter the business. There are competitors who I think are doing quite a fine job. All power to them." The notion of regulating the Yellow Pages has been taken up by public utilities commissions and the courts on a number of occasions, but in each instance (except in California, which is looking to soon cease regulation itself), it's been ruled that the Yellow Pages are neither a public service nor a public utility, and thus don't come under the umbrella of the commissions.

Outside of California, the parishioners of the individual telephone companies can fix advertising rates however their wallets desire. Rates giddy all over. They seem to reflect how much the market can bear. Many advertisers confess that they find themselves hopelessly bewildered when they pore over rate charts. "I feel like I'm reading my mother-in-law's checking account records," one advertiser said to me. Another ad executive told me, "They are like no other advertising medium, that's for sure. They don't follow any of the normal rules. Rates have nothing to do with circulation. They have nothing to do with anything that I can figure out. Yet you've got to be in them. Everybody reads them. In short, they're kooky."

For instance, a quarter-page display ad in the Manhattan Yellow Pages goes for $4,579 a year. In St. Louis, that sized ad fetches $4,680. In Houston, the rate is $6,300, steepest in the country. ("What do you expect in oil country?" a man at an advertising agency said.) Even rates in cities of identical populations fluctuate sharply. In Barnesville, Georgia (pop. 10,000), a quarter page ad is $472. In Southport, North Carolina (pop. 10,000), it is $468. In Liberty, Texas (pop. 10,000), it is $1,116. Moving up, in Tulsa, Oklahoma (pop. 331,000) the rate is $3,504. In Columbia, South Carolina (pop. 330,000), it's $2,325. "You want to know what determines rates?" an advertiser asked me. "I'll tell you. Good old American greed, that's what."

Anyone with a business phone gets himself a free one-line listing in the pages. Everything else costs. Ads can be listed in almost any form combining the "bold listings," "anchor listings," "space listings," "trade items," and "display ads." Every added detail pushes the rate a little higher. To compound the fun (and profits), the Bell companies offer their Yellow Pages advertisers a bewildering thirteen thousand different headings under which to appear. A furniture rental company, for example, has available to it no fewer than nine headings—from "Bedding" to "Tables." Headings come and go. Phone company people convene on an annual basis to toss around headings. Some fairly new ones include: Skateboard Parks and Rinks, Bagels, Spill Control Service, Industrial Hygiene Consultants, Roommate Referral Service, T-shirts, and Cave Exploration Equipment and Supplies. AT&T policy prohibits prices in Yellow Pages ads, something that had been allowed until the early 1950s. Thus, Bobo's Super-Duper Walnut Shop can't advertise "the tastiest walnut on this good earth for just two cents." The reasoning of the phone company is that prices change quicker than directories, and so the public might be too easily led down the wrong path.

The accuracy of Yellow Pages listings wavers from company to company. AT&T claims it does yeoman service in making the pages as accurate as possible, maintaining that its directories, lumped together, are 99.98 percent accurate. Working with a staggering number of listings, the directories do on occasion misspell names or omit a business altogether, and inaccuracies have spurred a tall stack of law suits. They usually flop, however, because the plaintiff is unable to prove "malicious intent."

Up until several years ago, I was intrigued to find out, the Bell System employed thousands of people who literally did nothing but go bleary-eyed proofreading directory pages. "We used to have zillions of these chaps," Ed Hancharik told me. "We couldn't find enough people to do the work. When a really big book was closing, we would have to hire part-timers from the Kelly Girl agency and whatnot." Now, however, directory data is stored in and printed by computer, and the proofreading calling has gone by the boards. The computers themselves are programmed to snoop for errors. "For instance, we have street tables stored in the computers," Hancharik said, "and the computer will validate that a street in an ad is actually a street and it's spelled right. We do still have a Quality Control Group in each operating company that checks the veracity of our display ads. Say a florist wants his ad to report that he's been in business since 1955 and he's open every night and he's a member of FDA. We make sure of these things. Our checkers take out any obscenities and we shun superlatives —the only, the best. We don't allow an ad that says, 'I'm the best plumber in town.' That knocks every other plumber, and how do we know who's the best plumber?"

There are some in this country who would like to see some massive changes in directory practices. One of these people is Eric Selten, who owns the Selten Agency, an ad shop in Los Angeles founded by his mother that does nothing but Yellow Pages advertising. Selten is peeved about a number of things—errors that he contends are as high as half of the listings he places, commissions that he says are lower for him than for others. Consequently, he filed an antitrust action against most of the Bell System operating companies and some independent phone companies in late 1977. Since then, he says some clients have been all but blackballed by certain Bell companies. Terry Breese, the ad manager for Miller's Outpost, a sizable retailing outfit that advertises in some one hundred directories, told me that he has been bumped out of a half-dozen directories with no advance notice because he's a Selten client. Jack Krinsky, president of Ad Visor, another specialist in Yellow Pages advertising based in Long Beach, California, who also has filed an antitrust suit against a number of telephone companies, told me, "There are loads of errors in those books. One year, they even printed our own address wrong."

Ed Hancharik is galled when the subject of errors is raised. When I spoke with him, he declared, with a smile glued on his face, "Errors are an unfortunate eventuality when you deal with this quantity of listings. I mean, imagine all the possibilities for errors.

When you consider how few we have, I think we do a hell of a job."

Apart from errors, a broad array of smoky disputes has been touched off over the years. One consumer complaint that keeps trickling in has to do with the fact that some companies get away with listing themselves under a batch of different names. They have the phone company install phones at assorted addresses where they may have nothing but that phone—and then arrange to have all the calls routed to one office. The phone company points out that there is nothing wrong with this, though consumers protest that they often wind up being misled. Some people have been disappointed with the work of a repair company, so next time they try another firm, only to find out that it's the same company bearing a different name so that it lands still another treasured directory listing. A Cleveland company called ABC Appliance was listed with as many as a dozen different addresses and names. Only one was, in fact, the ABC office. The remainder included an office building, a drapery company, a private home, and an apartment complex. As a result of an agreement struck with the Ohio attorney general's office, the company abandoned that practice and now lists only neighborhoods, such as "Broadway Ave. Area" alongside its phone numbers. The phone company, in an effort to stifle some of these problems, has begun to insert more warnings and disclaimers in directories. A few directories, for example, carry the caution that "business subscribers are sometimes known by more than one name and often do business and advertise under different names."

Businesses have come to exhibit an ineluctably stubborn passion to get top billing in the alphabetical listings in directories, figuring subscribers often call the first place they come across under a heading, rather than wear their fingers out moving any further down the list. Thus the Yellow Pages are packed with wacky names. In Oklahoma, there was a case involving a pest control company that wanted to land a choice spot in the directory by naming the company AAAAAAAAAAAAAAAAAAAAAAA Pest Control. The phone company said no way. It was expensive listing all those As (twenty-three of them) and others might soon follow with even more As. The pest control company sued. Ma Bell won. Several years ago, a crafty New Jersey sewer-cleaning outfit had no better success in trying to slip into the Yellow Pages simply as "A."

One of the oddest pages of directory history concerns the

escapades of the Krasilovsky family. Mike Krasilousky Trucking & Millwright Company (the "u" in Krasilousky is significant) is a large Brooklyn trucking firm that specializes in moving heavy machinery, huge statues, and other things even Hercules might have had trouble with. It once moved twelve tons of bells into a church. It moved an atom smasher into Mount Sinai Hospital. It swung four Univac computers through a third-story window at Remington Rand after they said it couldn't be done. The company originated in 1939, when the late Mike Krasilovsky broke away from his uncle's firm, called S. Krasilovsky & Brothers. The two Krasilovsky firms began to steal each other's customers, who rarely knew which Krasilovsky they were dealing with. So Mike began spelling his last name with a "u" so that he would vault ahead in the Yellow Pages' listings of riggers. "Krasilousky," his theory was, would stop anybody. Then one of Mike's cousins, Milton Krasilovsky, entered the moving business. A bright young fellow, he changed his telephone name to Mick, a misnomer that at first glance looks like Mike, and he dropped the "v" from his last name altogether, pushing him ahead in the "Krasilo(v)(u)sky" listings. Undaunted, Mike took over the Atlas-York Safe Corporation, leapfrogging ahead while retaining the "Krasilousky" listing. But then one of Milton's cousins acquired the Acme Safe Company. Mike retaliated with Ace Trucking Company, and for good measure, tossed in the J. P. Nolan Company, Inc. Then another bright cousin of Milton's, Marvin, inspired the AAA Acme Krasilovsky Safe Company. Mike unimaginatively threw in the towel. During the war of names, Mike managed to run his listings up to eighteen, five more than Milton. Many customers, needless to say, were totally baffled as to just who it was they were doing business with.

A private eye once resorted to legal action because the directory refused to include in his ad the fact that he offered the ability to "debug" a person's premises. The directory's grounds had been that he who can debug can also bug, and bugging happens to be illegal. The private eye sued. He lost. A Woodbridge, Connecticut, physician initiated a $100,000 damage suit against the Southern New England Telephone Company, accusing it of improperly listing his specialty in the Yellow Pages as "osteopath" instead of "obstetrician." The physician contended in the suit that the incorrect listing resulted in lost business and caused damage to his professional reputation. The case was resolved out of court. Among other things, the phone company promised to get the listing right the next time around. In July 1974, a woman lawyer accused the Illinois Bell Telephone Company of dropping her name from both the Chicago telephone directory and its information listing after she began to represent a small communications concern in legal actions against the telephone company. Charging harassment, she filed a lawsuit in Cook County Circuit Court seeking $750,000 in aggregate damages. Illinois Bell insists that the omission of her name from the phone book and information listing had been purely an accident. The case is still pending. In Victorian fashion, Ma Bell also spurned an ad submitted for one of its Yellow Pages by a Chinese restaurant that bore the headline: "Food and sex are human nature." The company blanched at the use of the word "sex," and suggested it might be changed to love. Ma Bell was totally unimpressed by the restaurant's explanation that the phrase had been uttered by Confucius in 500 B.C.

The enormous success of the Yellow Pages is in no small way traceable to the highly potent advertising campaign that has been craftily engineered for them. For most of a century, the pages have been assiduously calling attention to themselves with practically every known means of communications short of skywriting. The Bell System, all told, spends roughly $18 million a year breathlessly, earnestly, convincingly touting the Yellow Pages. For the last fifteen years, the campaign has been "Let Your Fingers Do the Walking Through the Yellow Pages," one of the most familiar slogans in America. The accompanying emblem, giant fingers traipsing through the pages, is one of the best known emblems. Not long ago, AT&T took the trouble to show an assortment of emblems to a sampling of the population, to see if they could match up the right emblems with the appropriate products. About 86 percent of them got the big fingers correct, more than identified any of the other emblems. The CBS eye was a distant second.

An AT&T ad manager told me recently, "The advertising to get people to use the Yellow Pages is very important, since this makes the books all the more valuable to advertisers. A likely side benefit, I need not mention, is that people will get on that phone more. Actually, we've begun to redirect the campaign from the idea of just urging people to look things up in the Yellow Pages to having them look something up, then phone ahead to make sure that the product they're interested in is in stock before they head over to the merchant. This means people will make more calls. Handling phone calls, after all, is our real business."

18

And at the Tone . . .

In New York City, the number is 936–1616. In Boston, it is 637–1234. In San Francisco, it's 767–2676. In Miami, it's 324–8811. And in Pocatello, Idaho, it's 232–4570. Dial any of them and you get the Time of Day. Forty-two million people—give or take a few thousand—call the New York number every year. Chicagoans, presumably more time-attentive, dial the time 57 million times a year. Every day, between 10 and 15 percent of all of the nation's telephones in some two thousand cities across the country are answered by a mellifluous voice that crisply recites the precise Time of Day.

To all callers, the telephone company gladly dispenses the time, the weather, and such dial service renditions as off-track betting dope, jokes, nursery rhymes, sports briefs, trivia, and the Dow Jones stock report. In New York, the dial-number capital, you can pick from fourteen different possibilities and spend the entire day on the phone listening to recordings. What it comes down to is show biz, AT&T sheepishly admits, but the money is good. All told, AT&T adds more than $100 million a year to its tills from the recorded messages, and being that the costs are fairly negligible, they are one of its most profitable services.

As it happens, Ma Bell doesn't make its own time machines, but rents them from a practically unheard-of little entity called the Audichron Company. Long curious about what was behind the Time of Day, I couldn't resist a diversion to Audichron. Its headquarters, wide and low, reach across a considerable stretch of asphalt in a bland industrial park north of Atlanta, Georgia. Walter Walker, the president of the firm, a husky, courtly man in a conservative gray suit, was all smiles when he greeted me. He had good reason to be pleased. For nearly half a century, his company has manufactured the Time of Day for just about the entire United States. If there were no more watches or clocks, the country would depend on Audichron to know what time it was.

Settled in his spare but comfy office, with its harmonious walls of unobtrusive beige, in a chair that seemed to envelop him, Walker ran down the company history for me with relish. The Audichron time machine, he explained, was the product of the mind of one man. His name was John Franklin. Franklin started out in the ministry and did things like work in the retail tire business. His hobby, though, was making clocks. For a period in the 1920s, he brewed a product called Tick Tock Ginger Ale, and to get people to drink it he concocted billboards that boasted working clocks, known as Tick Tock Clocks. Back in those days, when people were desperate to know what time it was, they would proceed to call up the telephone operator, and she'd take a peek at her watch, which might or might not have been wound that day, and report the time. Reasonably reliable. But it ate up precious time that the operator was supposed to be using to connect calls. The phone company was kind of miffed at all these operators peering at their watches and singing out the time. Franklin caught wind of the need for a time machine, and he looked into the matter. Inspiration struck. One momentous day in 1924, he recorded himself announcing the time, minute by minute, on the sound track of some motion picture film. Using a razor blade, he then sliced the sound track off the film and wrapped it around a chromium drum. He hooked up a motor-driven pickup head, connected a speaker, and had himself the very first time machine.

Initially, Franklin rented his time machines to local business-es. They would order additional phone lines from the phone company, hook up the time machines to them, and then devise promotional campaigns tied to the Time of Day. One of Franklin's first clients was the Coca-Cola Company. The machines were an immediate hit, and Franklin had no trouble wooing an avalanche of customers. People called in swarms. It seemed that nobody knew what time it was. Seeing all this action, the phone company shrewdly mentioned to Franklin that, by the way, it would be very happy to buy his machines and install them in its central offices.

Nope, nope, nope, Franklin said. He wasn't about to sell any of his time machines. He knew they were gold mines. Instead, he formed the Audichron Company and leased his gadgets to phone companies. The phone companies, in order to reap some revenue of their own, then went and sold commercial sponsorship of Time of Day recordings to businesses. These businesses then paraded over to Audichron and paid it to record the time and the commercial messages. (Only in a few big cities, like New York, does the time come free of commercial plugs.) Audichron had it made. Franklin died in 1962, and he left a trust that owns the majority of the company. The employees own the rest.

"We've gotten into more sophisticated eqiupment now, of course," Walker told me. "Our machines use a magnetic drum rather than film. Our top machine is accurate to within one millisecond. That's pretty damned good." Walker explained that there are three basic models. One employs a tone ("At the tone, the time is one fifty-three"), and is unadorned of commercials. It gets used in places like New York, Los Angeles, Chicago, and Washington, D.C. People in these places pay for all of their local calls, and there has been some nasty public reaction to getting a commercial on a call that you're paying for in the first place. A second model plays a new commercial for every hour and announces the time only to the minute. It's used in small towns. The third version, found in cities the size of Atlanta and Houston, switches on a new commercial every ten seconds and offers a choice of the time in seconds or minutes. The machines, half of which are leased to the Bell System, go for between $125 and $1,000 a month.

"We're about sixty percent saturated domestically," Walker said, "so we expect to do some more growing. We've got our machines in South America, the Philippines, Hong Kong, Singapore, Australia."

I asked Walker what kind of money could be made in time machines, and he replied, "Well, we're grossing about ten million dollars a year, and we net about a million and a half. So it's a pretty nifty business."

At Walker's invitation, I accompanied him across the street to another Audichron facility, where the machines were actually made. We moseyed over to a table on which a horde of glistening time machines stood. Each machine was light gray in color and about the size of a microwave oven. The commercial drum was affixed to one end, and the time drum to the other. The machines were engineered to work twenty-four hours a day, Walker explained, with a failure rate of just once every twenty years.

"We don't just do time," Walker pointed out, "although that's still the big one. We have weather machines. We've got a staff of meteorologists who do the forecasting for Bell for the whole state of New Jersey, among other places. All told, we do weather for fifty cities right now. We've got a Santa Claus announcement. And we do operator intercept announcements. You know, they go, 'I'm sorry, the number you have reached is not in service.' Then, when you've got a new listing, they report the new number. We also do recordings for coin phones. 'Your time is up, please deposit five cents for the next three minutes.' A brand-new product we have is an automatic wake-up machine for hotels. It can dial as many as twenty rooms simultaneously and wake you up with time and temperature. We've got one working at the Peachtree Hotel here in Atlanta."

Walker flicked on one of the machines and handed me a pair of earphones. I slipped them on and heard, "Cool tonight, sunny and warm tomorrow."

Satisfied with the forecast, I removed the earphones, and Walker quickly handed me a second set. "At the tone, time, four-sixteen and fourteen seconds," purred a female voice.

Walker hoisted the cover off the machine and pointed out the drums. "See, this belt is hours," he said. "It revolves one complete time every twelve hours. The middle belt is minutes and does a sixtieth of a revolution every minute. The third belt is the seconds and tones.

"For the weather machines, we have built in a thing called traffic load protection," Walker continued. "This automatically abbreviates the message when calling volume zooms to high levels. What we do is record the announcement in segments, such as today's weather, tomorrow's forecast, and the sponsor's message. When a storm, say, drives volume up for the weather, the load protection feature cuts down the length of the announcement cutting out, say, the forecast so we can still handle all the calls."

The deluxe model of the time machine, Walker explained, has a comparator unit in it to regulate its accuracy. A signal is beamed into the unit from WWV, the National Bureau of Standards shortwave station in Fort Collins, Colorado, home of an atomic clock by which the entire world sets its timepieces. WWV does nothing but broadcast the time all day. The Audichron comparator unit checks its time with the WWV time, and if they drift more than a few milliseconds apart, the unit automatically adjusts the machine's time so that it is just right. Interestingly, Walker told me, the Bureau of Standards uses one of the Audichron devices and master tapes for its WWV broadcast. Live announcers, no matter how hard they might want to break into the radio business, would find the job of announcing the time all day a bit onerous.

I asked Walker who the sponsors were, and he replied, "Most sponsors are financial institutions. The commercial length is just five seconds, which isn't adequate to really describe a product. People, we find, aren't going to listen for more than five seconds. So the medium is best suited to sponsors looking for institutional advertising. It's banks and savings and loan associations. We do get some others. We had a Baptist church in Memphis. Several used car dealers. A fried chicken place in New Orleans. An undertaker, too. But these are rare."

"What about the voices on the tapes?" I asked.

Walker said that the company has two male voices and one female. A sponsor gets his pick. Northwestern cities generally prefer a woman's voice, Walker said, while the western and southern cities go for the man. "The idea is to get a neutral voice and a voice that won't change. We have to constantly change the commercials, but we like to use the same time drums with the new commercials. If the voice doesn't match, we've got troubles." Don Elliot Heald, the general manager of WSB-TV in Atlanta, is the veteran voice of the crew, having recited the time for more than a quarter of a century. But the most famous voice, I knew, was that of Audichron's female announcer—Jane Barbe, the Time Lady.

Jane Barbe's voice is etched in the memory of almost everybody who calls up the time. Dial it up in more than half the cities that offer it and Jane's on the other end. A whopping 8 million people hear Jane on Time of Day every day. In a typical year in a typical city, the phone company has reported, she answers the phone about 100 million times. Jane has been recording the time for fifteen years now, and she shows no sign of slowing up.

In an affluent residential district of Atlanta stands 5055 Highpoint Road, on an avenue of comparably spacious split-levels and ranch homes with broad, tree-shaded lawns. Once my interviewing with Walt Walker came to an end, I packed up my notes, thanked him, and drove in my rental car up the winding driveway to 5055 Highpoint. I pressed the doorbell, and, after a long pause, there was a snapping of locks. The door opened wide to reveal a sunburnt redhead with blue eyes, a pretty face, and a perpetual smile. She made an immediate impression of contained energy and precisely focused intensity. She nodded and beckoned me in. This was Jane Barbe.

The living room included two fireplaces, and a white shag rug snuggled the floor. I eased into a love seat while Jane poured me some coffee. "I'm sorry, I've only got instant," she apologized. "I sure hope you don't mind." I had heard Jane's voice on innumerable occasions when I dialed the time or weather in New York, and I had heard it again just a few hours ago over at the Audichron studios. But now it sounded out of whack. Jane has a distinctive Southern twang. When she gives out the time or informs you that your best friend's phone has been disconnected, there's no accent. I remarked on this, and Jane explained, "This is me you're talking to now. When I'm working, I lose the accent. It's not very hard to do, if you're a professional. That's not me you hear on the phone. That's the working me."

Reassured by this explanation, I asked Jane how she fell into the Time of Day business.

She said she found time in 1962. She had met her husband, John, shortly before that, when the two of them were under contract with the Buddy Morrow Orchestra. John wrote commercial jingles (as he still does), and Jane did freelance voice work for commercials (as she still does). A friend brought her to the attention of the producer at Audichron, she took an audition, and the rest, as they say, is history.

"At first, it was such a complete switch from doing regular commercial work," Jane said. "You see, you don't record the time by saying, 'Four forty-eight.' What you do is you start with the hours. You say, 'Time one . . . time two . . . time three . . .' and go all the way through the hours before you start doing the minutes. You just count through them. 'Ten . . . eleven . . . twelve . . . thirteen.' In New York, they have the tone, and so for that I say, 'At the tone, the time is one . . . two . . . three.' And then you do the minutes separately also. Everything, you see, is done in little bits and pieces and then it all gets matched up."

"How often do you record?" I asked.

"I go in every week, sometimes several times a week," Jane answered. "It's mostly to do new commercials. About twice a year we have to redo the time, because the voice is always changing and you want the time tape to sound the same as the latest commercial tapes. The voice is such a funny thing, I tell you."

I asked Jane if she changed her voice at all to suit a particular area of the country.

"Not really," she said. "I do do what I call an attitude. For the Northeast, I make the delivery a little crisper and put a smidgeon more harshness to the voice, because people are always in a rush up there. They're scampering all over the place. Goodness, I don't know how they stay sane. In Texas, though, I'll try to make it a little softer and take the edge off the voice. They take life a little easier in Texas."

"Are there any tricks of the trade?"

"Yes, there are," she said. "I must concentrate and literally think of somebody to whom I'm speaking. I make up faces, names. I must be talking to somebody or I'll just sound like a machine. I'll sound like a robot. Nobody wants to pick up the phone and hear a robot. Goodness, I'd just hang up on me if I sounded like a machine."

"Who are these people you talk to?"

"Sometimes, it's a little old lady with her galoshes on. Sometimes, it's a business man with a gray pin-striped suit and a red necktie and black shoes. I get pretty specific. Sometimes, it's a little blonde-haired kid with his roller skates on. It could be anybody. Whatever pops into my head. You know, it pays to sound human, because I get calls and letters from people who want to know who the Time Lady is. I got a Christmas card from an old lady who said she called me every morning for the weather so she'd know how to dress. I got a letter from a blind woman who said she was lonely and she called me all the time, because I sounded nice and friendly."

"How do the temperatures work?" I asked.

"With temperatures, we start at forty below and go on up to a hundred and twenty above. Obviously, we don't use all of these all that much. I mean, that's pretty hot and pretty cold, isn't it?"

Jane chuckled to herself, and then she fairly burst out with, "Every week, I do slews of operator intercept messages. I do each number individually twice, once with a falling inflection and once with a rising inflection. That way, Audichron can mix them up so they sound human. When they had that big fire in New York, I did a thousand, just a thousand, intercept messages. 'Due to an emergency, this exchange is temporarily out of service.' I did Mrs. Santa Claus last Christmas in New York. I just can't keep track of the cities I'm in. I know I'm in Las Vegas, San Francisco, New York, Los Angeles. In Los Angeles, they used to call me the Popcorn Lady, because you would dial POPCORN to get the time. I'm also the wake-up voice in the Peachtree Hotel. I say, 'Good morning, Peachtree time is six twenty-two. Breakfast is now being served in the Carousel Lounge.' I could go there and wake myself up. I did horoscopes for a while, too, but we don't do that anymore. We had a little trouble with the horoscope writer. She was too specific. She would say things like, 'Go out and buy some railroad stocks.' Well, you can imagine Audichron's legal problems. Woowhee! So I rewrote them a little. But we don't do them anymore."

"How much longer will you do the time?" I asked.

"Oh, I don't know," she said. "As long as my voice holds up, I guess. I still love it. I'm never bored. You know, my daughter, Susan, who's seventeen, has done a couple of intercept messages that have been put into service. Audichron, though, says she needs to mature a little. I would be honored to have her succeed me someday."

"Did you ever dial yourself for the time?" I asked Jane.

"Well, I'll tell you," she said. "I've never been in the habit of dialing the time, because I always wear a watch and I'm very conscious of what time it is. If everyone were like me, I'd be out of business. I remember, though, the first time I got myself. I was calling Western Union about a telegram, and the number had been changed and, lo and behold, I got myself on the intercept announcement. Well, it's like the first time you look in a mirror and see yourself. I was so startled that I hung up and never got the new number."

19

Tomorrow

It grows even faster than the United States. Every working day its installers relentlessly plug in a hundred thousand more telephones, its customers moving so often that it must put in seven to gain one. Its long limbs connect 138 million phones (forty-eight thousand of them snuggled in cars and trucks), and by the year 2000 it confidently expects to have 100 million more. Long-distance gabbing, if the projections of its planners are on target, will swell by 8 percent a year for the next two decades, overseas chatter by a remarkable 21 percent. Its revenues stack up to 1.8 percent of the Gross National Product and are growing at double the rate of the GNP. It is awash with assets—its aggregation of phones and spaghetti strings of cable, its clicking electronic switching systems and hornlike microwave towers—which are valued at $114 billion. Planners expect that sum to balloon to $400 billion by the year 2000. These vast amounts might be dismissed as pure corporate boasting, except that AT&T functionaries qualify as dispensers of the most conservative projections on the business landscape.

Making a product that can't be bought and thriving on a commodity that can't be seen, the American Telephone and Telegraph Company keeps rolling along, getting bigger and richer. Meticulously going about its business, the phone company has proved repeatedly over a long period of time that it can withstand all abrasions and affronts. It has always hung tough. At one time or another, its loathers have tried to drop a wet blanket over it. Legislators and lawyers have attempted to sunder it for decades (it has forty separate antitrust suits pending against it right now), but it is still intact. Its pulse beats strong. It is a company that has never suffered a loss for any financial quarter, and perhaps never will.

In the more than one hundred years of its existence, the Bell System has resoundingly succeeded in its laudable mission of extending what it calls "P.O.T."—plain old telephone service—to virtually every American who desires it, at a price almost every American can afford. "We put in phones wherever there is a body who wants to talk," one AT&T executive told me in the course of my travels. "Phones are more pervasive than bathtubs. We're putting in phones in rural corners of Missouri. The lines alone are costing us nine thousand dollars, and the revenues on those lines are about twenty-seven thousand dollars a year. People don't talk much about those sort of things." In Egypt, you are lucky to ever get a phone call through. Telephones break down with the regularity of sundown in France. Forget about getting a private phone in China; the Chinese prefer to put booths on street corners for communal use. In Russia, it is all but impossible to call anybody because the government makes phone directories one of the scarcest commodities in the country. In the United States, service is nonpareil. Less than one in a hundred calls doesn't get through. The typical Bell phone needs to be repaired at most once every five years. Some service difficulties persist in Louisiana, where much of Bell's cable spends its life beneath water, and there are sporadic problems in the Houston area, where the population growth is still hairy, but otherwise service complaints from customers stand as low as they have ever been.

Yet having a phone is no longer enough. People want more. In the future, Bell promises, they are going to get it.

As the nation hurtles obstinately into the years of the "information society," phone company people say, all manner of ingenious capabilities will be common. The phone will automatically put through a wake-up call to you in the morning. It will electronically snap on your office lights and air conditioner (or heat) shortly before you saunter through the door. When you take off at the end of the day, the phone will lock up. Word-processing machines will be hooked into the phone system. Dash off a staff memo at your desk and it will be automatically transmitted to receiving devices attached to phones throughout your company. Your appliances will be wired to the phone. On your lunch hour, you'll call home and get the clothes washer going. Later on, you'll have to momentarily interrupt a meeting to call the dryer. An hour before you wrap up for the day, you'll phone the microwave oven to start the Yankee pot roast. Half of all gas station sales are paid by credit cards. The appeal of plastic payment will surely go up as bills get steeper. In the future, you may pull into the station and run your credit card through a device. The gadget will dial a number over the phone lines to a data base that validates your card. The pump unlocks. You put in your twelve gallons of unleaded and are charged $50.

Other things. There will be no need to trudge down to the local elementary school to vote in elections. You will vote by phone. Electric and gas companies will read meters over the phone. The traveling meterman will go out of business. The mail will come by phone; no more postman with pouch slung crookedly over his shoulder.

Still other things. "I'll want to repair my 1956 Granada," said Howard Anderson, president of the Yankee Group. "I'll call the specifics into a data bank and out will pour instructions on how to do it. I'll be out there in my driveway, flat on my back, all greasy, and I'll be shouting into my telephone, 'Now I've taken the wheel off, what do I do next?' And the phone will respond, 'Now take out the bearings.' At night, I'll be doing my income taxes and there will be a computer program I can call to explain the horrendous mess to me. All of this from AT&T. There will be remote diagnostics. The washing machine breaks down; you plug it into this black box that is your phone and a Sears person says, 'Aha, the fan belt is gone,' and when the Sears repairman comes by he will have the right part with him for the first time in his life. You can hold a team meeting with your Little League team by phone. You dial one number and the entire team picks up."

A visual display will probably be on everybody's phone to print out the number of the calling party. Oh, no, it's Aunt Corky again! Let it ring. Better yet, punch a button that causes the phone to deliver a recorded message reporting that you have, on short notice, been sent to prison. Matters may be arranged so that there will be no phone books and no directory assistance operators. You want a person's number? Dial the letters of the name on your phone and the number flashes on your display.

The phone will be wedded to the TV, or else to a wall screen (which, when not in use, can display an electronic picture of say, ships on a shimmering ocean; you may even, if you so desire, be able to sniff the salt air and hear the crash of the waves). That way, you can do your shopping at home by calling up mops and looking them over on your screen. Call up the Sears catalogue on the phone and order away. You'll pay two cents a page for the call, or whatever. Do your banking by phone. You want to read the newspaper? Dial it up on the phone. "The home of the future is going to be much more of an office of the future than it is today," Howard Anderson said. "You'll be able to see a horse race on your TV and there'll be a program to bet on the races through your phone. You'll be able to dial up recipes from a data bank and plan an entire meal for a dinner party. The uses will keep expanding. It's like when they first began to wire houses for electricity. Light was the first application. Now I'm sharpening my pencils with electricity, I've got entertainment hooked up, I've got security hooked up, I've got smoke detectors hooked up. There will be no standard phone in the future. Dozens of models will exist. If you want a polka-dot phone waking you up each morning to 'The Battle Hymn of the Republic,' be AT&T's guest."

It is probable—in the long run—that the telephone will no longer be called the telephone. And so the name, the American Telephone and Telegraph Company, will become a misnomer (the telegraph portion is already a misnomer) and it, too, will undoubtedly be changed in time. Perhaps to something like the American Communications Company? The Big Bell Company? Ma Bell, Inc.?

As it is, Ma Bell is expecting a child—the telecommunications industry has already dubbed it "Baby Bell"—that will take charge of the unregulated computer activities that the phone company is moving into. Like everything else Ma Bell conceives, it will be quite a child. It will start life with some 15 percent of its parent's assets—or about $20 billion—and it is expected, by 1985, to be raking in $10 billion in revenues. By itself, it would stand fortieth on the corporate totem pole. Baby Bell's precise birth date and configuration are still fuzzy. A gaggle of doctors must give their blessings. The FCC has already nodded its assent. But there are still Congress and the Justice Department, with its ongoing Federal antitrust suit, to be heard from. After five years of on-again, off-again wrangling with the matter the Senate, late in 1981, finally passed a massive deregulation bill that would certify the birth of Baby Bell. However, the House has been drafting somewhat different legislation that would clamp more severe restrictions on AT&T than does the Senate version. Many corners of the communications world are hanging on every move. Above all else, they want layers of safeguards that will assure that Ma Bell can't siphon profits from its regulated local and long-distance phone businesses and plow them into Baby Bell to crush competitors, since the FCC alone seems woefully inadequate to the task of policing Ma Bell and its progeny. Many fields are sweating over incursions from the awesome phone company. Cable operators fear that it will roll into their industry. Newspaper and magazine publishers fret that it will dip its toes into home information systems and that electronic Yellow Pages, with up-to-the-minute towel ads and the latest chopped meat bargains at A&P, will drain classified ads out of local papers. Already, Ma Bell has cooked up ambitious experiments with Knight-Ridder Newspapers in Florida and with CBS in Ridgewood, New Jersey, to test the appeal of a home information system. In deference to newspaper publishers, the phone company did consent to an amendment tacked on to the Senate deregulation measure that bars it from originating any material that will be sent over its network. While such sticky matters get thrashed out down in Washington, Ma Bell has been subjecting its sales soldiers to stiff tests to see if they can pass muster in the new competitive environment. Many seasoned Bell employees are said to be queasy. Little is being left to the imagination. Sales hands are being told that when they go out on calls they will dress in blue or gray suits; they are being instructed that they will arrive at clients in a four-door American car.

William Sharwell, AT&T's vice president in charge of planning, an easygoing, thoroughly unselfconscious man, sat in his office one afternoon and pondered the future: "When I was growing up in the 1930s, in a middle class family, we had one black telephone that was located on a window seat between the second floor and the first floor, because it was convenient to both the upstairs and the downstairs. Today, of course, no middle class family has that kind of setup. When I look at my kids, they use the telephone much differently from the way I used it. When I called up another teenager, it was a real event. Now, my teenagers seem to be on the phone half their waking hours. They're on the phone calling across the street. The telephone to them is like a toothbrush. What's going to be the standard in the future is clearly a two-way audiovisual system. One of the signal advantages we will get, I think, is control. I'll give you an example. I recently obtained a mortgage on a new piece of property. At once, I was besieged with telephone calls from all sorts of people who had something to sell that they were sure I couldn't do without. Window shade people, decorators, builders, *New York Times* purveyors. The telephone calls were a nuisance. Well, in the future, we should be able to shut off a certain number of calls. We'll be able to forward some calls to a recording. You'll be able to change your call patterns yourself. Nothing bothers me more than when I'm in a store being waited on and the phone rings and the clerk goes to answer the phone. That tells me the person on the other end of the phone is more important than the one standing in front of him. I don't like that. In the future, I think we can handle that with call storage or call-back procedures. The calls will be held until the salesman gets done with his live customer."

Sharwell scratched his head. "The mobile phone has got to be one of the big areas of expansion. Not only will there be phones in every car, but a cordless telephone that you can carry around with you in your pocket. A possibility is a national telephone number for everyone. Anybody who wants to reach you can dial that number, and the call will be forwarded to where you might be. You're shopping at the supermarket. You're sunbathing at the beach. You're in Beirut. You're climbing the Alps. The call will find you. The thing will look like your wristwatch. You'll probably be able to just speak into it, not even have to push any buttons. Give me the President, and you'll get the President. We may never have to dial any numbers again."

Testimony from the eternally clubbable Bill Ellinghaus, AT&T's president. He talks to me in his office on the top floor of 195 Broadway. He is a large, looming, beaming man, with an engulfing handshake. He gives me his account of AT&T's future: "We'll be providing service to the public. It'll be as good or better than it is now. I foresee that we'll be the carrier of last resort. Our emphasis will continue to be making available service to whoever wants it at low cost. We'll probably be the only one able to provide end-to-end service to the public. We'll be managing the nationwide network. Our growth rate will continue. We have a long-term growth rate objective of eight percent a year, and I see that continuing. A difference will be that competition will keep growing, and the marketplace will dictate more of what we can do. Telephone service will be provided in a way to meet your individual needs. There will be different types of rate plans. The telephone network will be a highly intelligent network, as opposed to one that is very efficient today. The phone will require low power, maybe power by light rather than electricity. There will be more cost pricing for a number of reasons, one of them being that we will have the wherewithal to record what everybody does on the phone. Those who incur the costs will pay the costs. More so in the future, the top management people here will have to have a broader understanding of the business than they have needed in the past. I was an installer way back when, who came up through the commercial department and then through marketing. I think the management employee ten years or so from now will have a sophisticated knowledge of the corporate world. He'll have to be much more of a marketer than in the past. We will have to take more risks. We will have to move faster. But will the basic mission of the phone company change? No. We will always be a service organization first. Earnings will not come at the expense of service. I think the Bell System has a great future. We're not the staid old monster that everyone perceives we are that takes years to turn around. Do we stub our toes every now and then, has our batting average sunk below one thousand? Sure, but so what. I've been in the business thirty-four years and I wish I could spend thirty-four more years. If any of my youngsters asked me if he should go to work for the telephone company, I'd say, 'You betya.'"

It seems inevitable to many Bell students, however, that the biggest company on earth must at some point finally address the question of how big is too big. If AT&T continues its unrelenting growth, by the year 2000 it may be 5 percent of the GNP. Bell watchers figure that the phone company might have revenues of $200 billion, earnings of $20 billion. Robert La Blanc, the vice chairman of Continental Telephone, says: "There's a social question in my mind whether any company can be five percent of the GNP. Man, is that big! I think they've done a pretty good job discharging their social responsibilities as big as they are now. I'd rather have them handle electronic mail than the Post Office, to take one example. But there's a legitimate worry whether this country will let something get as big as the phone company is going to get."

One reason often advanced for the phone company's remarkable vitality is the fact that its employees find themselves in more personal contact with their customers than is true in any other business. "As I often tell our fellows," an AT&T marketing man said to me, "we've got to sow the seeds of future sales. If we sow them well and fertilize them and nourish them, we'll have a happy time. We have to keep convincing people that the phone is their good pal." But those contacts will taper off in the future, as technology allows increasing numbers of people to put in their own phones, as it allows repairmen to cure sick instruments from remote locales, as it further obviates the need for operator assistance. "Yes, there will be less contact as we have known it," Bill Ellinghaus told me. "In the past, we had people located in every single community in the country. There was a telephone man or a telephone gal everywhere you looked. Obviously, we don't have that anymore. Does that cause us a problem? The answer is yes. We will have to conceive of other ways of keeping in touch—maybe more open houses at our facilities, more public speeches."

The phone company right now is drivingly busy trying to add spark to its brushes with customers. Make a credit card call, and the operator is as sweet as your grandmother. "Good morning, this is Mrs. Bell. . . . Thank you for using your credit card. Now have a nice day." Robert La Blanc said to me, "I think they're doing their damnedest to change their image. Talking to their operators today is a real delight. In the past, they were whipping people. Get so many calls per minute. Now they're breaking their backs to be nice. As they get farther and farther away from the customer, they've got to make the contacts that are left as sweet as sugar. They've really got to make them count."

The continuing dominance of AT&T in the world of telephony seems inevitable. Given the crossed purposes of all the big and little powers that would have to work together to accomplish any major dismantling (the Justice Department, on the one hand, boldly sues the phone company; meantime, the General Services Administration quietly negotiates a modernization of its phone system with its exclusive provider of service—AT&T), it would appear that the phone company is not very likely to be the subject of dramatic decrees or acts of legislation. Surely, more firms will be bidden to join the menagerie of phone company competitors. The phone company is a tremendous asset to society at large, but as it gets even bigger it will need to be policed all the more, restraints put on it, and competition, bets are being laid, will help out. The Bell System knows—it has had no choice but to know—that it does not need to build, own, and operate all of the nation's communications systems. It is not immoral for an ITT, a Hitachi, or an IBM to eat some of the cake. But AT&T —opportunistic—will go on being boomingly successful. It will always be rich, and it will always be scorned by some for its riches.

The question, though, is not so much whether it is good or bad as whether the country can live with the bad part—occasionally unfair pricing schemes, a bit too aloof an attitude, a pervasive influence that can sometimes get out of hand, a disingenuous preaching that profits mean nothing, a nasty operator now and then picking up your call—in order to have the good. The thing is, above all else, AT&T is a survivor. Nobody can come to any agreement on the morals of the phone company—and I'm dubious whether it can be said to be purely good or purely bad; there are exceptions to every rule, rules of exceptions—but there is no denying its unshakable ability to endure. As Charles Brown said to me, "If all the problems we face today are solved by the end of my term, I think it is accurate to say that just as many new ones will arise to replace them. And we'll have new solutions to run them down."

As I visited telephone people around the country, they kept asking me if I realized the amount of investment implanted in the telephone system and how damaging to that investment any major change in the industry's patterns could be. Did I realize just how massive this operation was? Did I realize how much more dependent on the telephone we were going to become? Of all the comments about the nature of the phone company that I had heard, the one I remembered best was from a veteran observer of the Bell System, who, over lunch one afternoon, when I pressed him about the company's character, said, "The Bell System is like the sea. Sometimes it is very quiet and peaceful. It's soothing to admire it. Other times it gets angry and rages up and occasionally wreaks havoc. And then it retreats again. We pollute it and we build barriers to it, but we can't live without it, and I'm not sure we can really control it. It is so big that no one can ever truly understand its immensity. No matter what else happens, though, it is always there. It is just always there."

Index

About the Author

Sonny Kleinfield is a financial reporter for *The New York Times* and has published widely in many other national periodicals, including numerous articles on book publishing. He is the author of two other books: *A Month at the Brickyard* and *The Hidden Minority*. Mr. Kleinfield lives in New York City.